STANLEY B. MARROW

PAUL

His Letters and His Theology

An Introduction to Paul's Epistles

PAULIST PRESS
New York/Mahwah

Maps by Frank Sabatte, C.S.P.

Library of Congress
Catalog Card Number: 85-61745

ISBN: 0-8091-2744-X

Published by Paulist Press
997 Macarthur Boulevard
Mahwah, New Jersey 07430

Printed and bound in the
United States of America

CONTENTS

iii

To . . .

σὺ γάρ μ' ἐβιώσαο

ACKNOWLEDGEMENTS

Much of the credit in this work belongs to those who would be most surprised to learn and least willing to believe that it is theirs: my students. To them first I wish to express my abiding gratitude.

The work on the composition and the preliminary redaction of the book occupied the major part of a sabbatical semester in Rome, where the facilities of the superb library of the Pontifical Biblical Institute were made available to me through the gracious and ready help of its librarian, Father Henry Bertels, S.J. To him, therefore, and to all the staff of the library I owe a debt of gratitude not easily absolved by this acknowledgement.

I owe a special thanks to Father Charles O'Neill, S.J. and the librarian of the Casa degli Scrittori, who very kindly permitted me the use of their library in the last days of my stay, when the summer had shuttered all institutions of learning in the Eternal City.

My return to Cambridge brought me face-to-face with the stern workings of the computer and its "Jesuit obedience" to even my most hesitant commands. As I wrestled with its unforgiving word-processor, the help and unfailing patience of Father Michael Doody, S.J. turned a despondent struggle into a cumulatively valuable learning experience. To him I owe a vote of thanks for showing me how to do in a few months what would easily have required more than a year to complete.

Finally, I wish to express my heartfelt gratitude to all those whose generosity and love made my sabbatical leave so pleasant and so productive.

Introduction

So now I seized greedily upon the venerable writings inspired by Thy Spirit, and especially upon those of the
apostle Paul. . . . Wondrously did these truths sink into
my very being when I read that least of Thy apostles and
looked upon Thy works and trembled . . . (Saint Augustine, *Confessions* VII.21).

What Augustine meditated upon and marveled at, what
nurtured and fortified untold numbers of Christians
down the centuries, what inspired saints and fired heretics,
remains, alas, very much a closed book to so many Christians
today. Paul and his writings reach many of these Christians,
either in the inelegant translations to which their liturgical
celebrations subject them, or in the current rant and cant of
disillusioned and dyspeptic self-appointed reformers, whose
misreading and misunderstanding of Paul would be dismissed lightly as an outlet for their disappointments and dis-
illusions, were it not for the fact of their obstructing thereby
the access of others to genuine Christian freedom.

There is, of course, a vast amount of literature on Paul,
and it continues to grow from year to year. But, between the
largely anodyne works of piety and edification, and the forbidding works of scholarship, there is, if not altogether a void,
then certainly a large place for works on Paul that put him
and his letters within the reach of so many Christians who admit they know little about him and yet are increasingly convinced of their need to know more. For such among them as
are looking for a work that would "introduce" them to the
apostle, his conversion, his life and his letters, and that would
provide them with some matter for reflection without pre-

1

suming on their part an unreasonable background either in theology or biblical scholarship, this book might prove usable and, perchance, useful.

There are many theologies of Paul, some of them more than deserving to be called classic. There are also many works on Paul the apostle, his life, his missionary activity, his background, and his conversion. But there are not many—certainly not many Catholic—works that take up Paul's life in conjunction with his theology, attempting to illumine and interpret one by the other, not by tracing individual themes across the Pauline corpus, but by singling individual themes within each epistle in its chronological order, and bringing the recurrence of such themes elsewhere to bear on understanding them within their context.

With this aim in view, the general pattern of the book, though easy to discern from the table of contents, might require some explanation of its parts. The first three chapters are really introductory. They serve to provide some understanding of Paul and his background and, against that background, to give some glimpse of that experience which we have come to call his "conversion." A proper understanding of the basic facts of the conversion remains essential to the comprehension of anything Paul says in any of his epistles about the mystery of Christ and the life of the Christian.

The subsequent chapters simply follow the order of the epistles. This, necessarily, results in a disproportion in their individual treatments, a disproportion that is in no way a reflection of their importance but a mere accident of their sequence. Since it seemed best to single out the major themes in each epistle, and since many of these themes are not exclusive to one epistle but often recur with regularity in subsequent epistles, the treatment necessarily anticipates later compositions and obviates the need of repetition when these later compositions come up for consideration. Thus, by the time one gets to Romans, the last of Paul's epistles, most of the major themes will have been treated already; or, when Philippians is taken up, one of its major themes, the conversion of Paul, will already have had a lengthy discussion in the introductory chapters.

But the purpose of all this has to be kept in mind in order to make any sense at all. The book is intended for the educated laity who, in today's vortex of ideas, find their knowledge of Paul inadequate, and that inadequacy no longer tolerable. Should the book prove to be of some service to them, its purpose will have been achieved if it makes the reading of Paul's epistles a bit easier and the access to his theology a little less forbidding. To that end, it would be best to look up, not only the larger context of the passages actually quoted, but those other passages cited from the other epistles of Paul as well as from the rest of the New Testament.

It is perhaps because we know Paul better than any other person in the New Testament, because we have so much from his own hand that reflects such a diversity of circumstances and was occasioned by problems we recognize as so startlingly our own today, that we can, like Saint Augustine, "read that least of Thy apostles and look upon Thy work and tremble," not with the servile fear that holds so many of us in thrall, but with that inestimable "liberty of the children of God."

ONE

Paul and His Background

1. The Name of Saul Paul

Though Christian piety often and exegetes sometimes have discoursed movingly on the name as destiny, and drawn out appealing parallels to illustrious figures in the Old Testament, the explanation of the "Saul Paul" is far less religiously inspiring. The Old Testament does give examples of individuals whose names were divinely ordained or altered at turning points in their lives in order to describe their God-given mission and destiny in the history of salvation. There was Abraham who at the time of God's covenant with him was told: "No longer shall your name be Abram [exalted father], but your name shall be Abraham; for I have made you the father of a multitude of nations" (Gen 17:5). There was also Jacob: "Your name shall no more be called Jacob [he takes by the heel or he supplants—see Gen 25:26], but Israel, for you have striven with God and with men, and have prevailed" (Gen 32:28).

The New Testament too tells of instances of a divinely decreed name, as in the case of John the Baptist (Lk 1:62–63). Of course the outstanding example is the name of Jesus:

> She will bear a son, and you shall call his name Jesus, for he will save his people from their sins (Mt 1:21; see Lk 1:31 and 2:21).

So it was quite understandable that a person as important as Paul should have had his double name of Saul-Paul provided with a similarly inspired and inspiring explanation.

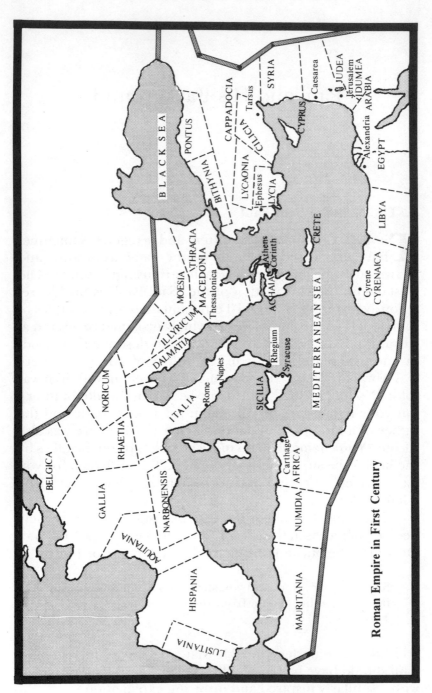

Roman Empire in First Century

The main source for this line of thought is the Book of Acts. It is quite evident that, from Acts 13:9 on, the person hitherto called "Saul" (Acts 7:58; 8:1, 3; 9:1, 8, 11, 22, 24; 11:25, 30; 12:25; 13:1, 2, 7) becomes "Paul." It seemed, therefore, quite natural to suppose that, with the commencement of the apostle's first missionary journey and at an important turning point in his career, the change of name from the very Semitic "Saul" to the Greco-Roman "Paul" should signal a far more significant change for the history of the world. Yet Acts 13:9 itself should suffice to temper such fanciful interpretation. Acts simply says, "Saul, who is *also* called Paul," and that is all there is to it.

For, like so many of his contemporaries, Paul had a double name, one Hebrew and the other Latin (or Greek). If anything is to be made of the fact that after Acts 13:9 the name Paul is used, while before Acts 13:9 Saul was used, then the simplest explanation is that the author of Acts used the Hebrew name in the Jewish part of his narrative, and the Latin name in the part given to the Gentile mission. So, however endearing such explanations as that of Augustine (*de Spir. et lit.* VII.12) are: that the name of Paul was chosen because he was the least of the apostles (*paulus* in Latin means "small"), we have to be content with the more pedestrian explanation as the more likely. Saul Paul was the double name of the man history knows as "Paul of Tarsus." We have in the New Testament similar binomials like Jude Thaddaeus (Mk 3:18), Thomas Didymos (Jn 11:16), and John Mark (Acts 12:12).

2. Tarsus, "No Mean City"

Palestine in the first century of our era constituted but a small part of the vast and sprawling Roman Empire; and though its capital Jerusalem boasted the largest single Jewish community, it was by no means unrivaled by the other metropolitan centers of the Roman world, where thriving Jewish communities prospered. Alexandria, Antioch, Damascus, Ephesus, Tarsus, and Rome itself were not only important cultural and economic centers of the Empire, they boasted large Jewish populations that contributed very significantly to the life and culture of those illustrious cities of the Empire. So, when Paul declares in Acts 21:39, "I am a Jew, from Tarsus in Cilicia, a citizen of no mean city," he is not merely indulging the rightful pride that becomes a citizen of a great city, but stating a fact well attested by history, however unkindly that history might have subsequently dealt with the fortunes of the place.

Tarsus in Cilicia, a part of modern day Turkey, in the northeast corner of the Mediterranean, was situated on the banks of the Cydnus River. Its history goes back to the third millennium (around 2300 B.C.). It is mentioned as "Tarsi" in the Assyrian records of Shalmaneser III (858–824 B.C.). In Roman times its importance was recognized when, in 67 B.C., it was designated the capital of the province of Cilicia. Like many other cities, Tarsus got caught in the struggle between Cassius and Mark Antony, and suffered the consequences. But eventually it had its full rights as a free city restored to it under Augustus Caesar. Such rights allowed its citizens to boast of their Roman citizenship, as did Paul in Acts: "I was born a citizen"—unlike the tribune interrogating him, who had "bought his citizenship for a large sum" (Acts 22:28).

Shortly before Paul was born, that "rare Egyptian," Cleopatra, paid a visit to Tarsus, where she "pursed up" Marc Antony's heart "upon the river of Cydnus." She sailed up the river in full regalia, "O'er-picturing that Venus where we see/ The fancy out-work nature":

> The barge she sat in, like a burnish'd throne
> Burn'd on the water; the poop was beaten gold,
> Purple the sails, and so perfumed, that
> The winds were love-sick with them; the oars were silver
> Which to the tune of flutes kept stroke, and made
> The water which they beat to follow faster,
> As amorous of their strokes (*Antony and Cleopatra* II.2).

Cicero too spent a year (50 B.C.) in the city as the governor of Cilicia. We do not know what Cleopatra thought of Tarsus, but Cicero felt that one more year there would have killed him. His attitude, however, is the comprehensible, if unkind, reaction of a Parisian compelled to serve as consul today in some bustling midwestern town.

Even the name of Tarsus has its share of legend. Though, in all likelihood, it was named after the local deity Tarkus, a better known and more famous legend surrounded its origins. In his third Satire, Juvenal speaks of a Stoic philosopher who "was brought up in Tarsus, by the banks of that river/Where Bellerophon fell to earth from the Gorgon's flying nag." The "nag" was, of course, Pegasus, and the word in Latin used for "Tarsus" is *pinna,* which can mean either feather or hoof, and translated the Greek *tarsos,* the flat of the foot.

Thus, Paul's pride in his native city was indeed justified, even as his Roman citizenship was ample reason for boasting. He was a citizen in an Empire at the apogee of its long-lasting glory. He was born a Jew in the complex and teeming world of a period in history designated by historians as "Hellenism." It is indeed arguable whether anything less than that rich and variegated background could have equipped him so admirably to carry out the task he undertook and the mission to which he was called. God's grace, after all, does not operate in a cultural vacuum.

3. Hellenism

Near the ancient city of Babylon, on the afternoon of the 10th of June 323 B.C., Alexander the Great died at the age of thirty-three. The world was never the same after that fateful event: the passing of a youthful Macedonian general who, perhaps uniquely in history, fully deserved the title "Great." A minor jewel in the crown of his world conquests was his defense of the prosperous city of Tarsus from the plundering designs of a Persian satrap named Arsanes. Many generals before and after Alexander aspired to conquer "the world," but none succeeded as he did, not merely in subjugating vast territories to his sway, but in imposing the indelible mark of his culture on peoples, their languages, their world views, their religious ideas, philosophies and arts. That pervasive and lasting phenomenon is globally described as "Hellenism":

an amalgam of the finest elements of Greek culture with all the myriad treasures of mind and heart of the lands where Alexander's armies trod. The phenomenon explains, among innumerable other historical facts, why our New Testament itself, though composed in the hour of Rome's glory, was written entirely in Greek, and why Paul himself addressed even his letter to the Romans in Greek and not in Latin.

But, long before the Christian era, the phenomenon called Hellenism had exerted its influence even on that bastion of intransigent conservatism, Judaism. Not only did the Judaism of the time feel the need to translate its sacred Scriptures from Hebrew into Greek for one of the largest Jewish communities outside Palestine, that of Alexandria, the most famous of the countless cities that bear the name of the Macedonian conqueror; but the very core of Jewish religion felt in varying degrees and in many subtle ways the effects of Hellenistic ideas and philosophies.

Indeed, the phenomenon of "Hellenization" was so extensive that it is often difficult to segregate and label concepts—as scholars were once wont to do—as either Jewish or Hellenistic. The path of Hellenistic incursions into the Jewish world of ideas was particularly uneven and obstacle-strewn, especially on Palestinian soil. But there is no denying the "profound transformation" (Hengel, *Judaism and Hellenism*, vol. 1, p. 311) of Palestinian Judaism during the Hellenistic period, which extends from the death of Alexander the Great in the last quarter of the fourth century B.C. down to about the end of the first century of our Christian era.

Though it is easy enough to underestimate the influence of this Hellenistic culture on Paul's life and thought, it is not easy at all to define its extent. While a form of "God speaks well of God" zeal prompts many to undervalue or even to deny the Hellenistic influences on Paul and to try to explain the New Testament exclusively in the categories and within the ambit of ideas of the Old Testament, the very complexity of the phenomenon of the interaction of Judaism and Hellenism compels us to consider seriously the extent and the implications of Hellenism in both the Old and the New Testaments.

The influence of Hellenism on all our New Testament is undeniable. Its influence on Paul himself, a native of one of Hellenism's great centers of learning—whose schools at one time rivaled those of Athens and Alexandria—extends far beyond Paul's imagery, rhetorical style, or vocabulary. There is no denying the Hellenistic factors in Paul's background; and it is certainly arguable that, were it not for that "mixture of elements" in him, he would not have been what he was: the great apostle of the Gentiles.

4. The Gentiles

There is in Galatians 2:7–8 a distinction that could facilitate our comprehension of the term "Gentiles." In the description of his journey to Jerusalem and his encounter with "those who were of repute" (Gal 2:2), Paul defines Peter's sphere of missionary activity as well as his own:

> I had been entrusted with the gospel to the uncircumcised, just as Peter had been with the gospel to the circumcised (for he who worked through Peter for the mission of the circumcised worked through me also for the Gentiles (*ta ethne*) (Gal 2:7–8).

Paul here sets the "uncircumcised" in parallel with the "Gentiles," thus equating the Gentiles with the non-Jews. So, in a manner of speaking, the religious world to someone of Paul's background was divisible into Jews and Gentiles. It is, of course, a good deal easier to describe what we mean by "the Jews" with their belief in the one unique God, their reverence of the sacred books of the Old Testament, and the variety of their religious practices and observances, than it is to describe what was encompassed by the term "Gentiles."

In attempting to describe that Gentile world, the nations (*ta ethne*), as the New Testament Greek calls it, we should first keep in mind that to regard that world as atheistic would be false, and to speak of it as polytheistic would be misleading. That, generally speaking, the Gentiles did worship some god other than the one worshiped by the Jews excludes them from being characterized as atheistic. That a Gentile worshiper honored his own particular god while doing reverence and paying homage to a variety of other deities is not the same as worshiping several gods indiscriminately at once. Indeed, the Gentiles did not regard such reverence of many gods as blasphemous, but they tended to view the intransigent exclusiveness of the Jews as tantamount to blasphemy. Our understanding of the Gentiles must therefore keep in mind that they were, strictly speaking, neither godless nor arreligious.

To get some idea of the complexity of the Gentile religious world, it would be helpful to divide it into the world of the philosophers and the world of religions. The first century of our era knew a number of philosophies and philosophical schools (Epicurean, Stoic, Cynic, Pythagorian, etc.), description of which lies beyond the confines of this particular exposition. But what must be noted here is that, however extensive their influence, such philosophies and their views of religion, of the gods, and of the problems of life and death fell within the grasp of the relatively few who were educated and literate. The influence of philosophical ideas inevitably percolated to the lower echelons of society; but, in themselves, such ideas remained confined to what we usually call "schools of philosophy."

One of the most popular of such schools was the Cynic. Attributed to Diogenes of Sinope, its reputed founder around the third century B.C., the school derived its unsavory name from his boast: "I fawn on those who give me anything, I yelp at those who refuse, and I set my teeth in rascals" (*Diogenes Laertius* 6.60)—like a dog, which in Greek is *kynos*, whence "Cynic." Cynicism was a widespread—one would almost say fashionable—philosophy of Paul's day. As a moral and philosophical system it had little to do with our current understanding of "cynicism." It had an elaborate system of moral precepts; and the *diatribe*, the rhetorical mode of argument it employed to propound them, left its unmistakable mark on Paul's style in his letters. This rhetorical mode of *diatribe*, like the Cynicism which employed it, is also far removed from our current understanding of the term. To get some idea of what the Cynic *diatribe* involved as a rhetorical mode of argument, one might—for instance—read carefully 1 Corinthians 9, and note there the easy and familiar address of the style, the questions punctuating the exposition, the brief sentences, the parallels drawn, etc. All these are rhetorical devices employed in the Cynic *diatribe* and found frequently in Paul's writings. So, however extensively Jewish his upbringing and background, Paul's education had had to comprise some schooling—formal or informal—in what was part of the normal curriculum of a lad brought up in Tarsus in Cilicia.

5. Religions in the Gentile World

In an age which deemed an attitude of intolerance to alien gods an impiety, and regarded as blasphemers, not those who believed in a god other than their own, but those who disdained and eschewed all other gods, it is not surprising to see religious tolerance held in such high esteem, or to find religion itself boasting of a well-populated pantheon. Each city had its own revered deity as well as a whole galaxy of other major or lesser deities. Even the emperors received their share of worship, and returned the compliment by erecting imposing monuments to the deities of the cities that so honored them. The list of the gods worshiped seems endless, but there was always a hierarchy of preference among them, Zeus/Jupiter usually heading the list. Appropriate sacrifices were made to specific gods and goddesses on designated feasts, in times of special need, and on occasions of national, family or personal solemnities.

The Roman world in general and the Romans in particular were especially prone to designate a tutelary deity for practically every aspect of life. Sir Frank Adcock once remarked that, had the Romans had bicycles in their day, they would surely have worshiped a goddess Punctura to preside over them. Analogies to this practice, however imperfect, are not altogether wanting in our own times. There are patron saints for everything imaginable—and indeed for some things hard to imagine; there are also a multiplicity of titles, sanctuaries, shrines and images to honor the Blessed Virgin

Mary throughout Christendom. This is not to suggest for a moment that either the Blessed Virgin or the saints are in any sense worshiped by Christians. The analogy—and it is no more than that—is of religious practices, not of the theologies underlying them.

Yet, however comprehensible the phenomenon from a human point of view, it ought not to diminish in our eyes the difficulties that a fiercely monotheistic religion like Judaism encountered in that world of Gentile tolerance. On the other hand, the very multiplicity of deities and religions opened the path to both Jewish and Christian missionaries in the Roman Empire. In a world that welcomed "Oriental" imports, they found ample proselytes. Thus, although the speech of Paul in the Areopagus of Athens is a set piece of rhetoric, the point it makes is certainly instructive: "What therefore you worship as unknown, this I proclaim to you" (Acts 17:23). According to the author of Acts, Paul prefaces his speech by the rhetorical *captatio benevolentiae* (winning the audience's good will): "I perceive that in every way you are religious" (Acts 17:22). That very religiousness, coupled with his audience's tolerance—even if it bordered at times on bored indifference (see Acts 17:32)—paved the way for the missionary labors of the apostle of the Gentiles.

Another striking feature of the Gentile world of religion was the mystery cults. In the already crowded world of Greco-Roman gods, Oriental importations of secret cults exercised their own irresistible allure. With specified annual periods of observance such cults involved the ritual worship of the god or goddess around whom the particular death-and-resurrection myth of the cult deity was woven. Among such cults as that of Cybele, Mithras and Orpheus, the mystery cult of Isis stands out. We know surprisingly little about the particulars of such cults. Yet, though their jealous custody of their ritual secrets has proved remarkably successful, we do possess, in a romance of the third century A.D., a moving picture of the devotion that a goddess like Isis could and did command in her devotees. Though the hero of *The Golden Ass* is a fictitious character, the author of the work, Apuleius, was not (A.-J. Festugière, *Personal Religion among the Greeks*, ch. 5, esp. p. 84).

The evident and moving piety of the prayer addressed by the hero at his deliverance from his long life of tribulations and at the time of his initiation into the cult of the goddess Isis is eloquent witness that the Gentile world was definitely not "pagan" and certainly not irreligious. If the "atheism" or unbelief of certain philosophers and writers of that period has impressed us, the mute witness of those silent masses who, in their miseries, turned to a particular god or goddess for salvation, relied on their deity for protection and succor, and strewed the length and breadth of the Roman Empire with the illiterate tokens of their gratitude carved in stones, must keep us ever conscious of the deep religious roots that waited to be tapped by the apostle of the Gentiles and by those who followed in his footsteps.

TWO

Paul's Life and Conversion

6. The Apostle of the Gentiles

Paul of Tarsus is a unique figure in our New Testament. Though anonymity shrouds such authors as the four evangelists and the writers of the Catholic epistles, the man to whom fourteen of the New Testament epistles are attributed is known to us with a certainty and a clarity far exceeding any other in the New Testament. The identity of such names as Matthew, Mark, Luke, John, James, Peter, and Jude has been—and continues to be—the subject of debate. But no such debate is possible about the identity of the man from whom we have the epistles to the Thessalonians, the Galatians, the Corinthians, the Philippians, the Romans, and Philemon. Not only does the author of these epistles reveal himself in them both directly and indirectly, but other New Testament writings—notably the Acts of the Apostles—furnish added biographical details about him, his mission and his apostolic labors. Of course, there are many and important points in Paul's life that are obscure to us; but, compared with our ignorance of the other New Testament authors, our knowledge of the life and person of this apostle can almost be said to suffer from an embarrassment of riches.

The source of this "embarrassment" is the Book of Acts which furnishes us with a host of details about Paul's life and journeys, his missionary toils and his sermons, and his relationship to the churches, to Judaism, and to the Roman authorities. It is therefore not surprising that, despite the accuracy of detail and the general reliability of the accounts in Acts, elements of conflict in the evidence and of obscurity in the data remain to plague us.

But any serious reader of the New Testament will be aware of the need to understand the aim and purpose of the author of Acts before passing judgment on the historical validity of his work. Vatican II's exhortation, "Those who search out the intention of the sacred writers must, among other things, have regard for 'literary forms' " (*Dei Verbum*, ch. 3, no. 12), can be a salutary corrective to our too hasty dismissal of the information which the Book of Acts provides about the life and work of Paul. It should also keep us aware of that intention of its writer which was operative in shaping his account.

Though individual points of disagreement between what Paul himself says in his letters and what Acts says about him will be noted when the need arises, it is useful to keep in mind a general working principle: When the Book of Acts and Paul concur on a point, the evidence of Acts is corroborative; when they dissent on a point, Paul's own statement is to weigh more heavily in the balance, while that in Acts is to be comprehended within the larger scheme and purpose of its author; and, finally, when there is no evidence to the contrary, the statements in Acts are to be taken at face value. This is not only a principle of common sense, but also one that takes seriously the true nature of literary compositions as well as their divinely appointed purpose: "For whatever was written in former days was written for our instruction, that by steadfastness and by encouragement of the scriptures we might have hope" (Rom 15:4).

7. The Acts of the Apostles as a Source

The Book of Acts informs us that Paul was "a Jew, born at Tarsus in Cilicia," "a citizen of no mean city" (Acts 22:3; 21:39). We have already seen the rightness of this latter boast about Paul's native city (see no. 2 above). We have also considered something of the Hellenistic background that such origin implied for a Jew in the Gentile world of the Diaspora

ROMAN EMPERORS	PAUL'S LIFE	PAUL'S LETTERS
27 B.C. Augustus		
14 A.D. Tiberius		
	30 Crucifixion	
	35 Conversion of Paul	
37 A.D. Caligula	**35–38** Paul in "Arabia"	
	38 Paul's visit to Cephas	
41 A.D. Claudius	**38–48** Paul in "Syria and Cilicia"	
	48 The "Apostolic Council" in Jerusalem	
	48 or 49 Paul's mission in Galatia	
	50 Mission in Philippi,	
May 51 Gallio, Proconsul of Achaia	Thessalonica, Berea, Athens, and Corinth	First Thessalonians
	autumn 50 to spring 52	
54 to 68 A.D. Nero	Paul's stay in Corinth	
	summer 52 to winter 55–56 Travel to Antioch and Ephesus;	
	visit to Galatia;	Galatians
	mission in	First Corinthians
	Ephesus;	correspondence of
	visit to Corinth;	Second
	imprisonment in	Corinthians
	Ephesus	correspondence of
		Philippians
	winter of 55–56	Philemon
	Stay in Corinth	Romans
	56 Journey to Jerusalem	
	58 Travel to Rome	
	60 Death of Paul	

(see nos. 3–5 above). One other implication needs explicitation here. Paul had to be at least bilingual. Greek, of course, is the language of his letters. Acts, moreover, tells how a Roman tribune reacted to Paul's question with: "Do you know Greek?" (Acts 21:37). It also has Paul himself speaking to the people of Jerusalem "in the Hebrew language" (Acts 21:40): "And when they heard that he addressed them in the Hebrew language, they were the more quiet" (Acts 22:2). Both "Greek" and the "Hebrew language," however, need some qualification. The Greek spoken was what is commonly referred to as the *Koine*, the common language of the people, the vehicle of ordinary daily intercourse. Our New Testament is itself written in this *Koine* Greek, and not in the classical language of Homer and the tragedians, nor of Plato, Aristotle and the great historians. Perhaps the two kinds of Greek could be compared—profitably if not altogether accurately— to the English of Chaucer and to that of today's newspapers.

What the author of Acts means by "the Hebrew language" however is not the language in which most of the Old Testament was written, but the Aramaic spoken in Palestine of the first century. To use yet another imperfect example, this Aramaic compares with Hebrew as Italian compares with Latin. Aramaic was the language current in Palestine after the return from exile in 538 B.C. It was sufficiently different from the Hebrew of the Old Testament to make a translation (*targum*) from one language to the other necessary:

> And they read from the book, from the law of God, clearly [with interpretation]; and they gave the sense so that the people understood the reading (Neh 8:8).

The Book of Acts, moreover, has Paul say that he was "brought up" in Jerusalem itself, "at the feet of Gamaliel," the famous Jerusalem rabbi of the first century, and that he was "educated according to the strict manner of the law of our fathers" (Acts 22:3). Here we run into a difficulty. The difficulty is not with the fact of Paul's orthodox Jewish upbringing but with the statement that it was acquired in Jerusalem rather than in his native Tarsus. Paul himself bears witness to his own strict Jewish upbringing: "circumcised on the eighth day, of the people of Israel, of the tribe of Benjamin, a Hebrew born of Hebrews; as to the law a Pharisee" (Phil 3:5). Yet he says nothing in his letters about his having been educated in Jerusalem. This silence is, in itself, of minor significance. But a Jerusalem upbringing would mean that Aramaic not Greek was his first language. Yet, given the fact that we have from Paul's hand much in Greek and absolutely nothing in Aramaic, we are left to wonder about the place of his upbringing. His Greek is certainly creditable and could well have been his first language, even if it is not the top grade literary *Koine* we find in Luke and Acts, for example. Moreover, if Luke's statement in Acts is not to be dismissed out of hand, we have to allow for a relatively rich Hellenistic education in Paul's background to explain his Greek imagery, his political and commercial terminology, and his rhetorical style which—as has already been remarked—shows the influence of the Cynic diatribe (see no. 3 above).

What the Book of Acts tells us about the events immediately following the conversion of Paul can be accepted at face value, with but minor reservations. The specific details of Paul's missionary activity and of his journeyings back and forth could also be taken, generally speaking, at face value. But whether or not the apostolic assembly at Jerusalem mentioned in Acts 15:2 is to be identified with that which Paul himself mentions in Galatians 2:1–10 remains—and in all likelihood will continue to remain—open to discussion. What ought to be kept in mind, however, is the overall impression which the author of Acts wishes to convey of what—already to his own generation—was a golden past of amity and accord within that blessed community of believers, a time of harmony with those in whose midst that community lived and grew in number in Palestine and in the rest of the Roman Empire.

8. The Conversion Accounts in Acts

Paul's conversion is, inevitably, of prime importance for understanding him, his mission, and his theology. Yet, despite the abundance of the material we possess about the event itself, our curiosity remains far from satisfied, and the attempts of interpreters over the centuries to satisfy it are a good deal less than satisfactory. Not only are the details of the event, despite—or perhaps because of—their number, difficult to reconcile, but their interpretation has been, and continues to be, a divisive issue. Yet one thing at least is certain: he "who made havoc in Jerusalem of those who called on this name" (Acts 10:21) became "a chosen instrument of mine to carry my name before the Gentiles and kings and the sons of Israel" (Acts 9:15).

Three different chapters in the Book of Acts offer three circumstantial descriptions of what took place on the road to Damascus. In chapter 9 we have a straightforward Lucan narrative in the third person; in chapter 22, an apology by Paul himself to his co-religionists in Jerusalem; and in chapter 26, a formal defense by Paul before King Agrippa and Festus in Caesarea. The accounts differ, as they should; for Luke is not ignorant of the rhetorical niceties that require the changes he rings on the one basic account of the incident. But, despite these changes, differences in the accounts persist even though the core of the account itself remains quite unaltered.

Thus, despite the diminishing role of Ananias or the differing reactions of the companions to the actual event, the three accounts in Acts agree on the fact that Paul persecuted "any belonging to the Way" (Acts 9:2; 22:4; 24:10). They also agree in situating the event: as Paul "approached/drew near to/journeyed to Damascus" (Acts 9:3; 22:6; 26:12). Above all, all three give an almost identical account of what happened.

In the description of what, according to Acts, happened on the road to Damascus certain points should be kept in mind. The event itself is narrated in a literary form already known in Old Testament accounts of the calling and mission of great figures in the history of salvation. There is the call of Jacob to return to his home (Gen 31:11–13) and to go down into Egypt (Gen 46:2–3); the calls of Abraham in Genesis 22:1–2, of Moses in Exodus 3, and of the young Samuel in 1 Samuel 3:4–14. All these accounts follow a pattern: the call by name, the response, and the mission. Thus, in the call of Jacob:

(a) God spoke to Israel in visions of the night, and said, "Jacob, Jacob."
(b) And he said, "Here am I."
(c) Then he said, "I am God, the God of your father; do not be afraid to go down to Egypt; for I will make of you a great nation" (Gen 46:2–3).

Similarly, in the call of Moses:

(a) God called to him out of the bush, "Moses, Moses!"
(b) And he said, "Here am I."
(c) "Come, I will send you to Pharaoh that you may bring forth my people, the sons of Israel, out of Egypt" (Ex 3:4, 10).

Now, if we compare the central event in the narratives of Acts with these Old Testament accounts, the parallelism becomes immediately evident:

(a) "Saul, Saul, why do you persecute me?" (Acts 9:4; 22:7; 26:14).
(b) And he said, "Who are you, Lord?" (Acts 9:5; 22:8; 26:15).
(c) "I am Jesus, whom you are persecuting; but rise and enter the city, and you will be told what you are to do" (Acts 9:6; 22:10); or, in the account in which Ananias plays no role at all, "But rise and stand upon your feet; for I have appeared to you for this purpose, to appoint you to serve and bear witness to the things in which you have seen me and to those in which I will appear to you, delivering you from the people and from the Gentiles—to whom I send you to open their eyes, that they may turn from darkness to light, and from the power of Satan to God, that they may receive forgiveness of sins and a place among those who are sanctified by faith in me" (Acts 26:16–18).

Of course, such similarity between the accounts is not accidental. It tells the reader of Acts how the author saw the event and how he understood its meaning in the life and mission of the great apostle of the Gentiles. Acts, moreover, had already set the stage for this in the account of Stephen's martyrdom when Luke first introduced Saul on the scene:

> They cast [Stephen] out of the city and stoned him; and the witnesses laid down their garments at the feet of a young man named Saul. . . . And Saul was consenting to his death (Acts 7:58; 8:1).

Should the point be lost on his readers, Luke comes back to it and makes it explicit later in the book:

> And when the blood of Stephen thy witness [*martyros*] was shed, I also was standing by and approving, and keeping the garments of those who killed him (Acts 22:20).

The death of Stephen is, like the death of Jesus in the Gospel of Luke, a martyr's death. Evidently, as less than two centuries later Tertullian was to remark—immortally: "The blood of martyrs is the seed of Christianity" (*Apology* 50.13). In the history of the Church as Acts views it, the death of that first martyr, "Stephen, thy witness" (Acts 22:20), sowed the seed of the great apostle whose mission was seen as on a par with that of Abraham, Jacob, and Moses. It would require peculiar obtuseness on the part of the reader to confound what are evidently theological reflections on an event with the historical components underlying it.

Therefore, Luke's purpose in writing the Acts of the Apostles must not be lost sight of when we assess the historicity, the did-it-really-happen quality, of his account. As a modern commentary on the Book of Acts justly remarks:

> The historical facts of the case do not indeed here stand revealed with complete clarity. That we can nevertheless to some extent guess them, however, is above all due to Luke's work. It remains a matter for astonishment that a man of the sub-apostolic generation can have sensed so much of the true state of affairs: he has left us a priceless gift (Haenchen, *Acts*, p. 299).

9. Paul's Own Account

Paul himself tells us very little about the Damascus incident, but in that little much is revealed. What impresses the reader of Paul's letters is his reluctance and reticence to speak about his inner personal experiences; and, of course, the Damascus incident was certainly such an experience. The author of Acts sees the incident as a vocation rather than a conversion, and the pattern of narrative he adopts bears this out. In Paul's writings, however, there are scattered references which often, though not always nor with certainty, refer to the Damascus incident rather as a conversion. Reluctant though he is to "boast" (2 Cor 12:1, 6; Gal 1:10; Phil 3:4), Paul refers to the Damascus incident as well as other past experiences in his life always in the context of his "defense and confirmation of the gospel" (Phil 1:7). It is with this fact in mind that we search his letters for references to the event on the way to Damascus.

First of all, it should come as no surprise that there is no mention in his epistles of Paul having been anywhere in or near Jerusalem prior to his conversion. Indeed, there is strong reason to suspect the contrary. In Galatians 1:22, speaking of his visit to Cephas in Jerusalem, Paul states that he was still "not known by sight to the churches of Christ in Judea"—something he could not very well have said had he been, as Acts has it, brought up in Jerusalem "at the feet of Gamaliel" (Acts 22:3) or had he been there to "consent" to the martyrdom of Stephen (Acts 8:1; 7:58; 22:20).

Secondly, though Acts and Paul agree on Paul's former life as a violent persecutor of the Church, there is no hint in Paul that he persecuted the Church in Jerusalem and Judea. There was no possibility of his ever having dragged anybody, bound or unbound, from Damascus to Jerusalem (Acts 9:2). Damascus was far beyond any jurisdiction of any Jewish court in Jerusalem. The Romans, to be sure, were often extremely tolerant in religious matters, but their tolerance did not take kindly to that sort of anarchy. Whatever the reasons behind the statement in Acts that Paul "received letters to the brethren, and . . . journeyed to Damascus to take those also who were there and bring them in bonds to Jerusalem to be punished" (Acts 22:5), historical fact could not be one of them.

Paul was impotent to act in that fashion both politically and legally (Haenchen, *Acts,* p. 298). Acts wanted to exaggerate the monstrous persecution which Paul conducted against the Christians prior to his calling so as to show with greater effulgence the "mighty works of God" in Paul's divinely operated transformation from the dreaded persecutor of the Name to its intrepid proclaimer.

There is, of course, the fact of Paul having persecuted the Christians—a fact on which both Acts and Paul agree: "I persecuted the church of God violently and tried to destroy it" (Gal 1:13; 1 Cor 15:9; Phil 3:6). But, despite the specific elements with which Luke, for his own theological reasons (Acts 7:58; 8:1, 3; 9:1–2, etc.), embellishes his account, we have to be content with the bare fact that Paul persecuted the Church violently, with fanatic zeal, and that he even tried to destroy it. In the final analysis, this is of more importance to understanding the incident on the road to Damascus than any theological or artistic embellishments of the event.

The Book of Acts, of course, is quite clear that the event took place on the way to Damascus. In the account in Galatians, Paul himself says, "and again I returned to Damascus" (Gal 1:17; see 2 Cor 11:32). This might very well indicate a link of the incident with the environs of that great city. Moreover, in his account of what happened afterward, Paul makes no mention of Ananias or anyone else as party to the incident, but states unequivocally, "I did not confer with flesh and blood" (Gal 1:16), and adds—contradicting Acts 9:26—"nor did I go up to Jerusalem" (Gal 1:17).

What Paul does say about the aftermath of the incident is: "I went away into Arabia; and again I returned to Damascus. Then after three years I went up to Jerusalem to visit Cephas" (Gal 1:17–18). About this considerable period of time, Acts is silent, Paul himself is not very forthcoming, and we are left to wonder what he did after God "was pleased to reveal his Son to [in]" him (Gal 1:15–16).

10. The Event on the Way to Damascus

Before attempting to say what happened on the way to Damascus, we have to keep in mind what has hitherto been said about the two kinds of evidence we have for the incident: the evidence in the Acts of the Apostles and that in the letters of Paul. Paul does not give an account of his own vocation even while acknowledging the fact that he is called by God, who "set me apart before I was born, and had called me through his grace" (Gal 1:15). He knows the "upward call of God in Christ Jesus" (Phil 3:14). He insists repeatedly that he is "called to be an apostle" (Rom 1:1), "called by the will of God to be an apostle of Christ Jesus" (1 Cor 1:1). But nowhere does he give the particulars of that call. Indeed, by acknowledging his having been set apart before his birth (Gal 1:15), he puts his vocation itself into the inaccessible realm of mystery—where any genuine vocation properly belongs.

In its triple recital of the Damascus incident, on the other hand, the Acts of the Apostles casts the account into the form of a vocation narrative very much along the lines of the Old Testament accounts of the calling of Abraham, Jacob, and Moses. In Acts, the account itself is not—strictly speaking—the account of a conversion, although Paul is presented as a vicious persecutor of "the Way" before the incident, and as a tireless and indomitable preacher "in the name of Jesus" (Acts 9:27) after it. Thus, to reassure the apprehensive Jerusalem Church about the dreaded Paul, Barnabas "declared to them how on the road [Paul] had seen the Lord, who spoke to him, and how at Damascus he had preached boldly in the name of Jesus" (Acts 9:27). But, as we shall have occasion to remark, a conversion is more than a mere change of attitude. The author of Acts, in pursuit of his own legitimate—and apologetically sound—theological goals, insists on the continuity between Paul's Jewish past and his Christian present. To speak of conversion, however, is to speak of a profound discontinuity, a rupture between what was and what has become.

Another—and no less important—point of difference between Paul and Acts has to do with the interpretation of the event itself. One has the impression from Acts that all that that fanatically menacing Jew needed was an encounter with the risen Lord to turn him into a zealously restless proclaimer of the Name. When his own fellow Jews found him "a pestilent fellow, an agitator among the Jews throughout the world, and a ringleader of the sect of the Nazarenes" (Acts 24:5), Paul hastened to reassure them:

> But this I admit to you, that according to the Way, which they call a sect (*hairesis*), I worship the God of our fathers, believing everything laid down by the law or written in the prophets (Acts 24:14).

According to Acts, far from having abandoned the faith of his fathers, Paul was all the more faithful to it by embracing the Way. Indeed, the real point at issue in Acts is reducible to faith in the resurrection. Paul, standing before "the chief priests and all the council" (Acts 22:30), flatly states: "With respect to the hope and the resurrection of the dead I am on trial" (Acts 23:6)—a hope which he, "a Pharisee, a son of Pharisees" (Acts 23:6), shared in common with them (see Acts 23:8). Therefore, Paul's "conversion" in Acts cannot be regarded as anything but the logical outcome of his fidelity to Judaism.

Consequently, when Acts recounts the Damascus incident it is eager to show God's mighty work in the calling of this great apostle. According to it, Paul saw "a great light from heaven" (Acts 9:3; 22:6; 26:13) and heard a voice. This was very much what is called a "theophany," the appearance of the glory of the Lord, much like the theophanies vouchsafed Abraham, Jacob and Moses, but quite unlike the appearances of the risen Jesus in the fellowship and intimacy which we find in Luke 24 and in Acts 1:3–4. This distinction too is part of Luke's theological point of view, where the function of witnessing to the resurrection belongs specifically—perhaps even exclusively—to the Twelve:

> So one of the men who have accompanied us during all the time that the Lord Jesus went in and out among us, beginning from the baptism of John until he was taken up from us—one of these men must become with us a witness to his resurrection (Acts 1:21–22).

According to these norms and within Luke's theological viewpoint, Paul does not qualify as an "apostle." Indeed, almost nowhere does Acts call him *apostolos,* except only in 14:14.

Paul himself, however, sees the turning point in his life very much in the light of a prophetic calling. He sees it in terms of a radical conversion. When he writes to the Galatians that God "set me apart before I was born, and had called me through his grace," he is harking back to Jeremiah:

> Before I formed you in the womb I knew you, and before you were born I consecrated you; I appointed you a prophet to the nations (Jer 1:5),

as well as to Isaiah:

> The Lord called me from the womb, from the body of my mother he named my name (Is 49:1);

> I will give you as a light to the nations, that my salvation may reach to the end of the earth (Is 49:6; compare 42:6–7).

It is to be noted that the word "nations" in the above passages in the Greek is *ethne,* which is usually translated "Gentiles." In the letters he addressed to the "Gentile" churches, Paul's whole life is seen as "set apart for the gospel of God, which he promised beforehand through his prophets in the holy scriptures . . . to bring about the obedience of faith for the sake of his name among all the nations (*ethne*)" (Rom 1:1, 5).

In the opening of his letter to the Romans, Paul insists on the fact that "grace and apostleship" came to him through "Jesus Christ our Lord" (Rom 1:4). He reminds the Galatians that the God who set him apart before he was born and called him through his grace "was pleased to reveal his Son to/in me" (Gal 1:15–16). He is more explicit still when, having listed the order of appearances of the risen Lord, he adds:

> Last of all, as to one untimely born, he appeared also to me (1 Cor 15:8).

He thus regards himself as on a par with those privileged to have seen the risen Lord:

> Am I not an apostle? Have I not seen Jesus our Lord? (1 Cor 9:1).

What precisely that "seeing" entailed, it is difficult to say and idle to speculate. Paul speaks elsewhere—again reluctantly, "there is nothing to be gained by it"—of "visions and revelations of the Lord" (2 Cor 12:1):

> I know a man in Christ who fourteen years ago was caught up to the third heaven—whether in the body or out of the body I do not know, God knows. And I know that this man was caught up into paradise—whether in the body or out of the body I do not know, God knows—which man may not utter (2 Cor 12:2–4).

The date of "fourteen years ago" is hard to fix but significant. There are in the Book of Acts references to incidents that took place after the road to Damascus, such as a "trance (*ekstasis*)" in Jerusalem (Acts 22:17–21), a "vision" in Corinth (Acts 18:9–10), a night when the Lord "stood by him" in Jerusalem (Acts 23:11), and, on the final voyage to Rome, one night "there stood by me an angel of the God to whom I belong and whom I worship" (Acts 27:23). But here we need to keep two things in mind: first, the experience Paul describes in 2 Corinthians 12 "cannot be equated with any recorded in Acts" (F.F. Bruce, p. 246); second, the "fourteen years ago" as well as Paul's description of the event itself precludes any connection with the Damascus incident (J. Hering, p. 91). It is doubtful, moreover, whether the vision mentioned in 2 Corinthians 12 is to be identified with any of the experiences mentioned in Acts, which has a tendency to multiply such phenomena.

To tell the truth, what Paul has to say about the "visions and revelations" is not very enlightening. His reference to "fourteen years" ago in a "boasting" contest with his Corinthian rivals would lead one to believe that the incident was unique and quite distinct from the Damascus incident.

11. Paul's "Conversion"

If by "conversion" we mean turning away resolutely from one cherished object in order to embrace another, then, so far as we can judge from Paul's own evidence in his letters, the Damascus incident was a conversion. As we have already had occasion to note, the Acts of the Apostles regarded the incident in quite a different light. It saw it rather as a vocation, a calling of Paul to be sent "far away to the Gentiles" (Acts 22:21). Of course, Acts does speak of Paul's former life as a persecutor of "this way to the death" (Acts 22:4; 9:5; 22:7–8; 26:14–15), but Paul remains, for all intents and purposes, what he was before: a pious and zealous Jew, even if his zeal thenceforth took a more positive character.

The picture we get from Paul's letters, however, is quite different. We see a radical break with the past, a fundamental change in outlook. It is, of course, misleading to imagine the change as instantaneous and the clarity of the vision as total. A period of time had to elapse (Gal 1:17–18) to allow for the maturation and the appropriation of the insight, as well as for the appreciation of its painful and exacting consequences. These consequences received even clearer expression in Paul's exhortations to the churches, in the debates with his opponents, and in the clashes with his erstwhile co-religionists, the Jews. Acts transforms all this into a different key, where harmony and accord sound the dominant motif.

But in order to understand the importance of the Damascus experience as a conversion, in the proper sense of the word, it is necessary to look at what Paul was before it and what he became after it. Paul himself describes well what he was before the experience:

> Circumcised on the eighth day, of the people of Israel, of the tribe of Benjamin, a Hebrew born of Hebrews; as to the law a Pharisee, as to zeal a persecutor of the church, as to righteousness under the law blameless (Phil 3:5–6; see Rom 11:1; 2 Cor 11:22).

Elsewhere, he speaks of his "former life in Judaism" as one in which he advanced "beyond many of my own age among my people, so extremely zealous was I for the traditions of my fathers" (Gal 1:13–14)—which is no idle boast, and certainly no small accomplishment. Reluctant though he was to boast (Gal 1:10; Phil 3:4), there can be no mistaking his pride in what he was. This, of course, is a point of the utmost importance. For, all too often, Paul's conversion is seen in the light of the great conversions of a sinful Augustine, a tormented Martin Luther, or an anguished Paul Claudel: guilt, anguish, and human frailty in quest of forgiveness, healing, and hope.

This was not the case with Paul. He was not having what in today's jargon is called an "identity crisis"—far from it. He knew all too well who he was, and was, moreover, proud of what he was. He was certainly not the philosopher embarking upon a tortuous and soul-searing quest for the truth; nor was he the religious fanatic tormented by self-doubt, hag-ridden by the scruples of his past, and convulsed by the nausea of self-disgust. Everything he tells us about the man on the road to Damascus points to a completely different image of a proud, self-assured and confident individual who knew precisely what he was about. He did not come crawling and begging to this turning point in his life, nor did he gradually grow into it as an anticipated and patiently awaited maturation, nor was he grasping for it as someone drowning reaches desperately for any hope of deliverance.

The picture we get from Paul was quite different. It was the Lord who encountered him, turned his plans upside down, and his life inside out. It was then that Paul began to realize that all he had striven for and achieved, all he had worked for and accomplished, all he had sought to be and had become—all that counted for nothing:

> But whatever gain I had, I counted as loss for the sake of Christ (Phil 3:7).

Paul's conversion was certainly not that of the religiously destitute. It was not the conversion of someone who had nothing and came upon unexpected riches. We misunderstand Paul and belittle divine grace if we imagine what he was before his conversion was bad or inconsiderable. His circumcision on the eighth day, his belonging to the people of Israel, his being a "Hebrew born of Hebrews," his Pharisaism, his zeal for the law, and his "blamelessness" under it (Phil 3:5–6) were inestimable assets of which he was rightly proud. They were a real "gain," genuine and solid accomplishments, of which he could justifiably boast. But—and this is crucial for understanding the conversion—by the grace of that singular encounter with the Lord, Paul came to regard all that as worse than worthless. He saw it as "loss."

The incident on the way to Damascus, judged by what Paul himself says about it, was a conversion, a complete turning away from what was genuinely good to its everlasting enemy, the better. To forget this is to reduce Paul's conversion to the penitence of a Mary Magdalene, the repentance of the good thief, or the bitter tears of a remorseful Peter. Paul's was simply not that kind of conversion. What he was and what he possessed before was neither bad nor nothing. It was simply "loss" or, as he himself more boldly says, "refuse" (*skybala* = dung) (Phil 3:8).

12. The Terms of the Conversion

To understand the conversion of Paul itself—not the event that triggered it, which remains ultimately beyond our grasp—we must examine a bit more closely its points of departure and arrival: From what and to what was Paul converted? To put it this way implies, of course, that the conversion was a process, and that, however compelling and overwhelming it might have been at its initial moment of impact, it took a good deal of time—indeed a whole lifetime—to unfold its significance and to reveal its implications. The rest of his life, in its trials and sufferings, in its controversies and confrontations, and in its untiring proclamation of the gospel of Jesus Christ, contributed to Paul's own comprehension of what it was that happened so long ago on the road to Damascus. Similarly, whatever he wrote to the various churches, his very understanding of the "insight into the mystery of Christ" (Eph 3:4), was directly attributable to that initial experience. If the conversion itself is dwelt upon at some length here, it is because a proper understanding of it is indispensable for any understanding of Paul's own gospel.

Thus, to understand the conversion as a process from a known point of departure to an even better known point of arrival, we have to look at what Paul himself says he was before it and what he became after it. For the former, we have those passages in which Paul speaks of his past life in Judaism (Phil 3:5–6; Gal 1:13–14; 1 Cor 15:9); and for the latter, we have not only these same autobiographical passages but also the whole collection of his letters, where in innumerable ways—both directly and indirectly—we get a glimpse of what he became.

What Paul was is best summed up in his own words:

> Circumcised on the eighth day,
> of the people of Israel,
> of the tribe of Benjamin,
> a Hebrew born of Hebrews;
> as to the law a Pharisee,
> as to zeal a persecutor of the church,
> as to righteousness under the law blameless (Phil 3:5–6).

This passage is straightforward enough not to require any elaborate interpretation. Yet it is a passage that has been prey to the temptation of facile dismissal as mere hyperbole, just another rhetorical device to serve the manifestly polemical and apologetic ends of the letter to the Philippians (see Phil 3:2–3). But, to do Paul justice, one must take him at his word. He knew, perhaps better than most, that there was nothing to be gained by boasting (2 Cor 12:1). What he says about his past is to be taken literally, even in—especially in—those assertions that most offend our theological or exegetical presuppositions.

If his Jewish descent poses no problem, and if his Pharisaic legalism and zealous persecution of the Church pose even less, his "blamelessness under the law" certainly does. The first is genealogically neuter, or so we think; the second is the very stuff of conversion stories, or so we like to think; but the third sounds too good to be true, or so have we been led to think. Paul's polemic against the law and against legalism has accustomed us to see the material impossibility of fulfilling "the law." We think too readily of passages in Paul's letters which lend force to such a view of the law:

> So I find it to be a law that when I want to do right, evil lies close at hand. For I delight in the law of God, in my inmost self, but I see in my members another law at war with the law of my mind and making me captive to the law of sin which dwells in my members (Rom 7:21–23).

We forget too easily that, precisely in passages such as this, Paul is speaking of his Christian present, not of his Jewish past.

Moreover, pious tracts and edifying biographies have made it difficult for us to imagine any conversion other than the one from hopeless sinfulness, or from despair at ever attaining genuine goodness. But Paul's conversion was different. Its starting point was not the "slough of Despond" or the "valley of Humiliation," but the high plateau of pride in genuine achievement. His boast, "as to righteousness under the law blameless," was no hyperbole. The law could be kept integrally and blamelessly—else it would have been but the cruel instrument of a capricious God. Others in Israel's long history did keep it. One has but to think of Hannah and Samuel in the First Book of Samuel, of Simeon and Anna in Luke 2, and of those numberless and nameless Israelites who could say with the psalmist and mean it:

> For I have kept the ways of the Lord
> and have not wickedly departed from my God.
> For all his ordinances were before me,
> and his statutes I did not put away from me.
> I was blameless before him,
> and I kept myself from guilt (Ps 18:21–23; see Ps 101:2, 6;
>   119:1, 80; Sir 15:15).

No, the law was not impossible to keep; and Paul was among those who did keep it, and could therefore rightly say "as to righteousness under the law blameless."

To add, as many readers of Philippians are inclined to do, that the law was impossible to keep *perfectly* would be either to misunderstand the law or to qualify its observance meaninglessly. Paul kept the law as "blamelessly" as he could keep it—not as someone else might keep it or imagine that Paul should keep it—and that was to keep it "perfectly." Nor was Paul unique in this. There were people who, like Zechariah and Elizabeth, walked "in all the commandments and ordinances of the Lord blameless" (Lk 1:6).

It was from that unexaggerated and accurately assessed position of moral integrity and spiritual achievement that Paul's conversion had its starting point. What Paul was, was good and laudable. He had every reason to be proud of it; for it was neither a trifling task to set for oneself, nor a distinction easily attained. Of course, once attained, such an ideal was not lightly relinquished; and it was perhaps the recollection of the price he had paid for that "blamelessness" that inspired and redoubled Paul's zeal in persecuting the Church.

Therefore, what is most astonishing in Paul's account in Philippians 3 is the radical change, the total reversal of values:

> But whatever gain I had, I counted as loss. . . . Indeed I count everything as loss . . . and count [all things] as refuse (Phil 3:7–8).

Here, in a nutshell, is the essence of Paul's conversion: all that he was, all that he had achieved, all that of which he was justly proud and in which he could rightly boast, he now counted as "refuse." What he aspired to and attained, what he worked for and accomplished, what he wanted to be and had become—all that was worthless nothing, even less than nothing.

Few are those who rightly appreciate, not the struggle itself, but the resolve to undertake it. Fewer still are they who can comprehend what is involved in such reversal. Most of us tend to view an event like Paul's conversion from our own pusillanimous point of view; and herein lies the danger of romanticizing the account to rob it of its compelling realism, or supernaturalizing it to deprive it of its challenge. Whatever happened to Paul on the road to Damascus altered his life radically, reversed the scale of his values, and made his vision of all things utterly new. Not the event itself, which in the final analysis lies shrouded in mystery, but the resulting conversion as such is where the meaning and the challenge of the account for the reader are to be sought.

Just a brief word about the event itself. The reluctance to specify it arises, not from any unwillingness to countenance the divine intervention, but from an acute awareness—in this case, as in any other recorded either in the Old or the New Testament—of its mysterious nature and its inscrutable workings, because, ultimately, those who, like Paul, had had such encounters in their lives possessed neither the words to describe them nor the means of communicating their real nature to others. We, on the other hand, lack the means of comprehending such privileged individuals even when they try to communicate their experiences. In other words, I can well understand what Paul means when he says he saw Cephas and James in Jerusalem (Gal 1:18–19). Encountering other living beings is the kind of experience I have daily in my life. But when Paul says that he saw Jesus our Lord (1 Cor 9:1), I—who have never had anything remotely resembling such an encounter—can only either believe Paul or refuse to believe him. Of course, those who do not see, or are unwilling to see, a difference between Paul meeting Peter and Paul encountering the risen Jesus will—in all likelihood—be baffled by this. Their bafflement will, I hope, be allayed when the question of the resurrection is taken up (see below, No. 28).

Furthermore, I myself have to confess to a prejudice on this point. Whenever anyone tries to explain an event like the encounter with the risen Jesus to me, I turn skeptical: not because no one can have such an experience, nor because of a reluctance on my part to believe anyone who does, but simply because anyone pretending to explain it could not have had the same kind of experience, consequently lacks the means to comprehend it, and, therefore, could not be talking about the same thing that Paul writes about. Paul's experience, like any genuine experience of the kind, is literally ineffable; it cannot be put into words.

Paul himself simply states the fact: that Christ "appeared" to him (1 Cor 15:8), that God was pleased to "reveal his Son to him"—or as the Greek more inscrutably has it, "in him" (Gal 1:16), that he had had "visions and revelations (*apokalypsis*) of the Lord" (2 Cor 12:1–4; compare Gal 1:12). He knew, as all those who have had the genuine experience must know, that it was a thing that "could not be told, which man may not utter" (2 Cor 12:4). And, as Wittgenstein says in his *Tractatus:* "Wovon man nicht sprechen kann, darüber muss man schweigen" (what is unutterable should be passed over in silence). To inquire further into it would be to inquire too curiously indeed.

Of course, this attitude need not and cannot prevent us from asking: What lay behind Paul's conversion?

13. Paul's Fundamental "Insight"

Given the above reservations about the ultimate knowableness of the event itself, it must be evident that the question "What lay behind Paul's conversion?" can only be answered by a consideration of what—for lack of a more accurate and appropriate term—we might call Paul's fundamental "insight." This is to ask a question that derives immediately from Paul's statement that he "saw" the Lord (1 Cor 9:1), that the Lord "appeared" to him (1 Cor 15:8). Our question is not "What did he see?" or "How did he *see* the Lord?" but rather "What did Paul make of the vision, the appearance, the post-paschal epiphany, or call it what you will? What was it that Paul grasped for the first time and with such vehemence that he underwent a conversion?"

This question of course is not peculiar to the case of Paul. Any one of those mentioned in 1 Corinthians 15:5–8 (Cephas, the twelve, the five hundred brethren, James, all the apostles) had to be more than the passive beneficiaries of such an appearance of the risen Lord. In the appearance, and through it, those so privileged grasped a fact that hitherto lay hidden from them, but which, once grasped, could not but alter their entire existence. Whoever the beneficiaries of those resurrection appearances were, they could not but understand the meaning of the life and death of Jesus of Nazareth in such a way as to feel the irresistible compulsion to proclaim the good news to the whole world. This, after all, is what we have grown accustomed to refer to as the start of the Christian mission. For it was ultimately those "happy few" who were responsible—in one way or another—for all the "early traditions," "pre-Pauline sources," "primitive Christian community," etc., which modern biblical criticism has made current and commonplace in the discussion of the New Testament message.

So when we ask a question such as "What lay behind Paul's conversion?" we single Paul out because, in his case, we are uniquely fortunate in possessing his own elaboration of that fundamental insight throughout a corpus of letters written to different churches, on different occasions, and in answer to a variety of questions—on faith and the life of faith—which arose out of the Christ event, out of the attempt to appropriate and translate it into various cultures, and out of the struggle to lead one's life in response to it. Nevertheless, in responding to this question, we shall limit ourselves to the Philippians 3 passage with which we have hitherto been dealing. But we have to keep in mind that, in fact, the discussion of any page of any epistle of Paul contributes inevitably, in some way, to the answer.

Having sketched his background in Judaism (Phil 3:4–6; see also Rom 11:1 and 2 Cor 11:22), and having stated the fact of his conversion (Phil 3:7–8; note also the past tense of "persecuted" in 1 Cor 15:9 and "my *former* life" in Gal 1:13)—Paul gives the reason behind it:

> Indeed I count everything as loss because of the surpassing worth of knowing Christ Jesus my Lord. For his sake I have suffered the loss of all things, and count them as refuse, in order that I may gain Christ and be found in him, not having a righteousness of my own, based on the law, but that which is through faith in Christ, the righteousness from God that depends on faith (Phil 3:8–9).

The "surpassing worth of knowing Christ Jesus my Lord" constitutes what we referred to above as the fundamental insight of the conversion. Paul himself speaks of it elsewhere as God being "pleased to reveal his Son to/in me" (Gal 1:16). It is because of this insight into, this revelation of, the "surpassing worth" that Paul had to reverse the scale of his values, to see all his hard-won righteousness "based on the law" as total loss. It was not a question of whether that righteousness was good or bad; it was simply worthless, even less than worthless, when compared to that righteousness which is now available "through faith in Christ, the righteousness from God that depends on faith" (Phil 3:9).

One can readily comprehend the convulsive violence, the cruel wrenching that such an insight was bound to produce. But one can also readily imagine the prior and protracted resistance to even consider its mere possibility. If Paul persecuted the Christians, then he must have had some idea of what they stood for, and that must have posed a considerable threat to him and to his prized spiritual possessions. It surely cannot be very difficult to see, upon brief reflection, that Paul, "a Pharisee" (Phil 3:5) who had "advanced in Judaism beyond many of my own age among my people" and who was "extremely zealous . . . for the traditions of my fathers" (Gal 1:13), could not and would not have been so fanatically roused by the proclamation of a truth which he, as a Pharisee, already professed.

This point, of course, was not lost on the author of the Book of Acts:

> But when Paul perceived that one part were Sadducees and the other Pharisees, he cried out in the council, "Brethren, I am a Pharisee, a son of Pharisees; with respect to the hope and the resurrection of the dead I am on trial." And when he had said this, a dissension arose between the Pharisees and Sadducees; and the assembly was divided. For the Sadducees say that there is no resurrection, nor angel, nor spirit; but the Pharisees acknowledge them all (Acts 23:6–8).

It is not very easy to imagine Paul persecuting the Christians just because of their faith in the resurrection, even the resurrection of Jesus of Nazareth. Had Paul, a Pharisee and therefore a believer in the resurrection of the dead, rejected specifically the belief in the resurrection of Jesus, it would still be hard to imagine his rejection of it on so monstrous a scale as to require persecuting the Church of God "violently" and trying to "destroy" it (Gal 1:13; see 1 Tim 1:13). The passage just quoted from Acts 23:6–8 shows an astute theological mind insisting that "the bridges between Jews and Christians have not been broken" (Haenchen, *Acts,* p. 643). Surely, the author of Acts could have entertained no such notion had faith in the resurrection of Jesus been *the* insurmountable obstacle for a Jewish believer. No! To explain the fanatic vehemence of Paul and his resistance to the new faith, the resurrection of Jesus of Nazareth had to signify a good deal more than the specific instance of what a Pharisee believed and hoped to be the lot of all the just. What alone could explain Paul's sworn enmity to and persecution of the nascent faith had to be the insight into the ineluctable consequences deriving from the resurrection of Jesus: consequences which, once accepted, would unsparingly overthrow and alter the meaning of Paul's hard-earned righteousness. It was that righteousness which had to be relinquished, that "blamelessness under the law" which had to be counted as loss and discarded as refuse.

Faith in that righteousness could not exist simultaneously with "the righteousness from God that depends on faith" (Phil 3:9). If Paul had any remote inklings of such unsparing consequences of the message preached by the Christians, then one can readily understand his zeal as a persecutor intent upon destroying the Church (Gal 1:13; Phil 3:6; 1 Cor 15:8). If, prior to his conversion, Paul had resolved to "destroy" the Church, that could only have been for a reciprocally destructive threat posed by the Church to Paul's cherished Jewish faith. Certainly, that is how his conversion was viewed by his fellow Christians:

> He who once persecuted us is now preaching the faith he once tried to destroy (Gal 1:23).

If Paul felt the need to add here, "And they glorified God because of me" (Gal 1:24), it was because the conversion was

God's work and no one else's. To God alone belongs the glory of Paul's transformation from the persecutor of the faith to its proclaimer. As Augustine put it so well, "What does he who reckons his merits before you do except number your own gifts?" (*Confessions,* IX.13.34).

What Paul proclaimed was precisely the righteousness "which is through faith in Christ, the righteousness from God that depends on faith," and no longer "a righteousness of my own, based on law" (Phil 3:9). In other words, what was radically altered was precisely Paul's view of salvation. The new understanding of salvation was so different that it rendered any prior understanding, not erroneous, but worthless, impotent, and helpless. What Paul grasped, or rather what took hold of him in his conversion, was precisely the new understanding of salvation made necessary by the death and resurrection of Christ. And this is what lay behind Paul's conversion.

14. Paul after the "Conversion"

Though we discussed at some length the "conversion" of Paul, we must not lose sight of the fact that—as we saw above in No. 10—he himself regarded the incident, not only as a conversion ("my former life in Judaism"—Gal 1:13), but also as a call. He spoke of it in the accents of the ancient prophets' call to ministry. Thus, he writes of God as having "set me apart before I was born . . . called me through his grace" (Gal 1:15), and, of himself, as "one untimely born" (1 Cor 15:8). Such statements are clear echoes of:

> The Lord called me from the womb, from the body of my mother he named my name (Is 49:1);

> Before I formed you in the womb I knew you, and before you were born I consecrated you (Jer 1:5).

Paul's call was to be "an apostle" (Rom 1:1), "an apostle of Christ Jesus by the will of God" (2 Cor 1:1). He had no

doubt that the purpose of God's revelation of his Son to him
was "in order that I might preach him among the Gentiles"
(Gal 1:16). He linked his apostleship, his call and his mission
by the Lord directly to that event which we have described as
his conversion:

> Am I not an apostle? Have I not seen Jesus our Lord? (1
> Cor 9:1).

Everything Paul did after that event was, in his own eyes, an
obedience to the God who revealed his Son to him and called
him to be a bearer of his name "among all the nations" (Rom
1:5; see Acts 9:15; 22:15; 26:16–18).

Here we have to admit that our information about what
Paul did between that momentous event and the first letter
we have from him is extremely scanty. The period of time is
not inconsiderable. Between fourteen and seventeen years
passed, years when a great deal must have happened to reduce the insight of the road to Damascus to the myriad details
of a life so lived that Paul could, without the slightest exag-
geration, say:

> By the grace of God I am what I am, and his grace toward
> me was not in vain (1 Cor 15:10).

Practically all we know about those years from Paul himself is what he tells us in Galatians:

> I went away into Arabia; and again I returned to Damas-
> cus.
> Then after three years I went up to Jerusalem to visit Ce-
> phas. . . .
> Then I went into the region of Syria and Cilicia. . . .
> Then after fourteen years I went up again to Jerusalem
> . . . (Gal 1:17–2:1).

The Book of Acts, of course, is more forthcoming. A good
deal of what it tells us could well provide some indication of
what Paul did after the incident on the road to Damascus. His
being "with the disciples at Damascus," his proclamation of

Jesus in the synagogues, and the foreseeable reaction of those who heard him (Acts 9:19b–21) give us a fair picture that is not contradicted by Paul himself. Even the plot to kill him and his escape "over the wall . . . in a basket" (Acts 9:23–35) might be said to find corroboration in 2 Corinthians 11:32–33:

> At Damascus, the governor under King Aretas guarded the city of Damascus in order to seize me, but I was let down in a basket through a window in the wall, and escaped his hands.

Moreover, the decade that passed between the first letter and his death is barely enough time to accommodate that daunting list of his sufferings and trials which he gives us:

> Five times I have received at the hands of the Jews the forty lashes less one. Three times I have been beaten with rods; once I was stoned. Three times I have been shipwrecked; a night and a day I have been adrift at sea . . . (2 Cor 11:24–25).

Even statistically such a list requires a good deal more than ten years, especially in an age when travel was slow, the pace of life relaxed, and time itself measured in days and weeks, and not in minutes and seconds.

But all this still leaves us in the realm of conjecture. What we have to deal with is almost total ignorance of those important years that elapsed between the conversion and the first letter we have from Paul's hand. In commenting on Acts 9, which tells us seemingly so much, Ernst Haenchen remarks that "where the tradition used by Luke was really deficient was in its total ignorance of Paul's sojourn in 'Arabia.' It can be easily understood that Christian tradition contained nothing about it." (Haenchen, *Acts*, p. 334). Of course, the vacuum left by the silence of the sources has been fancifully filled over the years by images of an eremitical Paul withdrawing into the desert to pray and meditate and—had common sense been less common—to make the "Spiritual Exercises." But it is the part of wisdom here to admit our ignorance and, however much biography may abhor a vacuum, to leave the vacuum unfilled. In this restraint is the asceticism of genuine scholarship.

It might be useful at this point to recall that the "Arabia" mentioned by Paul in Galatians was not the *deserta* but the *provincia*, i.e., not the forbidding Arabian Desert, but the Roman province comprising the region to the south and the southeast of Damascus.

The Book of Acts, however, was "entirely correct" in taking it for granted that "Paul after his conversion immediately began his missionary career" (Haenchen, *Acts*, p. 335). Furthermore, we see from Galatians that that initial stage of Paul's missionary career was centered around Damascus and in the region referred to as "Arabia." But what form that missionary activity took, what success it achieved, and what obstacles it encountered remains unknown to us. Even the most fervid historical imagination can get no purchase here.

THREE

Paul's Epistles

15. Chronology

The chronology of Paul's life is a problem that has eluded satisfactory solution. The Acts of the Apostles, which could have been of immense help toward that solution, does not altogether satisfy our curiosity, despite its seemingly great concern for historical accuracy. Paul's own dating of the events in his life is scanty. It comes down to this:

(1) the conversion (Gal 1:15–16);
(2) going away "into Arabia" and again returning to Damascus (Gal 1:17);
(3) "then *after three years*" going to Jerusalem "to visit Cephas, and remained with him fifteen days" (Gal 1:18);
(4) then going "into the regions of Syria and Cilicia" (Gal 1:21);
(5) "then *after fourteen years*" going up again to Jerusalem with Barnabas (Gal 2:1).

There are thus two distinct visits to Jerusalem mentioned by Paul. The first, that in Galatians 1:18, is doubtless the one mentioned in Acts 9:26. This visit—on Paul's own account—was his only visit prior to the Apostolic Council, so that the story told in Acts 11:27–30 about the famine prophesied by Agabus and the relief mission by "Barnabas and Saul" is in the end more confusing than helpful in establishing a chronology.

The second visit to Jerusalem, that "after fourteen years . . . with Barnabas, taking Titus along" (Gal 2:1), is the one for

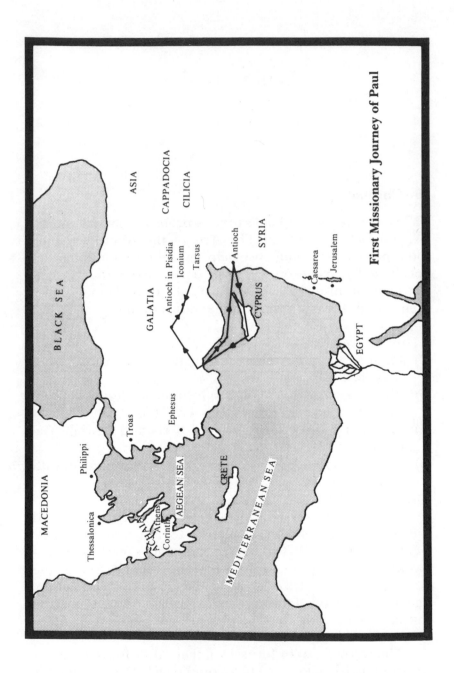

First Missionary Journey of Paul

the Apostolic Council (Acts 15). It provides a convenient dividing line in Paul's ministry, since all his extant letters date from the period following that Council. Unfortunately, the "after fourteen years" remains ambiguous: Is the count from the conversion, or from the first visit to Jerusalem? In other words, are we dealing with a period of seventeen years or fourteen? This ambiguity will necessarily affect any chronological listing of Paul's missionary activitiy. So what is needed is some solidly established calendar date on which to fix this sliding scale.

Here both the Book of Acts and modern archaeology conspire to provide just such a calendaric fix. In Acts 18, Luke recounts Paul's activity in Corinth and remarks:

> But when Gallio was proconsul of Achaia, the Jews made a united attack upon Paul and brought him before the tribunal (Acts 18:12).

This proconsulship of Gallio in Achaia, the region where Corinth is situated, can be dated fairly accurately, thanks to a discovery early in this century of four stone fragments at Delphi. The inscription on the fragments allows epigraphists to reconstruct the text as follows:

> Tiberius [Claudius] Caesar Augustus Germanicus, [Pontifex Maximus, in his tribunician] power [year 12, acclaimed emperor for] the 26th time, father of the country, [consul for the 5th time, censor, sends greeting to the city of Delphi].
> I have long been zealous for the city of Delphi [and favourable to it from the] beginning, and I have always observed the cult of the [Pythian] Apollo, [but with regard to]
> the present stories, and those quarrels of the citizens of which [a report has been made by Lucius] Junius Gallio my friend, and [pro]consul [of Achaea] . . . (see C.K. Barrett, *The New Testament Background*, pp. 48–49).

When account has been taken of the bracketed material as conjectural—which is not to say that it is either false or fanciful—three solid points call for attention: the name of the emperor, the number "26th time," and "Junius Gallio." Without going into all the details (see C.K. Barrett, no. 46, p. 48), the information comes down to this: that "Gallio must have taken office in Corinth (the seat of government for Achaea) about the first of May 51" (Haenchen, *Acts,* pp. 66–67). Thus the year A.D. 51 can serve as a fixed point in history from which a chronology of Paul's life after his conversion can be determined with relative certainty:

35	the conversion (or, if you choose to total up the "three years" of Galatians 1:18 with the "fourteen years" in 2:1, then adjust this and all subsequent dates by three years; i.e., read "32" rather than "35" for the date of the conversion, etc.);
35–38	"went away into Arabia" (Gal 1:17);
38	"went up to Jerusalem to visit Cephas" (Gal 1:18; Acts 9:26–30);
38–48	"went into the region of Syria and Cilicia" (Gal 1:21);
48	"went up again to Jerusalem with Barnabas" for the Apostolic Council (Gal 2:1; Acts 15); and shortly thereafter in
48 or 49	mission in Galatia (Acts 16:6);
50	mission in Philippi, Thessalonica, and Beroea (Acts 16:11–17:14)—traveling to Athens (Acts 17:15) and thence to Corinth (Acts 18:1), where *First Thessalonians* was written;
autumn 50 to spring 52	Paul stayed "a year and six months" in Corinth (Acts 18:1);

summer of 52 to winter of 55–56	traveled to Antioch and Ephesus (Acts 18); revisited Galatia; the mission at Ephesus (Acts 19:1); a visit to Corinth (2 Cor 13:1); and the imprisonment in Ephesus: to which period we owe the writing of *Galatians, First Corinthians,* the correspondence contained in *Second Corinthians,* and the "Captivity Epistles" (i.e., from the Ephesian prison): the correspondence in *Philippians,* and *Philemon;*
winter of 55–56	stay in Corinth, whence *Romans* was written;
56	the journey to Jerusalem;
58	"and so we came to Rome" (Acts 28:14);
60	Paul's death.

As can be seen from this chronology (adapted from Koester, *Introduction,* vol. 2, pp. 103 104), Paul's life as a Christian is divisible into two principal parts: from his conversion around the year 35, to the Apostolic Council in Jerusalem in A.D. 48; and from the Apostolic Council to his death around A.D. 60. His age at the time of his conversion is a matter of conjecture based largely on the legend about "a *young man* named Saul" being present at Stephen's martyrdom in Acts 7:58.

What is more important for a proper estimate of the dates assigned to the various events is their relation to the one fact from which they derive their significance: the death of Jesus. In the above chronological scheme, that event should be put around the year 30. Consequently, Paul's conversion would have taken place some three to five years after the crucifixion of Jesus of Nazareth.

We should remember furthermore that the letters we have from Paul, from the earliest (First Thessalonians) to the last (Romans), all date from the period after the Apostolic Council, when an agreement was reached between Paul and the Jerusalem "pillars," James and Cephas and John, that

Paul and Barnabas "should go to the Gentiles and they to the circumcised" (Gal 2:9). The subsequent decade was crammed with missionary endeavors, endless voyages, and what Paul himself calls "the daily pressure upon me of my anxiety for all the churches" (2 Cor 11:28).

16. The Pauline Epistles

There are in the New Testament fourteen epistles that bear, or once bore, the name of Paul in their titles: Romans, 1 and 2 Corinthians, Galatians, Ephesians, Philippians, Colossians, 1 and 2 Thessalonians, 1 and 2 Timothy, Titus, Philemon, and Hebrews. The title of the last in the list is rather inaccurate: it is not an "epistle," nor is it by Paul, nor is it "to the Hebrews." We could thus leave it out of consideration in the present discussion altogether, were it not for the fact that its case is quite instructive.

The Pauline authorship of Hebrews has to be decided on literary and critical evidence. It cannot be settled by a decision from any ecclesiastical or religious authority. To such ecclesiastical and religious authorities belongs the competence to insist on the canonicity of Hebrews, its inspiration or even its "apostolicity," but the fact of its *authorship* cannot be altered by any authority in heaven or on earth. If Paul did not in fact write Hebrews, then Hebrews was not written by Paul, and that is all there is to it. The authorship of any work can only be recognized or not; it is not subject to decree.

The compulsion to rewrite history is a trait shared alike by religious institutions and totalitarian regimes in our day. The churches knew the historical methodology of Oceania long before George Orwell's *1984*. But the Greek poet Agathon knew better when he wrote:

> This alone is denied even to God, to make what has happened into what has not happened (see Aristotle, *Nicomachean Ethics* VI.2.6).

This is why it is refreshing to know that, even in the heat of polemic, the Council of Trent—thanks to its saner elements—

forwent the opportunity to insist on Paul's authorship of Hebrews, an authorship that had been held suspect long before the Reformation and Erasmus denied it.

What is instructive in the case of Hebrews' authorship is this: Any reader of the New Testament must be careful to distinguish between what belongs to historically verifiable fact and what falls within the domain of dogma. The conviction that the two are contradictory or mutually exclusive has been rightly condemned under a variety of labels in the Church's history, but the subtle tendency to confound them has escaped condemnation. Such tendency lies at the root of a large variety of "fundamentalisms" throughout Christian history. To maintain the distinction between ascertainable history and asseverated dogma, however, is the indispensable first step toward rightly judging the biographical data in Paul's letters, properly valuing the narrative of Acts, and intelligently pursuing the meaning of works attributed to Paul, or James, or Peter, or any New Testament writer.

We turn, after this lengthy parenthesis, to the other thirteen epistles that claim Paul for their author. These can be conveniently divided into three groups, whose labels need not be as disconcerting to the religious sensibility as they might appear at first sight. The terms used for the three groups are merely technical labels for the sake of distinguishing, and not value judgments on any of the epistles:

(a) the genuine Pauline epistles, by Paul himself;
(b) the deutero-Pauline epistles, by followers or close associates of Paul;
(c) the pseudo-Pauline, later compositions claiming Paul for their author.

In the first category, the genuinely Pauline epistles, we have: Romans, 1 Corinthians, 2 Corinthians, Galatians, Philippians, Philemon, and 1 Thessalonians (and perhaps Colossians and 2 Thessalonians). In the second category are included as "deutero-Pauline": Colossians (most likely), Ephesians, and (perhaps) 2 Thessalonians. To the third category belong the so-called "pseudo-Pauline" letters which comprise the "Pastoral Epistles": 1 and 2 Timothy and Titus.

What must strike the reader immediately is the hesitation about two of the epistles in particular. The case of Colossians and—to a greater degree—that of 2 Thessalonians are not very easy to decide. They exhibit unmistakably Pauline characteristics, yet persist in posing serious problems to the exegete. These problems (which can be pursued in any good introduction to the New Testament such as W.G. Kümmel's or H. Koester's, or in any good commentary on the epistle itself, e.g., E. Lohse's on Colossians or E. Best's on Thessalonians) make one hesitate to include—without further qualification—either epistle in the category of the genuinely Pauline.

The distinction between the three categories is particularly necessary when we set out to understand the "mind of Paul," or when we wish to speak of his theology. Like all living thought, Paul's was bound to change, to evolve, and to grow in different ways and on different levels throughout his life. Because of his great influence and because of the importance "the churches" attached to his letters, that process was bound to continue uninterrupted. Of course, neither an inspired author nor an inspired idea is exempt from the laws that govern thought and reflection, whether they be profoundly religious, sublimely philosophical, or mundanely profane.

Paul's understanding of God's revelation of his Son underwent change and maturation over the years. That process did not cease with Paul's death. His epistles, or letters— the distinction, even if genuine, is of little practical value for our present purpose—were collected very early on. Even within the span of the New Testament itself, 2 Peter 3:16, which speaks of "all [Paul's] letters," gives some reason to believe that such a collection already existed. It existed because people respected and revered their author, and because they valued what he had to say about the Christian faith and the life of faith. That Paul enjoyed such popularity should come as no surprise to us. That that popularity gave rise to compilers of, commentators on, and imitators of his letters is but the corollary to the genuine popularity of any literary work in any age.

Pseudonymity

Perhaps we need be reminded only of this: In the early Christian centuries as well as in the centuries that preceded them, there was a widespread literary phenomenon called pseudonymity, i.e., the composing of a literary work under the name of a famous personage from the past. It would be more accurate to describe the procedure as "allonymity," since a pseudonymous work for us means that its author used a *nom de plume*, a fictive pen name. The phenomenon we are describing, however, claimed for its author some well-known personality from past history. It was as widely practiced as it was a generally accepted and ordinary literary device. Its modern equivalent would be, not so much Charles Lamb writing under the name of "Elia," but Robert Graves writing *I, Claudius*, or Marguerite Yourcenar, *Mémoires d'Hadrien*. But whereas such modern works are clearly works of fiction and were so intended by their authors, the works we are dealing with here were neither written as "fictions" nor regarded as such by those who read them—works like *The Testament of Moses, The Apocalypse of Baruch, The Book of Enoch*, etc.

As a matter of fact, all our New Testament—with possibly the sole exception of the genuinely Pauline letters—can serve as an illustration of the phenomenon of pseudonymity or allonymity. This fact does not diminish in the least the genuinity or the canonicity or even the "authenticity" of any of these works whose authorship remains a matter of dispute. The fact, therefore, that the Epistle to the Romans was written by Paul and that the Epistle to Titus was by someone else who used Paul's name makes the Epistle to Titus not one whit less divinely inspired, or less a part of the canon, or less "authentic" a book of the New Testament. But the distinction itself ought to keep us aware of the difference in provenance between Romans and Titus. It ought to alert us to the inevitable changes in the points of view, in the backgrounds, and even—or especially—in the theological perspectives between them.

In the final analysis, it is our fidelity to the New Testament as the inspired word of God that makes us apply the criteria and norms of historical and literary criticism to the individual works, and not the other way round. Our fidelity to the historical-critical method does not compel us to regard the New Testament as no more than "the word of man."

The Question of Unity

One additional point to keep in mind here is the nature of Paul's letters as we possess them. Whereas most of the letters are single compositions, two of them, 2 Corinthians and Philippians, are thought by many New Testament critics to be composite works, i.e., the result of joining together two or more letters of Paul into one letter. As the endless debate between scholars attests, the job of thus redacting the many into one was very well done. It is not always very easy to see the "sutures" between the joined sections, even where one would have thought the evidence compelling: as, for example, the break between Philippians 3:1 and 3:2 which, in the latest edition of the Greek New Testament that we have (the 26th edition of Nestle-Aland), is either typographically muffed or—to many scholars—editorially curious. The break, which ought to be between 3:1 and 3:2, comes between Philippians 2:30 and 3:1 in that highly regarded edition of our New Testament. This paragraphing is followed also by the Revised Standard Version.

Whether or not one accepts the unity of Philippians and of 2 Corinthians will necessarily affect the exegesis of a given passage in them. But accepting the unity of one or both epistles does not make the exegete a better Christian or a greater believer. To say, for example, that 2 Corinthians is a composite epistle in no way detracts from its canonicity or impugns its inspired nature. This is not an irrelevant point; for we need to be aware that, when we say that a book of the New Testament is canonical and inspired, we mean the book as we possess it now, as textually well-established as human knowledge and expertise allow. We do not mean some suppositious document constructed by a majority vote of a committee of exegetes who judge this view to be alien to Paul's thought or that opinion to be out of harmony with his theological scheme. What we have to look at is a given letter of Paul as it stands now in the New Testament, in the best text that textual criticism can provide on the basis of all the available manuscript evidence we possess. It is this text that we have to consider no matter what difficulties of interpretation it poses. Modern tastes and sensibilities are no more criteria of such textual criticism than are the dogmatic preferences of this or that church.

Belaboring this point, however, is not an idle exercise in recalling certain commonsensical presuppositions for interpreting the letters of Paul. The care to stress such a point is made necessary when approaching certain sensitive questions that arise in letters like 1 Thessalonians or 1 Corinthians, where other than strictly text-critical arguments are used to dismiss a given passage as "spurious" or a "later addition." What is essentially an instrument of clarification in the hands of the competent could, when wielded by the ignorant, become a tool of mindless obfuscation. For those with a "little learning" have a tendency to overvalue what smattering of truth they possess, imagining themselves to be the first to have discovered it and, consequently, going to great lengths to elucidate it to those they—mistakenly—suppose less fortunate than themselves. The danger of such ignorance, evident especially—though not exclusively—in the "semi-educated" incompetence so widely disseminated by the popular media, is doubly alarming today in biblical studies and in all the fields of Christian knowledge which utilize them.

17. Paul's Missionary Career

It is quite evident that Paul's life after his conversion was one of unceasing missionary labor on behalf of the gospel of Jesus Christ. A look at the chronology of his life shows the period from his conversion to his death to have covered a good quarter of the first century: the more than twenty-five years that are bisected by the Apostolic Council. As we have seen already, Paul's missionary labor began after his conversion, though the nature and extent of his activity during those first fourteen to seventeen years remains—to a large extent—hidden from our view. There are no letters to Damascus, to Antioch, or to "Arabia." The references to these places (Gal 1:17; 2 Cor 11:32; Gal 2:11) are no more than fugitive memories.

Nevertheless, the list of misfortunes and misadventures in 2 Corinthians 11:24–28, 32–33 (see 6:4–10; 1 Cor 4:11–13; Rom 8:35) cannot reasonably be dismissed as mere hyperbole. Even allowing for a natural proclivity to plaintiveness, beautifully captured in 2 Timothy 4:9–11—though Paul himself would euphemistically call it "glorying in the cross"—the picture we get of his missionary efforts is by no means a "pageant of uninterrupted triumphs."

Such at least is the impression one gets from the portrait of Paul in Acts: a miracle worker who, by blinding his opponent Elymas, converts the proconsul Sergius Paulus (Acts 13:7–12), who heals a "cripple from birth, who had never walked," and dazzles the Lycaonians to exclaim, "The gods have come down to us in the likeness of men!" (Acts 14:11 and 18), and who brings the hapless Eutychus back to life (Acts 20:7–12). When word spread in Ephesus that even an evil spirit acknowledged, "Jesus I know, and Paul I know," a number of magicians publicly burned their books, to the value of "fifty thousand pieces of silver" (Acts 19:11–20). No wonder "the word of the Lord grew and prevailed mightily" (Acts 19:20).

Moreover, according to Acts, it was not just Paul's miraculous power but his irresistible oratorical skills that won the world to Christ. The "Lucan" Paul is an *"outstanding orator"* (Haenchen, *Acts,* p. 114), addressing eloquently and cogently his fellow Jews at Antioch of Pisidia (Acts 13:16–41 and 42–43), or in Jerusalem (Acts 22:1–21; see 23:1–3), or in the presence of King Agrippa (Acts 26:2–23). He presents a compelling exposition of the case of Christianity to the Gentiles "in the middle of the Areopagus" (Acts 17:22–31).

This dazzling display of miraculous powers and oratorical skills must be weighed against the more sobering picture

in Paul's own letters. True, he says once that "the signs of a
true apostle were performed among you in all patience, with
signs and wonders and mighty works" (2 Cor 12:12; compare
Rom 15:18–19), though the meaning of the verse remains
hard to specify and its referent difficult to identify. But even
if Paul's words corroborate the list of miracles in Acts, the assessment of the "signs and wonders and mighty works" has to
be made in the light of his affirmation:

> For the sake of Christ, then, I am content with weak-
> nesses, insults, hardships, persecutions, and calamities;
> for when I am weak, then I am strong (2 Cor 12:10; see
> Gal 4:12–15).

As to his supposed oratorical skills—which should not be
confounded with the unquestionable mastery of rhetorical
principles evident in his writings—we have his own report of
his opponents' evaluation:

> For they say, "His letters are weighty and strong, but his
> bodily presence is weak, and his speech is of no account"
> (2 Cor 10:10).

Paul's enemies in Corinth had a better assessment of his abil-
ities. After all, one's enemies, the opponents one tries to win
over, are the best judges—almost by definition—of one's success as an orator. On their evidence, Paul was an ineffective
and unimposing speaker. This aspect of Paul's missionary activity needs stressing in every age when, as in our own, the
Christian proclaimers of the word have to compete with the
glossy illiteracy of contemporary hucksters of panaceas for
the human condition.

Of course, the fact that Paul writes so cogently and force-
fully is not altered by his unimposing stature and his negligible eloquence as an orator. For Paul to be the great person
he is, he need not have excelled in all the fields of human endeavor. To be a saint or a hero in any age, it is enough to have
excelled at doing one single thing conspicuously well: "The
single talent well employ'd." Our thinking otherwise has de-

prived us perhaps of both heroes and saints in our times; and, to satisfy our unappeasable need for them, we have been content to accept the brummagem specimens foisted on us by the restless fury of bankrupt fanatics.

As a matter of fact, Paul gloried in his oratorical inadequacy, and in the severe limitations on his skills as a speaker. It was an integral part of his insight, not that such gifts and skills are not to be valued or cultivated, but that they are not what ultimately matters in proclaiming the Gospel:

> For Christ did not send me to baptize but to preach the gospel, and not with eloquent wisdom, lest the cross of Christ be emptied of its power (1 Cor 1:17).

> When I came to you, brethren, I did not come proclaiming to you the [mystery] of God in lofty words of wisdom (1 Cor 2:1).

But the proper understanding of Paul's missionary activity has to be sought elsewhere than in the modes and techniques of oratory, the tactics of the super salesman, or the packaging and presentation of the message. To get an idea of how Paul understood his missionary activity, we would have to range over the whole collection of his letters, since each of them either deals explicitly with the question or indirectly provides some answer or illustration of its implications.

FOUR

The First Epistle
to the Thessalonians

18. Paul's Understanding of His Mission

To get some understanding of how Paul saw his missionary activity, we turn to the first letter we have from him, the First Epistle to the Thessalonians. This also happens to be the earliest composition in our New Testament, dating from the year A.D. 50.

1 Thessalonians, like all the genuinely Pauline letters with the exception of Galatians, follows its customary address and greeting with a "thanksgiving": "We give thanks to God always for you all . . ." (1 Thess 1:2). In this instance the thanksgiving happens to be a particularly lengthy one, extending from 1:2 to 2:16. It sums up here, as it does in the other letters, the basic theme(s) to be taken up in the main body of the letter. The thanksgiving in 1 Thessalonians is, moreover, an admirably composed unit whose recurrent triadic patterns lend force and clarity to its content:

> Remembering before God our Father
> (a) your work of faith
> (b) your labor of love
> (c) and steadfastness of hope
>   in our Lord Jesus Christ (1 Thess 1:3).

This, of course, is the faith-hope-charity formula with which we are familiar from 1 Corinthians 13:13, but in its—so to speak—salvation history sequence: faith regarding the past

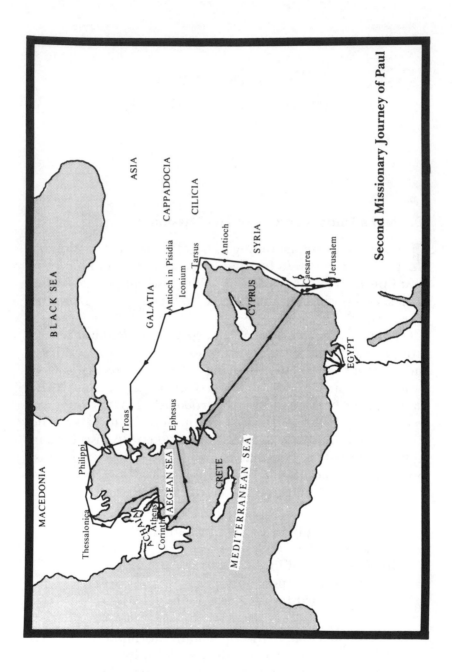

Second Missionary Journey of Paul

event; love operating here in the present; hope looking forward to the future (see 1 Thess 5:8; Col 1:4–5).

Paul goes on to remind his readers of what lay behind all their "work . . . labor . . . and steadfastness":

> For our gospel came to you,
> not only in word,
> but also in power
> and in the Holy Spirit
> and with full conviction (1 Thess 1:5).

This verse provides a major component of the answer to the question of how Paul understood his missionary activity. The answer, as is evident, is made up of one negative statement followed by the triad of affirmatives.

When Paul says that the gospel came to the Thessalonians "not only in words," he does not for a moment mean to say that words are of no use. He possessed far too much of that "endowment with words" to think that. Words are important as the means, the vehicle, by which the gospel is proclaimed, but they are not, and can never be, the operative force of the message. Their ill-use can hinder, and even altogether prevent, the efficacy of the gospel, but their right use is not and never can be the cause of the gospel's triumph in believers.

The Work of the Spirit

What brings that triumph about is the—almost pleonastic—triad of "power . . . Holy Spirit . . . and full conviction." The three expressions are nearly synonymous, for, as we shall have occasion to see, the Spirit (*pneuma*) is itself power (*dynamis*). We might recall such expressions as "God anointed Jesus of Nazareth with the Holy Spirit and with power" in Acts 10:38, and "by the power of the Holy Spirit" in Romans 15:13, 19. The "full conviction" is always used in the New Testament of a spiritual good; and here it is the eminent good of possessing the Holy Spirit, of preaching with its power and with the full conviction that could only come from possessing such power. "The declaration of the glad tidings by the apostle," wrote G. Delling, "took place, not in mere word, but in great 'fulness of divine working'. . . . The word [*plerophoria*, full conviction] is thus one of the terms which Paul uses to try to define linguistically the great richness of the divine work in the present life of Christianity" (G. Delling in *T.D.N.T.*, vol. 6, p. 311).

This mode of proclaiming the word "in power and in the Holy Spirit and with full conviction" is in marked contrast with the impotent bluster of those who "preach Christ from envy and rivalry . . . out of partisanship, not sincerely" (Phil 1:15, 17). Paul himself knew all too well:

> And I was with you in weakness and in much fear and trembling; and my speech and my message (*kerygma*) were not in plausible words of wisdom, but in demonstration of the Spirit and of power (1 Cor 2:3–4; see 2 Cor 6:6–7).

The proclamation of the Christian gospel is thus, first and last, the work of the Holy Spirit. This is what puts the efficacy of the gospel proclamation beyond the fads and techniques of the itinerant peddlers of wisdom in the marketplaces of the first century, as of the orotund vacuities of the communication media in the twentieth. Of course, the temptation to go to the other extreme and discard or disregard all human effort is—though perhaps understandable—inexcusable. The Holy Spirit will not and cannot act except in human beings who are, to the best of their ability, able to feel its "full conviction" and to communicate its power. Paul's statement is not a license for lazy habits of mind or for the sloppy use of words, but a challenge to every bearer of the Christian message to keep a just scale of values in, and an unblinkered vision of, the gospel and the true source of its efficacy.

Receiving the Word

But the proclamation of the gospel is a two-way process. It is not proclaimed at all, or proclaimed in vain, if the hearers do not "receive the word" (1 Thess 1:6–7). Paul employs another triad to describe this process:

You turned to God from idols,
to serve a living and true God,
and to wait for his son from heaven,
　　whom he raised from the dead, Jesus who delivers us
　　from the wrath to come (1 Thess 1:9–10).

The Thessalonians' response to the gospel message was a genuine conversion: a turning *from* idols *to* the service of the "living and true God." The conversion is, however, far more specific than this. In this context, to serve the living and true God necessarily involves all the specific items of the miniature creed enunciated here: the saving death ("delivers us") and resurrection ("raised from the dead") of Jesus, his function as the judge at the end-time ("who delivers us from the wrath to come"), and his awaited return "from heaven."

Thus, the object of Christian conversion was neither vague nor unspecific. It contained within itself all the constitutive elements of the Christian faith:

(a) the *Christological and soteriological* element: the saving significance of the death and resurrection of Jesus;
(b) the *eschatological* element: the final deliverance "from the wrath to come," which is already at work: "delivers" (a present participle in the Greek);
(c) the *apocalyptic:* the awaited coming of "his Son from heaven."

The Exercise of the Ministry
Paul then returns immediately to the theme of how his ministry was exercised among the Thessalonians. To this purpose he uses a double set of triads:

For our appeal does not spring
from error
or uncleanness,
nor is it made with guile. . . .
For we never used
either words of flattery, as you know,
or a cloak for greed, as God is witness;
nor did we seek glory from men,
whether from you or from others (1 Thess 2:3 and 5).

This double set of negative statements gives us indirectly a portrait of the itinerant preachers of rival philosophies and alien creeds in Paul's time. It also—and far more to our purpose—provides us with a nosology of all the ills that afflict Christian preaching in every age: the "error," whether of ignorance or of opinionated self-sufficiency; the "uncleanness" of using one's audience for one's own ends, of playing to the gallery; and the "guile" which is the recognizable twin of ministerial hypocrisy.

These negative traits are at the root of every misuse of rhetoric, of literary polish, and of all the accomplishments with which the minister of the word needs—each according to "his own special gift from God"—to be endowed. To declare the gospel of God with guile, with uncleanness, and out of error, is to use flattery to win the hearers to oneself, for one's own profit—whether spiritual or material (see 2 Cor 11:7), and in order to secure "glory from men." Indeed, what renders all preaching, all proclamation of the gospel, sterile and ineffectual is precisely this search for the "glory of men":

> They make much of you, but for no good purpose; they want to shut you out, that you may make much of them (Gal 4:17; see 1:10).

Paul, of course, does not deny that "for a good purpose it is always good to be made much of" (Gal 4:18), but that "good purpose" is easily lost sight of, and more easily still perverted into a subtle quest for the "glory of men." It is this quest for glory which, as John was to perceive so acutely, renders faith itself impossible:

> How can you believe, who receive glory from one another? (Jn 5:44; see Jer 17:5–6).

Of course, Paul's missionary activity has its positive traits, but they are traits that could be trusted as genuine only when the above negative elements are absent. Perhaps no field of Christian endeavor is so open to the temptation of hypocrisy as the ministry of preaching the gospel:

> We have renounced disgraceful, underhanded ways; we
> refuse to practice cunning or to tamper with God's word,
> but by the open statement of the truth we would com-
> mend ourselves to every man's countenance in the sight
> of God (2 Cor 4:2).

Only by the renunciation of underhanded ways, by the refusal to practice cunning or—most serious temptation of all—
to tamper with God's word can the apostle exercise that open-
ness of the truth and to the truth "before God and man."

It is that forthright refusal to use either the word of God
or his own hearers in order to serve his own interests which
ultimately enabled Paul to deal with the Thessalonians gently,
"like a child" (NEB). He had no need to use guile, or to "attempt to deceive" them. He knew, and they sensed, that he
imparted the gospel message to them with "yearning love"
and without any "base motive" (NEB). There was no doubt in
his mind that, as preacher of the good news, he was ready to
share with his hearers "not only the gospel of God but our
own selves" (1 Thess 2:7–8). Such an attitude surely precludes
any semblance of greed, whether material or spiritual:

> I preached the gospel without cost to you (2 Cor 11:7).

> Some indeed preach Christ from envy and rivalry, but
> others from good will. The latter do it out of love . . . the
> former proclaim Christ out of partisanship, not sincerely
> . . . (Phil 1:15–17).

Labor and Toil

Paul's mission among the Thessalonians was, in his
words, "labor and toil" and work "night and day" (1 Thess
2:9; see 1:3). It was not a part-time job, nor a sideline occu-
pation, even though he forwent his right to get his living "by
the gospel" (1 Cor 9:12–14). Paul was careful not to "burden"
(2 Cor 11:9; 12:13; 2 Thess 3:8) the churches to which he
"preached God's gospel without cost" (2 Cor 11:7). His action
was a free option on his part, not a denial of the "rightful
claim" (1 Cor 9:12; 2 Thess 3:9) which those who proclaim the

gospel have to earn their living by it. Nor did such "rightful claim" rest on human authority:

> Does not the law say the same? For it is written in the law of Moses, "You shall not muzzle an ox when it is treading out the grain" (1 Cor 9:8–9; see Deuteronomy 25:4).

> Do you not know that those who are employed in the temple service get their food from the temple, and those who serve at the altar share in the sacrificial offerings? In the same way, the Lord commanded that those who proclaim the gospel should get their living by the gospel (1 Cor 9:13–14).

Paul, however, of his own free choice, gave up that right simply to avoid putting "an obstacle in the way of the gospel of Christ" (1 Cor 9:12b). He did it also out of a polemical motive: to "undermine the claim" of the "false apostles, deceitful workmen, disguising themselves as apostles of Christ," who claimed that "in their boasted mission they work on the same terms as we do" (2 Cor 11:12–13). Thus, Paul's refraining from putting a burden on the churches was itself an apologetic for the genuinity of his apostolic mission. In Paul's eyes, it was enough "that in my preaching I may make the gospel free of charge, not making full use of my right in the gospel" (1 Cor 9:18).

How then did Paul manage to live? In two ways. First, he did not—as "the other apostles" did and had every right to do—"refrain from working for a living" (1 Cor 9:5–6). He labored, "working with [his] own hands" (1 Cor 4:12). He reminds the Thessalonians:

> We were not idle when we were with you, we did not eat anyone's bread without paying, but with toil and labor we worked night and day, that we might not burden any of you (2 Thess 3:7–8).

The Book of Acts faithfully echoes this when, in his speech to the Ephesian elders, it has Paul say:

> I coveted no one's silver or gold or apparel. You your-
> selves know that these hands ministered to my necessities,
> and to those who were with me (Acts 20:33–34).

Acts tells us, moreover, that Paul was by trade a tentmaker,
and that he stayed in Corinth with Aquila and Priscilla "because he was of the same trade . . . and they worked" (Acts
18:1–3).

Yet in Corinth itself, Paul was "in want" (2 Cor 11:9; Phil
4:11–12). So, to eke out his meager living, he "robbed other
churches by accepting support from them in order to serve
you . . . for my needs were supplied by the brethren who came
from Macedonia" (2 Cor 11:8–9). This, needless to say, was
not an isolated instance:

> And you Philippians yourselves know that in the begin-
> ning of the gospel, when I left Macedonia, no church en-
> tered into partnership with me in giving and receiving
> except only you; for even in Thessalonica you sent me
> help [or: money for my needs] once and again (Phil 4:15–
> 16).

But the church of Philippi was the only exception. Of course,
any reader of the Epistle to the Philippians would readily perceive that the bond that bound them to Paul was unique. The
thanksgiving in the first chapter of the Epistle would in itself
be sufficient to make anyone see how the relation between the
apostle and the church of Philippi precluded either of them
"taking advantage" (see 2 Cor 7:2) of the other. This is what
it is to preach the gospel without uncleanness and without
greed (1 Thess 2:3, 5): the uncleanness that would vitiate the
receiving, and the greed that would hamper the giving.

This aspect of Paul's missionary labor is salutary to ponder at a time when churches are run like corporations, when
church institutions advertise as "equal opportunity employ-
ers," and when ministers with their diplomas in hand jostle
one another for advantage in the job market. It is, of course,
equally salutary to ponder by all those whose "vow of poverty"
ought to have readied them to share with everyone, not only
the gospel of God, but also their own selves. Their "evangel-

ical" life, after all, was never meant to be such a travesty of "having nothing, and yet possessing everything" (2 Cor 6:10).

So Paul's "labor and toil" while he "preached the gospel of God" to the Thessalonians was marked by a "holy and righteous and blameless behavior" (1 Thess 2:10). Here again it is necessary to insist that this is no more hyperbole than his claim about his former life in Judaism (Phil 3:6). He was simply not the kind of man to leave things half-done in a variety of half-hearted ways.

Moreover, the nature of the Christian calling is such that he prays:

> May the Lord make you increase and abound in love to one another and to all men, as we do to you, so that he may establish your hearts *unblamable* in holiness (1 Thess 3:13).

> May the God of peace himself sanctify you wholly; and may your spirit and soul and body be kept sound and *blameless* at the coming of our Lord Jesus Christ (1 Thess 5:23).

He exhorts the Philippians:

> Do all things without grumbling or questioning, that you may be *blameless* and innocent children of God *without blemish* in the midst of a crooked and perverse generation, among whom you shine as lights in the world . . . (Phil 2:14–15).

Only a preacher who is aware that this divine calling to a life "in true righteousness and holiness" (Eph 4:24) is addressed, not just to apostles and evangelists and preachers of the word, but to *all* Christians, can aspire to conduct the ministry of the word in "holiness and righteousness and blamelessness."

Furthermore, the actual carrying out of this ministry of the word is once again described triadically in the letter to the Thessalonians:

> We exhorted each one of you
> and encouraged
> and charged you
> > to lead a life worthy of God, who calls you into his own
> > kingdom and glory (1 Thess 2:11–12).

This "appealing to you by encouragement, as well as by solemn injunctions" (NEB), was done in a manner that Paul describes as "gentle . . . like a nurse taking care of her children" (1 Thess 2:7), and "like a father with his children" (1 Thess 2:11). It reflected the tenderest care and the gentlest manner of parental solicitude.

The Word of God

Finally, to round off the protracted thanksgiving, Paul gives the essence of this ministry of the word. He sets down the very basis of his missionary activity, without which all the preaching and proclamation, all the exhortation and encouragement are but ploys in one oratorical performance among so many, just another performance clamoring for the attention and applause of the masses. To Paul's mind, what sets Christian preaching and the proclamation of the gospel apart from all trafficking in words is this:

> And we also thank God constantly for this, that when you received the word of God which you heard from us, you accepted it *not as the word of men* but as what it really is, *the word of God*, which is at work in you believers (1 Thess 2:13).

It is the faith of the believers that accepts the word proclaimed as the word of God, which it really is; and, to complete the circle, the believers can accept it as the word of God because it is already at work in them. Were this not so, Paul's address would have been rightly regarded as "of no account" (2 Cor 10:10). He was not competing with the accomplished and professional orators that crowded the philosophical and religious fora of his day. He was proclaiming a gospel whose true efficacy—he knew—came not from the proclaimer but from God, whose word it was.

Paul, therefore, regarded his missionary activity as the proclamation of the word of God. What efficacy the proclamation possessed and what success the ministry achieved were all due, entirely and wholly, to God's word "in power and in the Holy Spirit and with full conviction" (1 Thess 1:5). Human "error, uncleanness, and guile" (1 Thess 2:3) can hinder it and curtail its power; but "lofty words and wisdom . . . and plausible words of wisdom" (1 Cor 2:1, 4) cannot add to its efficacy:

> God chose what is foolish in the world to shame the wise,
> God chose what is weak in the world to shame the strong,
> God chose what is low and despised in the world, even things that are not, to bring to nothing things that are, so that no human being might boast in the presence of God (1 Cor 1:27–29).

The zeal Paul showed, the energy he expended, the talents he brought to bear, the gifts of mind and heart he exercised, were all single-mindedly directed to one aim: that "the word of the Lord" sound forth and "your faith in God" go forth (1 Thess 1:8).

19. Paul's Gospel

The "gospel" (*euangelion,* good news, whence "evangelical") is a comprehensive expression for the Christian faith. As we have already seen, 1 Thessalonians encapsulates it admirably when it specifies the object of the Thessalonians' conversion:

> How you turned to God from idols, to serve a living and true God, and to wait for his Son from heaven, whom he raised from the dead, Jesus who delivers us from the wrath to come (1 Thess 1:9–10).

This tripartite formula sums up God's deed in Jesus Christ: soteriologically, i.e., the death and the resurrection of Jesus in its saving significance; eschatologically, i.e., the inauguration of the time of final salvation already in the present (note the present and the future in "delivers . . . to come"); apocalyptically, i.e., the expectation of the return of the Son from heaven.

Two points are especially apt to be overlooked in the gospel thus proclaimed: (a) the unique agency of God, since it is he, "the living and true God," who raises Jesus to true life from death; (b) the apocalyptic expectation of the Son from heaven, since it is an aspect of the gospel that is likely not to be appreciated at its real worth by the modern believer. We shall have occasion to return to these sundry elements; but, before we do, we need to look elsewhere than in 1 Thessalonians at how Paul himself understood and described the gospel he proclaimed.

The Gospel of God

The gospel is, first and foremost, the "gospel of God" (1 Thess 2:2, 8, 9; Rom 1:1; 15:16; 2 Cor 11:7; 1 Tim 1:11). God is at its source; God is the author of the salvation it proclaims ("it is the power of God for salvation"—Rom 1:16); and God is the object of the proclamation in that the gospel proclaims him as the "living and true God" (1 Thess 1:9) in order that those who hear and accept its message may turn from their idols to serve only him. This of course is basically no different from the message of the Old Testament, which also proclaimed the glad tidings of a promised deliverance and called to the worship and service of the one God.

What makes the proclamation specifically good news in the New Testament is that it is the gospel "of Christ" (1 Thess 3:2; Rom 15:19; 1 Cor 9:12b; 2 Cor 4:4 "of the glory of Christ"; 9:13; 10:14; Gal 1:7; Phil 1:27; 2 Thess 1:8 "of our Lord Jesus"). It is the gospel "of his Son" (Rom 1:9); and—according to what exegetes judge to be one of the oldest credal formulae we possess in our New Testament—it is:

> The gospel of God
> which he promised beforehand through his prophets
> in the holy scriptures,
> the gospel *concerning his Son,*
> who was descended from David according to the flesh

> and designated Son of God in power
> according to the Spirit of holiness
> by his resurrection from the dead,
> Jesus Christ our Lord (Rom 1:1–4; see 2 Tim 2:8).

The very formulation of the statement makes clear the relation of "the gospel of God" and "the gospel concerning his Son." The good news that God "promised beforehand through his prophets in the holy scriptures" is now fulfilled and made a permanent reality proclaimed to all peoples and all nations. It is in this proclamation of "Jesus Christ as Lord" that there shines

> the light of the gospel of the glory of Christ, who is the likeness of God. . . . For it is the God who said, "Let light shine out of darkness," who has shone in our hearts to give the light of the knowledge of the glory of God in the face of Christ (2 Cor 4:4–6).

It is therefore more than understandable that Paul did all "for the sake of the gospel" (1 Cor 9:23), all "for Jesus' sake" (2 Cor 4:5). He speaks of "the grace given me by God to be a minister (*leitourgos*) of Christ Jesus to the Gentiles in the priestly service of the gospel of God" (Rom 15:16, see 1 Thess 3:2). Ephesians spells out even more emphatically what being a "minister" (*diakonos*) of this gospel means: "to preach to the Gentiles the unsearchable riches of Christ" (Eph 3:7–8).

Preaching to the Gentiles was Paul's special charge, his field of missionary activity in the period of the epistles. This is the reason why he speaks of "my gospel" (Rom 2:16; 16:25; "our gospel" in 2 Cor 4:3 and 2 Thess 2:14) as "the gospel which I preach among the Gentiles" (Gal 2:2). He saw his calling by God to be clearly directed to this end: "when he . . . was pleased to reveal his Son to/in me, in order that I might preach him among the Gentiles" (Gal 1:16; see Acts 26:16–18). He acknowledged this to be a "grace given to me" (Gal 2:9), that "he who worked through Peter for the mission of the circumcised worked through me also for the Gentiles" (Gal 2:8; "a light for the Gentiles"—Acts 13:47).

The important thing to keep in mind about the gospel, however it be qualified, whether "of God" or "of Christ," or "of Paul," is that it is always

> the power of God for salvation to everyone who has faith (Rom 1:16; 1 Thess 1:5; 1 Cor 1:18).

Of course, the gospel is "the power of God" first and foremost because it is "the word of God" (1 Thess 2:13; 1 Cor 14:36), the "word of the Lord" (1 Thess 1:8; 2 Thess 3:1), and "the sword of the Spirit" (Eph 6:17). It can be the word of God only to one who has faith, to one who hears the word with faith. Therein lies its true power and its efficacy unto salvation, an efficacy that resides permanently in the message itself, not in its proclaimers:

> For what we preach is not ourselves, but Jesus Christ our Lord (2 Cor 4:5; 1 Cor 15:10–11).

The gospel, moreover, is good news because it proclaims the salvation of God in the death and resurrection of Christ. The most eloquent preacher and the most accomplished missionary is utterly helpless unless the hearers accept the good news proclaimed, believe the gospel preached ("so we preach and so you believed"—1 Cor 15:11). It is then, and only then, that the gospel can be "the power of God for salvation to every one *who has faith*" (Rom 1:16). The gospel can be this because "in it the righteousness of God is revealed through faith for faith" (Rom 1:17).

Thus, the gospel of Paul is not—as centuries of debate might lead one to believe—*either* the gospel of the death and resurrection of Christ, *or* the gospel of justification by faith. It is not and cannot possibly be one without the other. If, however, we choose—wrongly, to my mind—to understand by "Paul's gospel" the message proclaimed insofar as it is marked by his own theological genius, by his peculiar circumstances, and by the emphases imposed on the proclamation by his polemics, then we ought to keep in mind that we are using the phrase in a very restricted sense indeed. In that case, the "gos-

pel of Paul" cannot be made synonymous or coterminous with
the "gospel of God" and the "gospel of Christ" without further ado. Failure to make the necessary distinction has resulted in endless and fruitless debates that persist to this day.

Therefore, the gospel as such is definable, and, consequently, the faith in the gospel has a definite content. It is a
faith in the gospel "concerning his Son . . . designated Son of
God in power according to the Spirit of holiness by his resurrection from the dead, Jesus Christ our Lord" (Rom 1:3–
4), "who was put to death for our trespasses and raised for our
justification" (Rom 4:25), and who is the awaited "Son from
heaven, whom [God] raised from the dead, Jesus who delivers
us from the wrath to come" (1 Thess 1:10).

Any "Other Gospel"

Indeed, the content of this gospel is so definite that the
believers can not only recognize it, but also reject any "other
gospel" as false:

> For if someone comes and preaches *another Jesus* than the
> one we preached, or if you receive a *different spirit* from
> the one you received, or if you accept a *different gospel*
> from the one you accepted . . . (2 Cor 11:4).

Paul himself recognizes, and the believers also should recognize, no other gospel (Gal 1:6–7), even though there were
then—as there are bound to be in every age—those "who
trouble you and want to pervert the gospel of Christ."

> But even if we, or an angel from heaven, should preach
> to you a gospel contrary to that which we preached to you,
> let him be accursed (*anathema*). As we have said before, so
> now I say again: If anyone is preaching to you a gospel
> contrary to that which you received, let him be accursed
> (*anathema*) (Gal 1:7–9).

This certainly cannot be put more clearly or more force-
fully. Yet a reminder is needed here: Since Paul was by no
means the only apostle preaching the gospel of Christ to the
world, his statement cannot mean to condemn all others who

were not of one mind with him. It could not conceivably have meant anathematizing of everyone who did not preach "the gospel of Paul," in the narrow acceptation of the phrase mentioned above (see 2 Cor 4:5). The agreement reached at the Council of Jerusalem ought to make this fact at least clear (Gal 2:1–10). What Paul meant to exclude categorically by his anathemas was any perversion, alteration, difference or departure from the "gospel of God," the "gospel concerning his Son," the gospel with which Paul, like so many others, "was *entrusted*" (1 Thess 2:4), which he, among innumerable others, had "also received" (1 Cor 15:3).

20. Beyond the "Gospel"

In a very real sense, the gospel allowed every latitude in the elaboration of its message, extending to every aspect of human life and, inevitably, coloring every department of human knowledge. The belief in the gospel reaches and, consequently, alters and modifies the deepest recesses of the believer's mind and heart. This is principally the reason why every generation must seek to express the meaning and implications of the good news in accents intelligible to the people of its own time. In the final analysis, that is why the letters of Paul are so peculiarly his, belong so characteristically to his time, and yet remain ever a source of understanding and life for every generation of Christians in every age. The real difficulty is in keeping clearly before one's eyes what is essential and—as it were—non-negotiable in the message, and what is time-bound and culturally conditioned, and hence can serve as pattern and model for adaptation rather than as creed and dogma for rigid imposition.

1 Thessalonians raises, among others, two problems that could serve as examples. Both problems arose quite naturally from the Christian's faith in the gospel. Now Paul not only preached that gospel to the Thessalonians but, having preached it, remained ever solicitous about their faith (1 Thess 3:5), that they "stand fast in the Lord" (3:8). He sent them Timothy from Athens (3:1) "to establish you in your faith and to exhort you" (3:2). Timothy, "our brother and

God's servant in the gospel of Christ" (3:2), brought back "good news of your faith and love" (3:6). But the good news of their faith and love did not preclude genuine problems. Judging by the evidence in the epistle itself, one of the most pressing was the problem "concerning those who are asleep (*koimomenon*, whence the English 'cemetery,' a sleeping place)," (4:13), i.e., the very genuine problem of the death of a Christian.

What then was this problem which Paul had to tackle in 1 Thessalonians? In Albert Camus' eponymous play, Caligula offers a fairly pithy reflection on the human situation: "Men die and they are not happy!" What another modern writer called "our unbecoming mortality" is a problem that has exercised the human race from the moment it first stared helpless before the irrevocable silence of death. This, however, is not the real concern of Paul in 1 Thessalonians, for the epistle does not offer a philosophical disquisition on human mortality, unbecoming or otherwise. The problem the epistle raises derives rather from the gospel which Paul proclaimed and to which the Thessalonians were converted:

> For since we believe that Jesus died and rose again, even so, through Jesus, God will bring with him those who have fallen asleep (1 Thess 4:14).

In other words, the problem arises out of the consideration of a fundamentally human event like death seen in the light of the gospel and its soteriological, eschatological, and apocalyptic aspects (see above, No. 18). If Jesus truly "died and rose again," if God has indeed "destined us . . . to obtain salvation through our Lord Jesus Christ, who died for us" (1 Thess 5:9–10; 4:14), and if "we who are alive" have to wait "until the coming of the Lord" (4:15), then what happens to the Christians who actually die in the interim, in the time between the resurrection of Jesus from the dead and his coming on "the day of the Lord" (5:2)?

Paul, evidently, judged the period between the two events to be within the span of a single lifetime; indeed, he expected "the day of the Lord" within his own lifetime: "*we* who are alive, who are left . . ." (1 Thess 4:17). Now, it really makes no difference whether the interim is very short, as Paul believed, or extremely long, as we know. What matters is the question itself: What happens to the Christians who die before the coming of the Lord?

The answer Paul gives to this question is valid regardless of the duration of the interim. It also happens to be the only thing that could be said with certainty on this matter; everything else—and that is a great deal indeed—is speculation. What Paul says about the problem of death—"falling asleep" is the biblical expression for it (see, e.g., Ps 13:3; 1 Kgs 2:10; 11:43)—is very simply this:

> We shall always be with the Lord . . . who died for us so that whether we wake or sleep we might live with him (1 Thess 4:17; 5:10; see Rom 6:8; Phil 1:23; Col 3:3).

For, even after Christ died and rose from the dead, Christians still have to die. So even though Christ by his death destroyed, as the author of Hebrews puts it, "him who has the power of death" and delivered "all those who through fear of death were subject to lifelong bondage" (Heb 2:14–15), those who believe in Christ still die. Yet all we can say about them with the certainty of faith is that they are "with the Lord." In a very real sense, that is all a Christian needs to know.

Of course, for those who are alive, death means the loss of a loved one, the irrevocable severance of a relationship— all the poetry and fancy notwithstanding. Death is irreversible, "The undiscovered country from whose bourn/No traveller returns." Therefore, we Christians, like everyone else, grieve at the sight of death. The death of another is our own loss, our diminishment. Therefore, we weep. But Paul adds the one single qualifier, not of Christian death, but of Christian grief: we do not weep "as others who have no hope" (1 Thess 4:13).

The hope that qualifies Christian grief and distinguishes believers from non-believers has its basis in the death and resurrection of Christ:

> For since we believe that Jesus died and rose again, even
> so, through Jesus, God will bring with him those who have
> fallen asleep (1 Thess 4:14).

> For God has not destined us for wrath, but to obtain sal-
> vation through our Lord Jesus Christ, who died for us
> that whether we wake or sleep we might live with him (1
> Thess 5:9–10).

To both these statements Paul adds, "Therefore, comfort one another with these words . . . encourage one another and build one another up" (1 Thess 4:18; 5:11). In this faith, and nowhere else, lies the true comfort of the bereaved.

A look at the history of Christian thought shows how little satisfied Christians have been with this response of Paul. They have sought, by every means available to them, to discover what Paul did not in fact say, and could not have said, simply because he himself did not know. Such eager expectations of specific answers to the inscrutable mystery of death proved wish-fulfilling; and there has never been a dearth of theologians and visionaries and philosophers and charlatans to cater to the insatiable demand. Few have been content to say, "I simply believe that the dead are *with the Lord* . . . and, as to the rest, I simply do not know"—as indeed no one does know, not even Paul.

21. "Until the Coming of the Lord"

The "coming of the Lord" is a translation of a Greek vocable, *parousia*, which has become part of the technical theological vocabulary in English. In classical Greek, the verb whence the noun derives means "to be present"; the noun itself has the sense of "active presence." But later, in the Hellenistic period, *parousia* came to be a technical term used, principally, either of the visit of a ruler such as the emperor, or of the visitation of a god such as Aesculapius in a dream or Dionysus in the cult. Though the notion is, of course, present in the Hebrew Old Testament, the technical term *parousia* finds no strict equivalent there. Yet the Old Testament does speak of God's presence, whether enthroned upon the ark of the covenant, or in the "tent of meeting," or in the history of Israel, or as in the passage in Deuteronomy:

> The Lord came from Sinai, and dawned from Seir upon us; he shone forth from Mount Paran, he came from the ten thousands of holy ones, with flaming fire at his right hand (Dt 33:2).

Of course, the prophets also speak of the "coming" of the Messiah:

> There shall come forth a shoot from the stump of Jesse, and a branch shall grow out of his roots . . . (Is 11:1–3; see 9:1–2; Gen 49:10).

> Rejoice greatly, O daughter of Zion! Shout aloud, O daughter of Jerusalem! Lo, your king comes to you; triumphant and victorious is he . . . (Zech 9:9; see Micah 4—5, especially 5:2–4).

Moreover, *parousia,* the "coming" of our Lord Jesus Christ (1 Thess 5:23), is not merely a technical term in the New Testament, but one of the foundation stones—some would insist, the very cornerstone—of its theology:

> This Jesus, who was taken up from you into heaven, will come in the same way as you saw him go into heaven (Acts 1:11).

This message of the "two men in white robes" in the opening of the Book of Acts might well be a relic of "the original interpretation of the Easter faith." For "the central significance of belief in the parousia is incontestable" in primitive Christianity, which "waits for the Jesus who has come already as the One who is still to come" (A. Oepke, *"parousia," T.D.N.T.,* vol. 5, pp. 867 and 865). Indeed, we should not allow our own greatly attenuated expectations of this coming to blind us to the preponderance of the notion in the portraits of Jesus presented, for instance, by the Synoptics:

> You will see the Son of man seated at the right hand of
> Power, and coming with the clouds of heaven (Mk 14:62;
> Mt 26:64).

Concerning *parousia,* more than half the instances of its occurrence (fourteen out of twenty-four times) are found in the Pauline epistles, and it is used more times in 1 Thessalonians than in any other book of the New Testament. There is no doubt in 1 Thessalonians that Paul himself counts on being present at the parousia:

> We who are alive, who are left until the coming of the
> Lord (1 Thess 4:15, 17).

Though it varied in intensity at different moments of crisis in his life, that expectation of the imminent parousia never really left him. When martyrdom threatened, his desire was "to depart and be with Christ" (Phil 1:23). Yet it is one of the best arguments against the unity of Philippians that in the very same epistle we have Paul saying—perhaps once the threat of martyrdom had momentarily receded:

> But our commonwealth is in heaven, and from it we await
> a Savior, the Lord Jesus Christ (Phil 3:20),

or affirming more unequivocally still: "The Lord is at hand" (Phil 4:5).

Conversely, one of the least suasive arguments for denying the Pauline authorship of 2 Thessalonians (see above, No. 16) is precisely the one based on the expectation of the parousia in 2 Thessalonians 2:1–12: "Now concerning the coming (*parousia*) of our Lord Jesus Christ and our assembling to meet him," when compared with that in 1 Thessalonians 4:13—5:11. It is undeniable that there is a change from one passage to another, but it is a change in concentration. It is perfectly natural to experience variations in the intensity of our expectations of an event we are certain will come to pass, yet are ignorant when exactly it will do so. The adjustment of one's sight after the disappointment of a miscalculated hope is natural and requires surprisingly little time in one and the same individual. Anyone who has waited for a loved one will have first-hand experience of this, and anyone who has not, ought to read Antoine de Saint-Exupéry's *The Little Prince,* and there learn the lesson from its fox.

If 2 Thessalonians interposes premonitory signs of the parousia (2 Thess 2:3–4), it does not thereby deny the imminence of the event. What it denies vehemently is that the event has *already* taken place:

> We beg you, brethren, not to be quickly shaken in mind or excited, either by spirit or by word, or by letter purporting to be from us, to the effect that the day of the Lord has come (2 Thess 2:1–2).

There is no denying the difficulty of interpreting the aggregate of signs in 2 Thessalonians that must come to pass before the parousia. But one may justly wonder if this difficulty cannot be sufficiently explained merely by the common obstacles inherent in this genre of apocalyptic literature, without necessarily requiring a different author for the epistle. If 2 Thessalonians is classed as a "deutero-Pauline" epistle, the reason lies elsewhere than in its teaching on the parousia.

But however one may resolve the question of the authorship of 2 Thessalonians, one point is certain. The conviction of the imminence of the parousia remained with Paul to the end. The idea is not abandoned even in Romans:

> For salvation is nearer to us now than when we first believed (Rom 13:11b; see 8:19, 23).

If this statement is anything more than a jejune truism, its reference must be to Paul's expectation of the parousia. Indeed, the expectation of the coming of the Lord is essential to the Christian gospel in any age. Paul's permanently valid contribution to this essential element of the Christian gospel is precisely this: "that the day of the Lord will come like a thief in the night" (1 Thess 5:2), and that therefore any attempt to calculate "the times and seasons" is to be resolutely avoided.

The unwavering expectation of the parousia must go hand-in-hand with the resigned ignorance of its appointed time. The Christian community that worships the Lordship of Jesus is the community that proclaims "the Lord's death *until he comes*" (1 Cor 11:26).

In the gospel of Paul the parousia is not only the basis of genuine hope but also the true source of "comfort" and "courage" for the Christian community as it lives its life, welcomes new members, or confines to the dust those who fall asleep in the Lord. Paul's answer to both problems of the Thessalonians, that of the death of the Christian and that of the parousia, concludes with the same words:

Therefore, comfort one another (1 Thess 4:18; 5:11).

To those who do not believe in the gospel, this is meager comfort indeed, but to those who do believe, it is a great deal, if only because it rests not on speculation and conjecture, but on faith:

Now faith is the assurance of things hoped for, the conviction of things not seen (Heb 11:1).

FIVE

The Epistle to the Galatians

22. The Gospel and Authority

It is a common enough truism that to understand a letter you have to know something of the circumstances that occasioned it. More often than not, Paul's own letters were written, either to meet specific needs arising from within a given community of believers, or to fend off threats and attacks on that community's faith and its living out of that faith. Though the needs of a given community can be quite fairly surmised from the nature and content of an individual letter, the threats and attacks upon its beliefs and its life of faith are not always easy to specify. The process involves the identification of "Paul's opponents" in Galatia, or Corinth, or Philippi; and this is by no means so simple to do. The very limited quantity of information about those opponents that can be sorted out and reconstructed from Paul's letters should keep us on guard. For not only is the information insufficient to give us a complete picture of them, but most of that information comes from their avowed enemy. This, by the way, is what has assured the perdurance of the interminable debate on the identity and the teachings of Paul's opponents, whether in Galatia or elsewhere.

Nevertheless, in any attempt to identify those opponents, two points should be kept in mind: (1) Paul was by no means the only Christian missionary evangelizing the Gentiles, nor did he himself work alone and unassisted in Gentile territories. (2) The earliest converts to Christianity were all Jews, like Paul, like the other apostles, and like Jesus' own disciples. They may have come from cities other than Jerusalem and

from regions far away from Palestine—as the Pentecost cat-
alogue in Acts so graphically describes them (Acts 2:9–11)—
but they were all Jews nevertheless.

It was some twenty years after that scene of Pentecost, as
the Book of Acts describes it, that an agreement was reached
at the Apostolic Council of Jerusalem (Gal 2:1–10; Acts 15)
which gave the missionary movement of the nascent faith a
fresh impetus and extended it far beyond the territories of its
inception and initial growth, beyond Palestine, Syria, Arabia,
Cilicia and Asia Minor. That agreement reached at Jerusalem
between Paul and Barnabas on the one hand, and James and
Cephas and John on the other, was an accord between equals,
not a unilateral decision imposed by main force of "It has
seemed good to the Holy Spirit and to us" (Acts 15:28 and see
15:25):

> But on the contrary, when they saw that I had been en-
> trusted with the gospel to the uncircumcised, just as Peter
> had been entrusted with the gospel to the circumcised (for
> he who worked through Peter for the mission to the cir-
> cumcised worked through me also for the Gentiles), and
> when they perceived the grace that was given to me,
> James and Cephas and John, who were reputed to be pil-
> lars, gave to me and Barnabas the right hand of fellow-
> ship, that we should go to the Gentiles and they to the
> circumcised (Gal 2:7–9).

So, in his travels back and forth in that Mediterranean
world, Paul must have gradually perfected his method of approach to the Gentiles, his plans for their conversion and the
establishment of communities among them, and eventually
his fashioning an eminently effective "instrument of ecclesiastical policy" (H. Koester, *Introduction*, vol. II, p. 110) out of
the ancient genre of the literary epistle. He had "fellow work-
ers" like Timothy (1 Thess 3:2), Titus (2 Cor 8:23), "Mark,
Aristarchus, Demas and Luke" (Phlm 24), Euodia, Syntyche,
Clement and "the rest . . . whose names are in the book of life"
(Phil 4:3). Paul went up to Jerusalem with Barnabas (Gal 2:1,
9), employed Timothy as his messenger to Philippi and Thes-
salonica (Phil 2:19; 1 Thess 3:6), and had Titus act as his li-

aison with Corinth in particularly delicate circumstances (2 Cor 7:6, 13b, 14; 8:16). Paul's was a large-scale, well-organized operation, and, like so many of its kind, it ran into difficulties, encountered obstacles, and did not escape rivalry from the descendants of the ape.

It is to be expected that, since the first Christians were "Jews by birth" (Gal 2:15), one of the first problems to beset the nascent faith had to do with its relation to the parent stock, Judaism. The law, God's saving word to his people Israel, would have to come under scrutiny, and circumcision, the visible sign of belonging to God's holy people and so of being subject to the law, provided the ostensible principal issue for the dispute. So far as we can judge from the evidence available to us, it was Paul's genius that grasped the problem most firmly and responded to it most uncompromisingly. He saw that, at least in the case of the Gentiles, there was no room for doubt: the gospel set believers free from the law. It was not, and could not have been, a question of "both . . . and," but only of "either . . . or." Paul's decision was not the impulse of a moment but the result of lengthy reflection on the "revelation of Jesus Christ" (Gal 1:12). Yet his missionary experience during that crucial period in his life which preceded the Council at Jerusalem remains obstinately hidden from our eyes (see above, No. 15):

> Then after fourteen years I went up again to Jerusalem with Barnabas, taking Titus along with me. I went up by revelation (*apokalypsis*); and I laid before them (but privately before those who were of repute) the gospel which I preach among the Gentiles, lest somehow I should be running or had run in vain (Gal 2:1–2).

What Paul laid before those in Jerusalem who were of repute could not have been the gospel which "I did not receive from man, nor was I taught it, but it came through a revelation (*apokalypsis*) of Jesus Christ" (Gal 1:12). That was the gospel which Paul preached (1:11); and there was, and could have been, "no other gospel" (1:7). (See the discussion of Paul's gospel, No. 19 above.) Such a gospel could not have been the result of a consensus by a committee, nor was it subject to arbitration by anyone, not even by "those who were of repute" (2:2, 6, 9).

But in the encounter with the ever-changing situations of life, the gospel inevitably requires elaboration in application. This part of the process is not "through a revelation of Jesus Christ" (Gal 1:12), but through the ordinary human course of trial, adaptation, arbitration, consensus, and the ever-present risk of error. Because of this factor in the proclamation of the gospel, Paul was anxious to lay "the gospel which I preach among the Gentiles" (2:2) before the "pillars" (2:9) of Jerusalem. That he went up to Jerusalem "by revelation" (2:2) is a much needed reminder of how necessary the human process is in God's saving design, and how indispensable it must be for the preservation of the "gospel of God."

Circumcision

The specific point at issue was circumcision, i.e., the need to comply with the ritual requirements of Jewish law as a necessary condition for accepting the gospel of Christ. There was no question whether circumcision was good or bad (Gal 5:6; 6:15), but simply whether it was *necessary,* under any circumstance, for a Gentile convert to Christianity. Paul, evidently, had reached the conclusion that it was not, and that was "the gospel which *I preach* among the Gentiles" (2:2), and on which he needed the assurance of the Jerusalem leaders "lest somehow I should be running or had run in vain" (2:2).

If there is a middle ground between anarchy and authority, it could not have found better definition than in this narrative section of Galatians. The half-hearted anarchists as well as the vacillating totalitarians in today's Church will do very well to make Galatians 2 the subject of long and silent reflection.

What Paul did was to take with him to Jerusalem a test case, Titus; and Titus "though he was a Greek . . . was not compelled to be circumcised" (Gal 2:3). There the matter would seem to have been settled, had it not been for

false brethren secretly brought in, who slipped in to spy
out our freedom which we have in Christ Jesus, that they
might bring us into bondage—to them we did not yield
submission even for a moment, that the truth of the gospel might be preserved for you (Gal 2:4–5).

It should be noted that Paul "did not yield submission even
for a moment" to those "false brethren," whoever they were.
This is quite a different thing from his attitude to "those who
were reputed to be something (what they were makes no difference to me; God shows no partiality)" (2:6). Seeking to preserve "the truth of the gospel" is never a dispensation from
courtesy at all times, nor from deference when it is due. Nor
should courtesy or deference be the excuse or the justification
for sycophancy—as Paul's conduct in Antioch (Gal 2:11–14)
well illustrates.

Paul's actions throughout the encounter in Jerusalem
should not blind us to the all-important motives that
prompted them. First of all, "the freedom we have in Christ
Jesus" is something to be ever defended against all those who
would "bring us into bondage," whether by the hectoring
brute force of authority, or by the subtler tyranny of current
fashions; secondly, the refusal to "yield submission even for
a moment" was not a vain show of force, nor the petulant in-
transigence of a jealously guarded jurisdiction, but solely
"that the truth of the gospel might be preserved for you" (Gal
2:5), i.e., for the Gentiles. Indeed, the "truth of the gospel"
can be preserved by no other means except this all too human
process where individual wills, blinkered self-interest, and
perceptive altruism jostle for vantage without the certainty of
victory being either immediately evident or always assured on
the side of the right.

The "Apostolic Council"

It would have made the course of events so much clearer
to us had we but had some clue to the identity of the "false
brethren secretly brought in, who slipped in to spy out our
freedom" (Gal 2:4). But, terse and obscure though the phrase

is, it is clear enough at least to dispel the aureate image of a primitive Church where "those who believed were of one heart and soul" (Acts 4:32). Yet, despite the scheming and the intrigue, the truth of the gospel was preserved. The outcome of what is commonly referred to as the "Apostolic Council of Jerusalem" was a compromise:

> When [those who were of repute] saw that I had been entrusted with the gospel to the uncircumcised, just as Peter had been entrusted with the gospel to the circumcised (for he who worked through Peter for the mission to the circumcised worked through me also for the Gentiles), and when they perceived the grace that was given to me, James and Cephas and John, who were reputed to be pillars, gave to me and Barnabas the right hand of fellowship, that we should go to the Gentiles and they to the circumcised (Gal 2:7–9).

Unsurprisingly enough, the compromise in Jerusalem was accompanied by a financial statement:

> Only they would have us remember the poor, which very thing I was eager to do (Gal 2:10).

This is not unimportant, because Paul's account of the events here is in reality a defense of himself and his actions. The Galatians could not have been ignorant of the financial assistance to "the poor among the saints at Jerusalem" (Rom 15:26), and, sooner or later, they too would have to contribute their share (see 1 Cor 16:1—"as I directed the churches of Galatia"). In that way the Gentile churches gave a concrete sign of their becoming "executors of the Jerusalem agreement" (H.D. Betz, *Galatians,* p. 101), and, on a still profounder level, manifested their gratitude for having come to share in the "spiritual blessings" of the saints at Jerusalem by being of "service to them in material blessings" (Rom 15:26–27). So all in all, the Jerusalem agreement was—if not in the judgment of the jaded cynic, then at least to the eyes of faith—a way "to maintain the unity of the Spirit in the bond of peace" (Eph 4:3).

Alas, the compromise did not last long. Peter, who at first saw no difficulty about eating with the Gentiles in Antioch, "drew back and separated himself" (Gal 2:12) when certain men came from James, who himself must have had a change of heart in Jerusalem. We possess no solid reasons for that change on the part of James, though in Jewish Jerusalem, where the Christian identity had not emerged as a new religion distinct from Judaism, such reasons are not hard to guess. But the motive behind Peter's action in Gentile Antioch was nothing more exalted than fear of "the circumcision party" (2:12). Therefore, Paul opposed Peter "to his face, because he stood condemned," and because with him "the rest of the Jews," i.e., the Jewish Christians, "acted insincerely, so that even Barnabas was carried away by their insincerity (*hypokrisis*)" (Gal 2:11, 13). Those who were reputed to be something were simply, in Paul's words, "not straightforward about the truth of the gospel" (2:14).

Even after due allowance is made for the apologetic purpose behind the account, the events narrated by Paul in Galatians 2:1–10 (in Jerusalem) and 2:11–14 (in Antioch), together with the remarkable concordant and accurate narrative in Acts 15:1–29, provide a relatively clear picture of the Apostolic Council and its immediate aftermath. But for this picture to yield its true significance, it must be seen in the light of subsequent developments in and beyond the New Testament. For, *pace* Aristotle, history is a bit more than "what Alcibiades did and what Alcibiades suffered" (*Poetics* 1451b).

One of the most recent commentaries on Galatians, for example, assesses what happened in Jerusalem thus. Three factions took part in the Jerusalem negotiations, (A) Paul and his group, (B) the "pillars" at Jerusalem, James and Cephas and John, and (C) those characterized by Paul as "false brethren." Party C, the "conservative faction," which demanded circumcision of all converts to Christianity, non-Jews and Jews alike, was defeated. This excluded faction continued its activity and caused severe problems for Paul in Galatia and elsewhere (see Gal 1:6–9). Party B, the Jerusalem leaders, the "middle position" which hammered out the compromise, eventually found its position untenable and changed it (see

Gal 2:11–14). Party A, the Paul and Barnabas faction, won what they came for: the acknowledgement of "the right of Gentile Christianity and its theological message to exist." "Thereby," concludes H.D. Betz, "the future course of the church was determined. . . . The ultimate result of the conference is the fact that the Christian churches today are culturally Gentile and not Jewish" (Betz, *Galatians,* pp. 82–83).

The question is: Are they? Did Paul and his understanding of the gospel really win the day? True, Christians no longer require circumcision; but was that the real point at issue? Or was it, as Galatians 3:1–14 (compare Rom 2:25–29) shows, the whole question of the law and its observance *as a means of salvation?*

> I testify again to every man who receives circumcision that he is bound to keep the whole law. You are severed from Christ, you who would be justified by the law; you have fallen away from grace (Gal 5:3–4).

To be sure, circumcision, dietary restrictions and the like are no longer in force, but was the law confined to them? Did they even constitute its core? In other words, was the dispute about the law simply a question of what part of it to keep and what to omit with impunity?

Christianity might well be "culturally Gentile" but, in another optic, it is theologically very Jewish. Paul's faction, in the end, was not victorious except that it won the right for the new religion to break through the constricting borders of Judaism. But Paul's principal insight did not win the day. Times of crisis and impending catastrophe made the young Church grasp for the securest way to unity and order: the faithful observance of the law and, with the triumph of Christianity in the Gentile world, the power—whether religious or secular—to insure compliance with its demands. Not even the ages of faith lived by faith alone. The history of heresies in the Church is but the map of peaks and excrescences: Encratites, Pelagians, Albigenses, Puritans, Jansenists, "Semi-Pelagians," etc.; but they are only the visible high points in the ordinary, unquestioned assumptions of Christian life, the excesses of assiduously pursued virtues and values.

There is a way of viewing the outcome of the Apostolic Council that reveals Paul to have been the ultimate loser, the mediating Jerusalem faction as the real winners, and the so-called "conservative" group as the qualified winners who paid a price for their victory: they lost their name, but their ideas triumphed. Christian Jews became an extinct minority, but Jewish Christianity won the day. If the struggle was between Jerusalem and Antioch, then Jerusalem ultimately won, even if its name became Rome or Geneva or Canterbury.

This digression is necessary because the issue at stake is ever so important. The view of what happened in Jerusalem and the consequences deriving therefrom affect not only our understanding of Paul's writings and of the rest of the New Testament, but also the assessment of our own situation in to-day's Church.

An eminent exegete once expressed his satisfaction at the triumph of Jerusalem's way: "You couldn't run a Church otherwise!" Perhaps, after all, he was right—if you have to "run" a Church.

23. The Law

In order to deal better with the complex question of what Paul understood by the law, we might do well to distinguish between "the Law" (in upper case) as part of the Sacred Scriptures, and "the law" (in lower case) as a God-given means of regulating the conduct of his people and of defining the terms of their fidelity to his covenant. In a way, this would be to distinguish the "Law" as a literary entity from "law" as an institution of salvation. Such a distinction, however, is merely a matter of convenience, a *distinguo ut intellegam* (I distinguish in order to understand).

When the New Testament speaks of the "law" (*nomos*), it refers principally to that part of God's revealed word in the Scriptures which, together with the prophets, form the chief components of what we call the Old Testament. The phrase "the law and the prophets" is familiar to any reader of the

New Testament. It is a reference to the entirety of the Scriptures, which comprised principally the Law (the Torah as it is called in Hebrew, or the Pentateuch as it is in Greek) and the Prophets (Rom 3:21; see, e.g., Mt 5:17; 7:12; 11:13; Jn 1:45). The five books of the law not only tell the story of how God created, chose, delivered and made a covenant with his people Israel, but they also spell out how God's people, those who believe in Yahweh as Creator and Redeemer of Israel, ought to respond, confessing him as their God and serving him all the days of their life. This is the law of the Lord, his word, his testimonies, his ways, his precepts, statutes, commandments and ordinances (see Ps 119).

> And now, O Israel, give heed to the statutes and the ordinances which I teach you, and do them; that you may live.... Keep them and do them; for that will be your wisdom and your understanding in the sight of the peoples, who, when they hear all these statutes, will say, "Surely this great nation is a wise and understanding people!"... And what great nation is there that has statutes and ordinances so righteous as all this law which I set before you this day? (Dt 4:1, 6, 8; see 4:40; 13:4; 26:18–19; Ex 19:5; 15:26; Lev 18:5).

The Lord gave Israel "the law and the commandment . . . for their instruction" (Ex 24:12). As Paul reminds them, this is their badge of honor and distinction among the nations:

> But if you call yourself a Jew and rely upon the law and boast of your relation to God and know his will and approve what is excellent, because you are instructed in the law, and if you are sure that you are a guide to the blind, a light to those who are in darkness, a corrector of the foolish, a teacher of children, having in the law the embodiment of knowledge and truth . . . (Rom 2:17–20).

The books containing this law of God for his people are collectively called the "Torah" in Hebrew, which is a more general and less strictly juridical term than its Greek equivalent *nomos*, which is translated "law." The Torah is really not so much a law digest as a set of instructions. Its narrative sections, no less than its explicit legislation, are meant to regulate the Israelites' conduct in relation to the Creator, Redeemer and Lord of Israel, as well as their dealings and relationships with their fellow Israelites, with aliens, enemies, friends, foreigners, neighbors, and all the other creatures on the face of the earth. Thus, the religion of the Old Testament, like any genuine religion, involved the whole of one's existence. The Torah provided the instructions and guidelines to direct aright the Israelite's conduct as a creature of God, as a member of his people, and a party to his covenant. Because of this Paul speaks of the law as "holy . . . spiritual . . . good," and of the commandment as "holy and just and good" (Rom 7:12, 14, 16). The requirements of the law are "just" (Rom 8:4). It finds its ultimate fulfillment in love:

Therefore love is the fulfilling of the law (Rom 13:10).

A. *An Institution of Salvation*

Seen in this light, the law is very much an institution of salvation ordained by the God who shows "steadfast love to thousands of those who love me and keep my commandments" (Ex 20:6). To regulate one's conduct by this law, to live one's life according to its teachings and precepts, is to be pleasing to God, to stand in right relation to the Lord of the covenant, and to find life:

> I call heaven and earth to witness against you this day, that
> I have set before you life and death, blessing and curse;
> therefore choose life, that you and your descendants may
> live, loving the Lord your God, obeying his voice, and
> cleaving to him; for that means life to you and length of
> days (Dt 30:19–20; see Am 5:4—"Seek me and live").

To seek the Lord, to seek his face, and in New Testament terms—to seek his "kingdom" (Mt 6:33) are all expressions of the profoundly religious search for life with God, for true "eternal life."

Of course, in this context, the temptation to abuse this

God-given gift is a bit more comprehensible and a good deal less surprising. What can go unnoticed, however, is the fact that such abuse arises as much out of outright violations of the law's precepts as from wrongheaded observance of its every command and ordinance. If creatures sin often by a rebellious denial of their creaturehood and by their refusal to obey the law of God, they sin as often and as persistently by a subtle and insidious pretense to attain by faithful observance of the law, if not at divinity itself, then at least to some equality with it: "You will be like God" (Gen 3:5).

If our reading of the New Testament has left us with the image of a world over-concerned with the observance of every "iota and dot" of the law (Mt 5:18) and the excessive "legalism of the Pharisees," then we do well to remember that such phenomena were the culmination of a trend, echoes of which are heard throughout the Old Testament, whether in the prophets' polemic against merely external observance:

> For I desire steadfast love and not sacrifice, the knowledge of God, rather than burnt offerings (Hos 6:6; see Mt 9:13; 12:7);

or in the Psalms' insistence on a religion of the heart:

> Sacrifice and offering you do not desire. . . .
> I delight to do your will, O my God (Pss 40:6, 8; 51:16–17).

Thus, the tendency to "void the word of God through your tradition which you hand on" (Mk 7:13) was not a phenomenon peculiar to the Judaism of the first century, nor is it unknown in the Christianity of the twentieth. An ineradicable desire for life, coupled with a limitless capacity for self-deception, can turn the holiest of divine gifts into instruments of servitude both for ourselves and for others.

In Paul's letters, such trends in creative disobedience to the word of God find expression in his bitter and protracted struggle against the opponents of the gospel. The law, of course, could be regarded as a set of ritual prescriptions (circumcision, the sabbath, abstention from meat offered to idols, etc.), which not only make the worshiper pleasing to God but also ensure divine help and protection. Paul's opponents in Galatia seem to have been of this variety of Jewish Christians. They offered Christians an "added plus" to their all-sufficient faith in the gospel. They were astute propagandists ("They make much of you"—Gal 4:17), and evidently successful enough in their efforts among the Galatians to cause Paul to be "perplexed about them" and to be "in travail" with them (Gal 4:20, 19).

The question came down to whether non-Jewish converts to Christianity needed to keep, not the whole gamut of the complicated ordinances of the law, but merely the ritual of circumcision, as some guarantee of belonging to God's people. But of course, as Paul is quick to point out:

> I testify again to every man who receives circumcision that he is bound to keep *the whole law* (Gal 5:3; see Rom 2:25).

Paul's "testimony" in Galatians 5:3 is more than a theological conclusion from the nature of the law. It is a wholly justified observation on the human willingness to embrace ritual servitude. So he has to remind his readers that the question is not whether or not circumcision is better for a Christian believer; it is simply that henceforth circumcision is irrelevant:

> For in Christ Jesus neither circumcision nor uncircumcision is of any avail (Gal 5:6).

> For neither circumcision counts for anything nor uncircumcision (1 Cor 7:19; Gal 6:15).

Therefore, whether or not they reflected on the human penchant for added religious security by means of ritual observance, Paul's opponents must have insisted on the need for, and the usefulness of, such a divinely ordained institution as circumcision toward salvation.

B. A Way of Perfection

Another way of regarding the law is to see it as a way of perfection, a means of attaining a set ideal. This is the familiar path trodden by the seekers after "perfection" in every age: the anxiety to attend to the minutest details, the bookkeeper's mind and method of dealing with the deity, the impatience with imperfection—whether one's own or, more especially, someone else's. Perhaps this view of the law as a way of perfection characterized Paul's opponents in Philippi. Such a way of seeing the law finds a familiar echo in the prayer of the Pharisee in Luke:

> God, I thank thee that I am not like other men, extortioners, unjust, adulterers, or even like this tax collector. I fast twice a week, I give tithes of all that I get (Lk 18:11–12).

This view of the law is not very far removed from the one that sets a high price on punctilious ritual observance. For, whether by fidelity to ritual requirements or by careful observance of every quillet of the law, the individual's aim is ultimately to secure some hold on the divinity, to make a just God obligated to render earned rewards and requite merited blessings. Neither tendency, however, is in itself reprehensible. It is only when either ritual observance of the law or its perfect fulfillment is regarded as a complement to, or a necessary condition for, the gospel of salvation in Jesus Christ that it poses a threat to the truth of that gospel, and subverts the freedom it proclaims. It is this which made Paul expostulate with the Galatians:

> You were running well; who hindered you from obeying the truth? . . . I wish those who unsettle you would mutilate themselves (Gal 5:7, 12),

and to warn the Philippians:

> Look out for the dogs, look out for the evil-workers, look out for those who mutilate the flesh (Phil 3:2).

C. *The Law as Wisdom*
     A third view of the law that is reflected in Paul's polemic against the Jewish-Christian opponents of the gospel is the

one least recognized by the casual reader. It is more a temptation to "eggheads" than to dealers in vigil lights and votive candles. It is the temptation to regard the law as the key to a superior wisdom, the *grimoire* to conjure open the locked doors to the storehouses of light. It sees the Scriptures as a book of "hidden truths" (H. Koester, *Introduction*, vol. II, p. 118) accessible to the philosophers, the Spinozas of every enlightened age. Quite likely, the correspondence gathered in 2 Corinthians shows Paul dealing with this kind of "wisdom."

Here again the threat to the gospel is very real, since such an attitude to the law not only views it as a primer to true wisdom, but pretends to attain salvation by means of that wisdom. This is what, in its more primitive sense, *gnosis* (whence we have "gnostic" and "gnosticism") means. It is not the quest for knowledge (*gnosis*) as such that is perilous—far from it; it is the view of its acquisition as salvation that is pernicious. Paul's unsparing polemic against this threat posed by Jewish Christianity is reflected—as we have seen already—in his attitude toward those who would preach the gospel "by earthly wisdom" (see 2 Cor 1:12), "the wisdom of man . . . of this age or of the rulers of this age, who are doomed to pass away" (1 Cor 2:5–6).

Whether, then, the law was regarded as ritual prescriptions to be carried out, or ordinances to be faithfully obeyed, or clues to be studiously pursued in search of a hidden wisdom, it is always regarded as a means of salvation, of pleasing the deity, of becoming a preferred friend of God. This use of the law as a means to personal salvation is the common denominator to all three attitudes that constituted the real threat to the gospel in all the propaganda of Paul's opponents. To Paul himself, any such attitude to the law compromised the unique all-sufficiency of the gospel of Jesus Christ. A non-Jewish Christian, a Gentile converted to Christianity, had no need whatsoever of becoming a "Christian Jew" in any manner or form, either by undergoing circumcision, or by obeying the law, or by seeking a hidden wisdom in its pages. The gospel of Jesus Christ in itself brought salvation to those who believed—and there was neither room for, nor possibility of, adding anything no matter how "holy and spiritual and good."

This understanding of the gospel explains not only Paul's relentless struggle against any and all of its perverters, but also the intemperate fury of his attacks against his opponents:

> I wish those who unsettle you would mutilate themselves (Gal 5:12; see 6:11–13).

> Look out for the dogs, look out for evil-workers, look out for those who mutilate the flesh (Phil 3:2).

> Where is the wise man? Where is the scribe? Where is the debater of this age? Has not God made foolish the wisdom of this world? (1 Cor 1:20).

What was at issue in all these remonstrations was whether anything ought to be, or could ever be, added to the salvation already brought about by the gospel of Christ. So, once the option was seen within this soteriological context, there was neither hesitation nor compromise possible between the gospel and the law. This was an outright and decisive choice that had to be made, as Paul knew at first hand from the history of his own conversion. It is precisely this decisive option which he relates at such great length in the account of his conversion precisely in the letter to the Galatians (1:11–24; see above, No. 13). Such a need for a clear option resulted in that ineluctable struggle between Judaism and Christianity among the "circumcised," and between Jewish-Christianity and Gentile-Christianity among the "uncircumcised."

The intemperate language of Paul in this bitter polemic might disconcert, disappoint, or even scandalize some. But they would do well to remember that the greatness of Paul does not depend on his conformity to the arbitrary norms of our social mores. He is great not because he meets the standards and requirements of our modern image-makers, the public relations pundits who manufacture our instant ersatz heroes, but because he transcends them. The undeniable harshness of Paul's langauge, if it requires explanation at all, ought to be seen against his own Jewish background. That background must have prepared him well both for the intemperate language of Israel against its enemies and for the excoriating objurgations of Israel's prophets against Israel itself. Any reader of the Bible will not be—or at least ought not to be—surprised at any of Paul's outbursts. A cursory reading of Psalm 109 or of Ezekiel 16 should check most urges to expurgate Paul and rid his epistles of "offensive" passages.

Such is the way of religious polemic. Temperate language has not often been the idiom of religious debate, and the history of opposition to the new religion goes back to its very inception—as witness Paul's own persecuting of the Christians before his conversion. In his first letter, he comforts the Thessalonians by reminding them that they were not alone in suffering. This is the timeworn commonplace of all would-be comforters:

> For you, brethren, became imitators of the churches of God in Christ Jesus which are in Judea; for you suffered the same things from your own countrymen as they did from the Jews, who killed both the Lord Jesus and the prophets, and drove us out, and displease God and oppose all men by hindering us from speaking to the Gentiles that they may be saved—so as always to fill up the measure of their sins. But God's wrath has come upon them at last (1 Thess 2:14–16).

This passage, to cite a well-known example, is so opposed to the pretended tolerance of the present age that some scholars feel the need to trundle out the whole creaky apparatus of Teutonic scholarship in order to excise it from the text. Though the textual evidence for its belonging to 1 Thessalonians is as solid as anything else in the epistle, the arguments propounded by these scholars seek to demonstrate that the verses are a later interpolation, and hence not by Paul himself. The suggestion—and it is hardly more than that—might well be true; but if it were true, then what do we do with these and other similarly "unfit" verses that are either incongruent with our image of Paul or offensive to our current sensibilities? What does it mean to say this or that verse is not by Paul even though it is attested in the most ancient manuscripts of our New Testament?

To decide to exscind a word, a verse, or a whole passage (e.g., Mk 16:9–20 or Jn 7:53—8:1) for lack of textual evidence is quite different from deciding, on other than text-critical grounds, that a verse or a passage or a whole work (like 2 Thessalonians or Ephesians) could not have been by Paul himself. Whether by Paul or by someone else, these verses or passages or works are part of the New Testament, and their authority is not diminished one bit by their different authorship. But the "scientifically" excised passages are relegated to the limbo of irrelevance simply because they do not fit our view of Paul's theology, or prove rebarbative to our social sensibilities.

Such attempts at "expurgating" the New Testament text are sophisticated—if not immediately evident—forms of a fundamentalism that sees in the New Testament an unexceptionable code of conduct and the unfailing justification for all our espoused causes. The intention behind such bowdlerizing zeal is laudable, if misguided. It pretends, in the case of 1 Thessalonians 2:14–16 for example, to combat the persecution of the Jews by depriving their patently unjust oppressors of a justifying "word of the Lord." But then what do you do with Matthew 27:25 or Romans 10:2–3, or indeed with the whole Gospel of John? Similarly, to right an evident injustice, modern scholars try to excise 1 Corinthians 14:34 ("the women should keep silence in the churches"); but, here again, what do you do with 1 Timothy 2:11–12. "These," retort the scholars, "are non-Pauline," and thereby imply that they are either irrelevant or departures from a pristine ideal. The process is endless, and human ingenuity before the unpalatable fact is inextinguishable.

No! The only honest and truly "scientific" way of dealing with such verses and with the difficulties they very obviously raise is to leave them in their attested context, and deal with them as one would with a genuine problem, not by pretending that they were not written by Paul and therefore do not really matter. Paul, of all people, did not mean his every "jot and tittle" to be taken as law. It would be more honest to say,

"Hier irrt Paulus!" (Paul is wrong here!) And when Christians or the Christian churches use Paul or any other part of the New Testament to perpetuate their injustices, it is the true courage of genuine scholarship to remind them that they are perverting the gospel, not to show them that their injustice has no basis in Scriptures.

In the final analysis, it is a worse and subtler "fundamentalism" that would require, not merely infallibility, but perfection of character in the sacred authors. It is one thing to be reassured that a given author communicates the revealed truth inerrantly; it is quite something else to suppose that such author's tastes and preferences and prejudices conform to a foreordained norm set up by our own prejudices and preferences and norms. Paul was capable of rage and anger, of writing words that others, in his time or in subsequent generations, might find regrettable. Worse still, his words are apt to be, and have often been, used by morally blind, so-called Christians to persecute Jews, to be unjust to women, or to subjugate "those who have a different complexion or slightly flatter noses than ourselves." Of course, it is not the least reason for the phenomenon of fundamentalism that people regard the New Testament as a source of answers to moral questions and guidelines to our—often perverted—human conduct. But it is no less fundamentalist to imagine that by excising this or that verse from 1 Thessalonians, or 1 Corinthians, or Philemon, we will have struck a blow against anti-Semitism, or for women's rights, or against slavery. In a sense, such an attitude would be to regard the New Testament as a new version of the law from which Christ has set us free.

24. "The Freedom for Which Christ Has Set Us Free"

It is hardly a coincidence that the epistle where the word "law" (*nomos*) occurs with striking frequency (thirty-two times in Galatians out of a total of one hundred and nineteen times in Paul, of which seventy-two times are in Romans, a much longer epistle) should also have a high frequency of the word "freedom" (*eleutheria*) and its cognates (which total forty-one instances in all the New Testament, twenty-eight of which are in Paul, and of these eleven are in Galatians). To cite these statistics is merely a way of saying that Paul's concern with the topic of law and freedom is a major theme occupying most of the letter to the Galatians, which has been called "the magna carta of Christian freedom." Indeed, "*eleutheria* ('freedom') is the central theological concept which sums up the Christian's situation before God as well as in the world. It is the basic concept underlying Paul's argument throughout the letter" (H.D. Betz, *Galatians,* p. 255).

The converts in Galatia had evidently grasped the meaning of freedom. They had enjoyed the blessings and "satisfaction" (Gal 4:15) which its gospel brings. They started out with flying colors, ran so well (5:7), and experienced so many things (3:4); yet, in a remarkably short time, their pace slackened, their fervor cooled, and all seemed lost. Paul remonstrates with them:

> Did you experience so many things in vain? . . . What has become of the satisfaction you felt? . . . You were running well; who hindered you from obeying the truth? (Gal 3:4; 4:15; 5:7).

They who had had a taste of the exhilarating freedom of the gospel were all too willing to "submit again to a yoke of slavery" (Gal 5:1). Other missionaries had come in the wake of Paul and "bewitched" them (3:1) and made them turn to "a different gospel" (1:6), a gospel "contrary" to that which Paul himself had preached (1:8). Those who had known the freedom of the gospel were all too ready to believe that "a man is . . . justified by works of the law" rather than "through faith in Jesus Christ" (2:16). They were willing to nullify the death of Christ on the cross, to bow to the yoke of a gospel of justification "through the law":

> For if justification were through the law, then Christ died to no purpose (Gal 2:21).

We should not be too quick to judge the Galatians; their history, after all, is the history of Christians through the ages, the biography of each one of us. To understand the gospel of freedom and the fate it suffered in Galatia—and thereafter in Christendom—we should keep in mind that Paul speaks in the letter to the Galatians of the believers' freedom principally from "the law." If his polemical needs forced him to stress this particular aspect of Christ's death for us, then we should not forget that freedom from the law is but one aspect of the redemptive work which set us free from death and sin as well as from the law. Indeed, a Christian's freedom from the law is but a corollary to his freedom from sin and from death (see No. 31 below).

In order to drive home to the Galatians the meaning of his gospel of freedom, Paul, a Jew "by birth" (Gal 2:15) and "as to the law a Pharisee" (Phil 3:5), says some harsh things against the law: its curse (Gal 3:10), its impotence to "make alive" (Gal 3:21), and the "yoke of slavery" it imposes (5:1). Of course, he recognizes all too well the positive aspects of the law: its divine origin (3:19), the fact that it does not "contradict the promise of God" (3:21 NEB), and the pedagogic role it played "until Christ came" (3:23–24).

Seen in this light, the law as *paidagogos* not only could be but should be used in the proclamation of the gospel. So did Paul rightly use it. For the genuinely Christian alternative to seeing the law either as a set of ritual prescriptions, or as a guide to perfection, or as a code enciphering a hidden wisdom is to see it as the book of the saving events and promises which find their culmination and ultimate fulfillment in Christ Jesus. The course of the argument on behalf of Christian freedom in Galatians provides excellent examples of this use of "the law" by Paul (Gal 3:15–29; see also 4:21—5:1; Rom 4:1–15; 10:5–13).

In the letter to the Galatians, Paul's argument for Christian freedom is, principally, an argument for freedom from the "yoke of slavery" (Gal 5:1) of the law. His own conversion did really mean tearing down (Gal 2:18) the whole secure structure of the law which he had erected like some secure bulwark around himself. His conversion meant that "through the law" he "died to the law" (Gal 2:19). So the price he had to pay for that freedom in Christ Jesus was high indeed; and, as a consequence, the impelling ardor of his argument against the slavery of the law is not only comprehensible but compelling. What is not so comprehensible is the Galatians' ready willingness to assume the yoke of slavery to the law after they had had their first taste of true Christian freedom.

Nevertheless, the success of Paul's opponents in Galatia is not all that difficult to understand. The Galatians' willingness to barter away their freedom in Christ and to embrace the slavery of the law is but one instance of a common enough human phenomenon throughout history. For all their claptrap and overblown rhetoric, men prefer a slavery of their own choosing to paying the high price which genuine freedom exacts. Few indeed are the unwilling slaves in this world when compared to all who willingly embrace servitude. Willing slaves are always the hardest to set free. The seductions of tangible and measurable achievement, the facility of foreordained rules over the heavy burden of personal decision, and the temptation to obligate the divinity by an "I give, you give" (*do ut des*) mentality have always proven too strong to resist for the believers in the gospel of freedom.

The "False Brethren"

The "false brethren," the "Judaizers," or the "party of the circumcision," could argue convincingly from the very premises Paul would never deny: that the law is God-given, is spiritual, good and holy (Rom 7), and that it is certainly not "against the promises of God" (Gal 3:21), which find their fulfillment in the gospel. But, of course, that was not the point, any more than was circumcision itself the point. What was at issue was the way in which salvation is attained: whether "by works of the law" or "by faith in Christ" (Gal 2:16; 3:2; Rom 3:28; 5:1; Phil 3:9) (see Nos. 12 and 13 above). Paul knew all too well that "neither circumcision counts for anything, nor uncircumcision" (Gal 6:15; 5:6; 1 Cor 7:19; Rom 2:25). He also knew that "every man who receives circumcision . . . is bound to keep *the whole law*" (Gal 5:3); that "circumcision indeed is of value *if you obey the law*" (Rom 2:25). But it was precisely from that law that the gospel set the believers free.

It was the freedom "which we have in Christ Jesus" (Gal

2:4) that was threatened by the "bondage" of the law in Galatia, by the Galatians' "desire to be under law" (4:21). The curious thing about this is that, as H.D. Betz remarks, "the concept which best sums up the Galatians' basic self-understanding is the concept of 'freedom' " (*Galatians,* p. 29). What made them so ready to relinquish it was the persistent quest for the tangible in religious life, the compulsive need for the reassurance of a prescribed course of action—both ritual (Gal 4:10) and moral (Gal 2:16; 3:2, 5, 10), and the restless urge to discover at every moment just how they stood in relation to God.

It has also been argued that what rendered the Galatians so receptive to the arguments of the "opponents" was their awakening to the fact of sin within a community still in the afterglow of its conversion. The opponents proffered the "adequate and effective" means of Torah and circumcision as the surest safeguards to the new Christian life of the community and its members (Betz, *Galatians,* p. 29). This would be an alluring and plausible solution to the problem of sinfulness within any community, but in actual fact it has never put an end to sin in the Christian community, any more than it did in the Jewish community.

What the law and its requirements do is define more sharply the sphere of sin:

> Yet, if it had not been for the law, I should not have known sin (Rom 7:7).

> For no human being will be justified in [God's] sight by works of the law, since through the law comes knowledge of sin (Rom 3:20).

Thus, the law shackles the believer to a set of rules and norms, violation of which could be righted by compliance with specified prescriptions, which in turn beget new norms and rules, etc., etc. In other words, all that the return to circumcision and the law does is provide the believer with a means of assuring or at least of checking how well one's own account stands with God. No amount of preaching that we are "not justified [reckoned righteous] by works of the law but through faith in Jesus Christ" (Gal 2:16) could outweigh the deep-felt satisfaction of knowing oneself to be "as to righteousness under the law blameless" (Phil 3:6), or at least of knowing specifically what one has to do to get there.

Anyone who has ever tried to explain this simple fact to Christians could imagine, even if confusedly, what a struggle Paul had on his hands in Galatia. It was—if one can put it thus—more difficult for Paul to draw Christians away from the seductions of the law than for the prophets to keep Israel free from alien gods. What was at issue was remarkably similar in both instances: a visible idol is more reassuring than an invisible God, especially if this God stubbornly refuses to be according to his worshipers' image: "I am God and not man" (Hos 11:9). So, too, working to prescribed rules and earning quantifiable merit is more reassuring than belief in the fullness of a free gift requiring nothing in return and demanding only faith, especially when the required faith remains refractory to our preferred methods of verification. Belief in the gospel does not banish sin visibly from the world, nor does it alter the sinner. Belief that Christ died for me and set me free from the bondage of sin and of the law ("For sin will have no dominion over you, since you are not under law but under grace"—Rom 6:14) somehow does not satisfy me as much as my doing something for myself, lending a hand, contributing my share, however negligible, toward my salvation.

Law and Sin

The God of Israel gave his people a law to keep them close to him; they made the law into a means of getting a hold on him, to "boast of [their] relation to God" (Rom 2:17).

> For he is not a real Jew who is one outwardly, nor is true circumcision something external and physical. He is a Jew who is so inwardly, and real circumcision is a matter of the heart, spiritual and not literal. His praise is not from me but from God (Rom 2:28–29; see Jer 4:4; Dt 10:16).

The law was thus perverted into a means of sinning, not indeed by obeying God's word, but by imagining that the obedience itself gave one a title to God and to his gifts. "But sin, finding opportunity in the commandment, deceived me," is how Paul puts it (Rom 7:11, 8). "The very commandment which promised life proved to be death to me" (Rom 7:10; 4:15).

It was, one might say, inevitable that sin found "opportunity in the commandment," that "apart from the law sin lies dead" (Rom 7:8). The fault, of course, was not in the law itself; it was rather in man and in man's irrepressible grasping for divinity on his own terms: "We know that the law is spiritual; but I am carnal (*sarkinos*)" (Rom 7:14). The "carnal," used here in its pejorative sense, means the realm of the "flesh" (*sarx*), the domain of all that in the creature is insubordinate and contrary to the Creator. Thus, it was not the keeping of this or that commandment that was the sin; the sin was in imagining that obeying a positive commandment and avoiding a negative one gave the believer some title to justification before God, some right to boast, some secure grip on life.

In order to get at the root of this perversion,

God sent forth his Son, born of a woman, born under the law, to redeem those who were under the law (Gal 4:4–5).

What the creature had persistently grasped for is offered freely and unconditionally: the "adoption as sons" (Gal 4:5). This ought to set the believer free, free from keeping this set of rules, avoiding that list of prohibitions, or fulfilling that series of ritual prescriptions, in order to get into a right relationship with God. That relationship has been set right once and for all in the death of Christ upon the cross. Therefore, you have no need to earn a salvation already freely and irrevocably given; you are incapable of meriting what is already gratuitously yours; and there is no room to strive to get where God has already set you.

Such is the freedom of the gospel. Those who enjoy it will "run in the way of thy commandments" (Ps 119:32). Indeed, they will do things no law could require anyone to do. They are free not only from the law but also from the need to interpret it, and, above all, from the need to subject themselves to the tyranny of its expert interpreters. They do all things not *in order* to be saved, but precisely *because* they have been saved:

> For in Christ Jesus you *are* all sons of God, through faith (Gal 3:26).

And there's the rub! It is only "through faith." There is no other way to salvation except faith in the gospel of Jesus Christ. Such faith offers no palpable guarantees, and leaves no room whatsoever for "boasting."

What the gospel proclaims is no more than the fact that Christ has redeemed us and set us wholly free to live, not for ourselves, but for him and for others. Nevertheless, the persistent clamor of demurs, of objections, or sometimes even of zealous outrage, which greeted and continues to greet what Paul says about our total freedom from the law seems incomprehensible. To proclaim that Christ set us free from death is cause for rejoicing, however obscure the meaning of the affirmation must remain for those who necessarily have to die one day. To preach that Christ set us free from sin is always welcome, however uncertain the hearers might be of its true import. But to state, or even to quote Paul as saying, that Christ set us free from the law rouses the deepest indignation of believers and casts the shadow of suspicion on the proclaimer. Any such statement about Christian freedom from the law seems always to be regarded either as incitement to rebellion, or as the opening gambit in a seduction.

Why being set free from the law should be so generally taken to mean abandoning God and turning against one's neighbor is a riddle. To the mind of most Christians, lawlessness seems to be the only meaning that freedom from the law can possibly have. To preach the gospel of our freedom from the law, which Paul proclaimed so persistently, is to court the risk of having both freedom and the law misunderstood. Paul's experiences with the Galatians and with the Corinthians in particular illustrate this double misunderstanding well.

One tendency among Christians is to argue that the believers will not "lead a life worthy of the calling to which [they] have been called" (Eph 4:1) unless there is a law detailing precisely how they are to do so. Another tendency is to understand freedom as irresponsibility, as unchecked license. The first, which might be called an "ascetic" tendency, is the prevalent Jewish-Christian type of Christianity where law regulates every aspect of life and thought and worship. The second, which might be called "libertine," has surfaced from time to time in the history of Christianity, but, very early on, it was dealt a blow from which it never fully recovered. Those who embark upon this "libertine" interpretation of freedom from the law often leave the Christian community before they have had time to elaborate theological claims for their position. Perhaps, however, today's reluctance to name anything "sin" might well be the subtle re-emergence of just such a tendency in the Church.

The Call to Freedom

Paul's position, however, was unequivocal. To recall the Galatians to their senses, he reminds them:

> For you were called to freedom, brethren; only do not use your freedom as an opportunity for the flesh, but through love be servants of one another (Gal 5:13).

The freedom Christ won for us is not a freedom *from* all responsibility and *for* one's ends. It is a freedom conferred upon Christians so that they can be more free to give of themselves in the loving service of others: "against such there is no law" (see Gal 5:23). The discussion of the love commandment in 1 Corinthians and in Romans (see below, Nos. 27 and 33) should bring this particular element to the fore. What is needed at this point is a reminder—a plea would be more accurate—that Christian freedom is infinitely more exigent than any law was or could ever be, that the responsibility it lays squarely on the individual believer is both weighty and, ultimately, inescapable, and that this freedom is really the only true way which a Christian has to proclaim to the world the good news: "For freedom Christ has set us free" (Gal 5:1).

"Freedom from the law," comments Heinrich Schlier, "thus means specifically freedom from the moralism which awakens hidden self-seeking. It means freedom from the secret claim which man makes on himself in the form of legal demand. It means freedom from the meeting of this claim in the form of legal achievement. It means freedom from self-lordship before God in the guise of serious and obedient responsibility towards Him" (H. Schlier, *"eleutheria," T.D.N.T.,* vol. II, p. 497).

Paul never conceived freedom from the law as anything but a gift which, like all gifts, must be put at the service of others in a life expended for others. Yet, even "the law of Christ" (Gal 6:2; 5:13; 1 Cor 9:21; Rom 13:10) has been perverted into a means of self-preservation and self-seeking. The temptation to be one's own master, to "self-lordship," "not by transgressing the Law, but by fulfilling it according to [one's] own interpretation" (H. Schlier, p. 497), has proven too strong to resist. We always play the casuists with God's law, whether we be masters in Israel or Christians in the pew. In the observance of the law there is really no difference. All, Christians and Jews alike, observe the law in their striving after "recognition in the sight of God," and "all the striving is aimed at winning this recognition in God's sight" (Rudolf Bultmann, "Christ the End of the Law," p. 43).

What the gospel of freedom proclaims is that God has already granted us this "recognition":

> For in Christ Jesus you are all sons of God, through faith (Gal 3:26; see 4:7 and Rom 8:15).

This Christ is quite simply "the end of the law" (Rom 10:4) as a way of, or a means to, salvation. Therefore, to belong to Christ is to be the master of all things: "All things are yours" (1 Cor 3:21). To belong to him sets us genuinely free from all the shackles that bind us to the drudgery of our self-strivings and to the tyranny of the expectations of others. The freedom that is ours "in Christ Jesus" relieves us of the enslaving need we all have to "boast of men" (1 Cor 3:21a). It sets us free from the bogus standards and norms they set for belonging to this or that category of Christians, from the counterfeit ideals they erect for recognition by this or that sacred authority. But, above all, the freedom we have in Christ Jesus relieves us of the need for self-deception (see 1 Cor 3:18), whether it be the hypocrisy of our dealing with others (see Gal 2:13), the severity with which we judge ourselves (see Rom 14:22), or the awkward posturings we assume before God:

> So let no one boast of men. For all things are yours, whether Paul or Apollos or Cephas or the world or life or death or the present or the future, all are yours; and you are Christ's; and Christ is God's (1 Cor 3:21-23).

With good reason did Bultmann call this "the mightiest expression of freedom" (R. Bultmann, *Theology*, vol. I, p. 331).

SIX

The First Letter
to the Corinthians

25. The Limits of Christian Freedom

Drawing what seemed like the inevitable conclusion from the gospel of freedom, some in Corinth boasted: "I am free to do anything" (1 Cor 6:12 NEB). In his letter to the Corinthians, Paul does not deny this. He only qualifies it:

> "All things are lawful for me," but not all things are helpful. "All things are lawful for me," but I will not be enslaved by anything (1 Cor 6:12).

Paul's concern is that the gospel itself should not be made into an instrument of subjection, that the freedom it proclaims must not be perverted into a slavery. This is more than a question of avoiding excesses, of seeking the golden mean. It is rather a question about the very nature of freedom. For, like all gifts, freedom confers a responsibility, and, like all responsibilities, it commands a price.

The responsibility that the gift of freedom confers is, of course, the responsibility of personal decision, the burden of option, and the consequent onus of accountability. This is what distinguishes true freedom from "libertinism," which is the unbridled exercise of reckless irresponsibility. The price which such libertinism exacts is the constraints it sets on the freedom of others. One is always free at somebody else's expense. Without a consideration of the freedom of others, the exercise of my own liberty is tyranny, pure and simple.

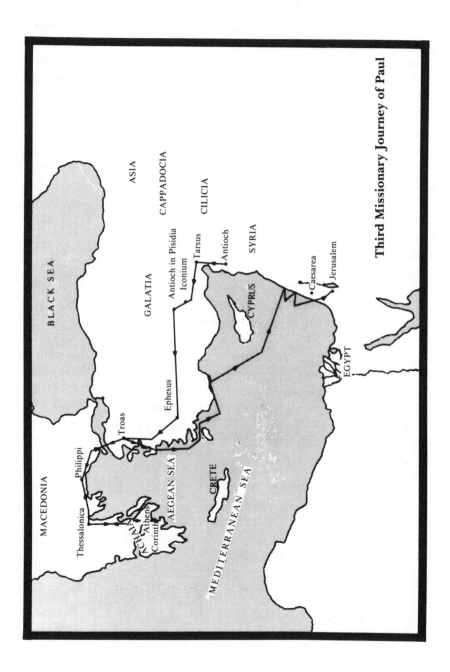

Third Missionary Journey of Paul

The responsibility imposed on the individual by the gift of freedom and the price it commands are but common sense born out of reflection on the human experience in history. Both the responsibility and the cost of freedom receive their peculiarly Christian hue from the light shed by the gospel on their exercise. In dealing with both these qualifications of freedom, the responsibility of personal decision and the respect for the other, Paul provides in 1 Corinthians an answer to the question about the limits of Christian freedom. It should be kept in mind here that to set limits is to define and not to curtail the exercise of freedom.

The dealings which Paul had with the "church of God which is at Corinth" are in themselves a paradigm of what the Latin Vulgate translates as his "daily solicitude for all the churches" (see 2 Cor 11:28). 1 Corinthians is not the first letter Paul wrote to Corinth: "I wrote to you in my letter . . ." (1 Cor 5:9), a letter which, unfortunately, is lost to us. In the time between that (now lost) letter and 1 Corinthians, Paul received news of the Corinthians by word of mouth ("It has been reported to me by Chloe's people"—1 Cor 1:11; see 5:1) as well as by letter ("Now concerning the matters about which you wrote"—1 Cor 7:1). It was quite likely that this letter which the Corinthians addressed to him provided the more immediate occasion for Paul's writing what we have come to call the "First" Epistle to the Corinthians. He must have composed it just about the time he was getting ready to leave Ephesus:

> I will visit you after passing through Macedonia. . . . But I will stay in Ephesus until Pentecost, for a wide door for effective work has opened to me, and there are many adversaries (1 Cor 16:5, 8–9).

So, the winter of the year 53–54 is a very likely date for the epistle (H. Koester, *Introduction,* vol. II, p. 121).

A report—it is not said by whom—had brought Paul the disturbing information of "sexual irregularity" (*porneia*) in the community at Corinth (1 Cor 5:1). This was not altogether new, for Paul had already had reason to discuss the matter in his previous letter:

> I wrote to you in my letter not to associate with immoral men (1 Cor 5:9).

Evidently, such a warning was not about life in a city notorious in the ancient world for its vice, and whose name had become synonymous with sexual immorality. In fairness, however, it should be added that Corinth, the "City of Aphrodite," was probably no worse than most large port cities of the world, then or now. Paul, of course, was not repeating the then current proverb that Corinth was no place for boys—girls it had aplenty, more than one thousand courtesans, according to the geographer Strabo (*Geography* 8.6.20). Nor was Paul advising the Christians against contact with the people of the city. He was perfectly clear that he was not talking about the Christians' life in, or their dealings with, a sin-ridden Corinth, but about their life as a community of believers:

> I wrote to you in my letter not to associate with immoral men, not at all meaning the immoral of this world, or the greedy and robbers, or idolaters, since then you would need to go out of the world. But rather I wrote to you not to associate with anyone who bears the name of brother if he is guilty of immorality or greed, or is an idolater, reviler, drunkard, or robber—not even to eat with such a one (1 Cor 5:9–11).

It is evident, then, that Paul is not talking about the Christians' dealings with their non-Christian fellow citizens. His concern was the order of the Christian community, the proper conduct of "anyone who bears the name of brother." Paul's intention is "not to shut Christians off from the world, but to clarify their standing in the world" (H. Conzelmann, *1 Corinthians*, p. 100). In this same commentary, Conzelmann goes on to say about 1 Corinthians 5:10: "The community practices not an ascetic ideal, but that freedom which includes freedom to separate itself from vice. It is of the very essence of the community to manifest its freedom from sin *in* the world, not alongside of it. We do not have to depart from the world in order to be able to believe" (Conzelmann, p. 100).

Paul, therefore, is not urging the Christians to "flee the world" (the *fuga mundi* of later Christian asceticism, which drove monasteries and convents and seminaries into the backwoods). He is simply reminding the Corinthians that their life as Christians in the world must seek to preserve its freedom, including its freedom to keep its community holy in the midst of this world, in the heart of its cities, and not in some Thebaid of the religious imagination. Paul's concern here is not with what the "outsiders" do or do not do:

> For what have I to do with judging outsiders? . . . God judges those outside (1 Cor 5:12–13).

but with a member of the community who has done something that requires prompt and decisive action by the community itself:

> Let him who has done this be removed from among you. . . . Drive out the wicked person from among you (1 Cor 5:2c, 13b; see Dt 17:7).

What had this person done to merit this? He was "living with his father's wife," a biblical term for "stepmother" (1 Cor 5:1b; see Lev 18:7, 8). Therefore, it was a case of incest which Paul describes as "of a kind not found among pagans" (5:1a). It would be relatively easy to let it go at that: the unqualified condemnation of the heinous crime of incest. But to do this would be to miss the real point of Paul's argument.

Were incest the main concern, the woman partner would also have had to be "removed from among you." But she is not even dealt with at all. What required immediate and firm action on the part of the community was a far more serious matter. It was not the incest as such, odious though it was, but the Corinthians' "arrogance" (5:2), their "boasting" (5:6), their gross misuse of Christian freedom to "deliberately set aside one of the most sacrosanct moral prohibitions of both

Jews and pagans" (J. Murphy-O'Connor, *1 Corinthians*, p. 40).
They considered their behavior as a reason for boasting of
their newfound "maturity and freedom." "Consequently,
they had only praise for the man who entered into an incestuous relationship 'in the name of the Lord Jesus' " (Murphy-
O'Connor, p. 40). Murphy-O'Connor, therefore, considers
the RSV translation, "I have already pronounced judgment
in the name of the Lord Jesus on the man who has done such
a thing" (1 Cor 5:3–4), to be "inaccurate." Thus, the abuse was
not in the commission of the sin as such, no matter how ex-
ecrable, but in the committing of it "in the name of the Lord
Jesus," in the name of Christian freedom from the law.

A. The Limit to Freedom

Such sinful abuse of freedom is not a personal matter
that terminated with the sinner. "A little leaven leavens the
whole lump" (1 Cor 5:6). Sin, all sin, has a social dimension.
So, no matter how free Christians might be, no amount of
freedom can possibly relieve them of their responsibility to
the community. Chapter 5 of 1 Corinthians is not dealing with
the incest taboo as such, but with the exercise of Christian liberty and the consequent responsibility of the individual sinner to the community, the responsibility of the community to
itself (to cast out "the old leaven, the leaven of malice and
evil"—1 Cor 5:8), and of both the individual and the community to the world in which they live ("celebrate . . . with the
unleavened bread of sincerity and truth"—1 Cor 5:8).

Every member of the community who was "washed . . .
sanctified . . . justified in the name of the Lord Jesus Christ
and in the Spirit of our God" (1 Cor 6:11) bears in the very
exercise of his or her freedom a heavy burden of responsibility toward every single member of that community. The
Christian community in the midst of this world has a responsibility toward it too: not to judge it (1 Cor 5:12–13), but to be
"sincere" and "true" (1 Cor 5:8) in every aspect of its life
within it. This is why Paul has no hesitation about what ought
to be done, and why he summarily invokes a sentence of holy
law:

Drive out the wicked person from among you (1 Cor 5:13;
see Dt 17:7b).

B. A Second Limit to Freedom

In addition to this first limit set upon the exercise of
Christian freedom, namely, the responsibility to the truth of
the gospel and to the community of believers, there is a second limit: the price that the gift of freedom commands. The
specifically Christian element is still more to the fore in the
nature of this price, in the cost of this freedom in the life of
the believer. A second question that was put to Paul by the
Corinthians illustrates this point admirably.

The question concerned the eating of food offered to
idols. "Now concerning food offered to idols" is how Paul
opens the discussion of the topic (1 Cor 8:1). This is the device
used by him to tick off one by one the questions the Corinthians had asked (see 1 Cor 7:1; 8:1; 12:1; 16:1). They had
written to inquire about a problem which, to the neophytes of
Corinth, must have been particularly acute in a city where
practically all the meat on sale had first been sacrificed to the
pagan deities, its choicest morsels cast into the sacrificial fire,
and the remains sold in the nearby marketplace or served in
banquets or in "temple restaurants" (H. Conzelmann, *1 Corinthians*, p. 148).

The Corinthians—who, in their irrepressible penchant
for slogans, ought to be the patron saints for many Christians
today—had another slogan ready to back up their "All things
are lawful for me" (1 Cor 6:12). The slogan was "All of us possess knowledge" (1 Cor 8:1). Since they believe "there is no
God but one," the Christians of Corinth *know* that "an idol has
no real existence" (8:4). Any idiot could see that; at least so
the Corinthians reasoned, and went on with utter insouciance
to attend the banquets of their pagan friends, buy meat sold
in the temple market, and eat in temple restaurants.

Paul, however, responds to their "All of us possess knowledge" by making a necessary distinction:

"Knowledge" (*gnosis*) puffs up, but love (*agape*) builds up
(1 Cor 8:1b).

He then adds a most important qualification:

> However, not all possess this knowledge (1 Cor 8:7a).

The distinction Paul makes is between "knowledge" and "love." All Christians believe as the principal article of their faith that "there is no God but one" (1 Cor 8:4; see Rom 3:30; Eph 4:6). But, fundamental though this "knowledge" is, it is not what ultimately matters. The reason for this is twofold. Such "knowledge," first of all, is relative, admitting of both progression and regress:

> If anyone imagines that he knows something, he does not yet know as he ought to know (1 Cor 8:2).

Secondly, though all Christians have this "knowledge," not all can make the same progress in it. To some, it would be almost elementary to conclude from "there is no God but one" to "an idol has no real existence" (1 Cor 8:4). Such (Gentile) converts need hardly be reminded:

> Formerly, when you did not know God, you were in bondage to beings that by nature are no gods (Gal 4:8).

But, alas, knowledge is not very democratic, and not even the cross could do away with its inequality. True, all believers know:

> For us there is one God, the Father, from whom are all things and for whom we exist, and one Lord, Jesus Christ, through whom are all things and through whom we exist (1 Cor 8:6).

But it is by no means true that all believers comprehend, grasp, or appropriate this truth with equal intelligence.

In the context of salvation, however, what matters more than "knowledge" of God is the love of God:

> But if one loves God, one is known by him (1 Cor 8:3; 13:12; Gal 4:9).

To be "known by" God is to be recognized by him, to be chosen by him: "The Lord knows those who are his" (2 Tim 2:19; see Num 16:5). In this love of God no one has an advantage over the others, no one is in any way handicapped. Each one can go as far as his generosity will take him. The great theologian is no better off than the incult mumbler of rosary beads, the prelate no better off than the dumbest sacristan, and the mightiest in the Church no better advantaged than the humblest and most helpless of their subjects. In any community of believers this love is what matters above all else:

> Love never ends; as for prophecies, they will pass away;
> as for tongues, they will cease; as for knowledge, it will
> pass away (1 Cor 13:8).

In their transitoriness lies their indifference, just as in the abiding nature of the love of God lies its permanence eternally.

Having made the distinction between knowledge and love, Paul goes on to add the very matter-of-fact qualification:

> However, not all possess this knowledge (1 Cor 8:7).

Needless to say, this is not the sardonic, porcine wisdom of some being "more equal than others." It is the very realistic acknowledgement of the undemocratic quality of knowledge in any human community. The community of believers is no exception. But what the believers have to be aware of is that the disparity in knowledge inevitably leads to the existence in one and the same community of those who are "weak" and those who are "strong," "the men of knowledge" (1 Cor 8:7–13; Rom 14:1–3; 15:1–3). And this is precisely where the burden of personal liberty exacts its price:

> Only take care lest this liberty of yours somehow become
> a stumbling block to the weak. For if anyone sees you, a
> man of knowledge, at table in an idol's temple, might he
> not be encouraged, if his conscience is weak, to eat food
> offered to idols? And so by your knowledge this weak man

is destroyed, the brother for whom Christ died (1 Cor 8:9–11).

We who are strong ought to bear with the failings of the weak, and not to please ourselves; let each of us please his neighbor for his good, to edify him. For Christ did not please himself (Rom 15:1–3).

Of course, "an idol has no real existence" (1 Cor 8:4); of course, meat offered to an idol is no different from any other; of course, as a free, intelligent Christian, I can take it or leave it:

Food will not commend us to God. We are no worse off if we do not eat, and no better off if we do (1 Cor 8:8).

But what of the others who lack the courage of my convictions? What of the brother or sister who lacks my "knowledge," and whose "conscience, being weak, is defiled" (1 Cor 8:7)? In one and the same community, "one believes he may eat anything, while the weak man eats only vegetables" (Rom 14:2). Could a Christian be so reckless as to let his liberty "somehow become a stumbling block to the weak" (1 Cor 8:9)?

And so by your knowledge this weak man is destroyed, the brother for whom Christ died. Thus, sinning against your brethren and wounding their conscience when it is weak, you sin against Christ (1 Cor 8:11–12).

This is the knowledge that the strong must keep constantly before their eyes. This is the heavy burden that accompanies every exercise of Christian freedom; and, should the exercise of this Christ-won freedom prove harmful to another, then the price it exacts is nothing short of the sacrifice of my own freedom for the sake of the other:

Therefore, if food is a cause of my brother's falling, I will never eat meat, lest I cause my brother to fall (1 Cor 8:13; 10:28–29).

No law could ever demand this; no one can oblige you to determine your liberty "by another man's scruples" (1 Cor 10:29b); but the gospel requires it. According to this gospel the limit to the exercise of Christian freedom is always the good of the "weaker" other.

Few teachings of the New Testament have suffered the neglect at the hand of the sloganeers of our age that this simple—though far from easy—Pauline instruction has. The sloganeers have been far too concerned to shed the shackles of *their* slavery, far too busy campaigning for *their* "rights," to pay much attention to the true burden of Christian freedom and the self-sacrificing price it exacts. As has already been said, one is always free at the expense of another. In the political arena, in the marketplace of ideologies, this simple fact could be, and all too often is, overlooked. In the Christian community it must be a fundamental and determinative factor in every exercise of freedom. For in the Christian scheme of things where a new category of "sin against Christ" (1 Cor 8:12) has emerged, it is a factor which—more often than Christians would like to believe—calls for the sacrifice of one's own freedom for the sake of "the brother for whom Christ died" (1 Cor 8:11):

> Only take care lest this liberty of yours somehow become
> a stumbling block to the weak (1 Cor 8:9).

26. Marriage, Divorce, and Celibacy

The questions concerning marriage or non-marriage, divorce and remarriage are among the questions put to Paul by the Corinthians in their letter: "Now concerning the matters about which you wrote . . ." (1 Cor 7:1). As one might have expected, the tendency to "libertinism" among the Corinthians, the desire to live out the slogan of "I am free to do anything" (1 Cor 6:12 NEB), was accompanied—as it so often is—by a reverse insistence on extreme ascetical practices that regarded all sexual activity and even marriage itself as evil. Thus, in one and the same Christian community at Corinth, there were those who, "in the name of the Lord Jesus," practiced an immorality "of a kind that is not found even among pagans," while others considered sex even within marriage itself to be reprehensible. Both one group and the other based their "morality" on the principle of Christian freedom. Those who opposed marriage where not the forerunners of Malthusian theoreticians, but Christians who misunderstood their freedom in Christ Jesus as a freedom from the ordinary demands of human nature, as a triumph over the "flesh," a blow dealt to their "baser" selves.

Once again, Paul does not respond to the question by outright denial of the premise of the ascetic-minded Corinthians. He concedes, "It is well for a man not to touch a woman" (1 Cor 7:1). He agrees, moreover, that "he who marries his betrothed [*parthenos*, virgin] does well; and he who refrains from marriage will do better" (7:38). But he insists:

> If anyone thinks that he is not behaving properly toward
> his betrothed [virgin], if his passions are strong, and it has
> to be, let him do as he wishes: let them marry—it is no sin
> (1 Cor 7:36).

Even though Paul is convinced of the urgency of the "[impending] distress," even though he thinks "the appointed time has grown very short" and "the form of this world is passing away" (7:26, 29, 31), he still insists:

> If you marry, you do not sin, and if a girl [*parthenos*, virgin] marries she does not sin (1 Cor 7:28).

Paul's reason for his position is at once clear and realistic. His were not the theories of primary and secondary ends of matrimony, nor the highfalutin jargon of modern sociology and psychology. To Paul's mind, people should get married for no more sublime or holy a reason than "the temptation to immorality," the possession of "strong passions" and the "lack of self-control" (1 Cor 7:2, 36, 5):

> It is well for a man not to touch a woman. But because of
> the temptation to immorality, each man should have his

own wife and each woman her own husband. The husband should give to his wife her conjugal rights, and likewise the wife to her husband. For the wife does not rule over her own body, but the husband does; likewise the husband does not rule over his own body, but the wife does (1 Cor 7:1b–4; see 11:11).

These verses hardly need explanation, but they might require an often forgotten reminder. Paul's equable and equitable treatment of both sexes throughout this chapter cannot be bettered by any of the willfully blinkered propagandists who have found in Paul their favorite whipping boy. Yet, in their even-handedness, Paul's statements were nothing less than revolutionary in their age. They remain no less so in every age willing to pay heed to what Paul says and how he says it.

Moreover, as Conzelmann comments on these verses (1 Cor 7:1–4), "the equality results from the limitation of freedom which is given with the presence of the partner" (H. Conzelmann, *1 Corinthians*, p. 117). In its exercise, genuine Christian freedom always requires the sacrifice of oneself for the other (see No. 25 above). This, and only this, can result in genuine "equality" between the sexes, between the races, and between the various strata of society. The remedy of self-centered aberrations is in their opposites.

A. Sexual Abstinence

This equality is further demonstrated in the case of the married partners who wish to abstain from sexual intercourse to "devote themselves to prayer." Paul is careful to lay down surprisingly commonsensical rules for their behavior. His prime care is to safeguard the freedom of both the wife and the husband, and to preserve the holiness of the bond that binds them together. He can envision a situation where sexual abstinence might be desirable. If it is, then it has to fulfill all three of the following conditions: (a) it has to be "by agreement," (b) "for a season," i.e., for a specified period of time, and, when this specified period elapses, (c) the partners have to "come together again, lest Satan tempt you through lack of self-control" (1 Cor 7:5). Sexual abstinence, even for so holy a reason as devoting oneself to prayer, is not free from temptation.

Such is the realism of Paul that it refuses to subjugate the freedom of the Christian even to the holiest of ideals. Actual Christian practice, alas, has not paid much heed to this Christian realism, nor has it always had as its primary concern the preservation of the individual Christian's freedom. These instructions of Paul are not the substitution of one law for another, a new law for the old. They are not an exercise in "legalism," as would have been, for example, the forbidding of sexual intercourse to all married people during, say, Lent, or on Fridays and Sundays of every week, or whatever. Paul's are simply exhortations born of a true appreciation of the human condition, from an awareness of the Christian cost of discipleship, and from a solicitude to prevent either the loss of Christian liberty in the individual or its encroachment upon the freedom of others for even the holiest of motives.

Above all, however, Paul is perfectly aware that what he is saying is "by way of concession not of command" (1 Cor 7:6). And here is where we come to the consideration of a legitimate and highly desirable "asceticism" in Christian life. For, Paul explains,

> I wish that all were as I myself am. But each has his own special gift (*charisma*) from God, one of one kind and one of another (1 Cor 7:7).

Put very simply, sexual abstinence is a gift of God, a "charism," given to some and not to others. Some have this gift and some do not, and there is no authority on earth powerful enough to alter the fact by fiat.

If those who have the special gift of sexual abstinence wish to remain single, then "it is well for them to remain single as I do" (1 Cor 7:8):

> But if they cannot exercise self-control, they should marry. For it is better to marry than to be aflame with passion (1 Cor 7:9).

The surest indication of someone not having this "special gift from God" is the inability to exercise self-control. Such a person, says Paul, "should marry." To some, this view is so down to earth as to seem almost cynical. But Paul realizes, as few after him in the Church have realized, that the gifts of God are distributed variously and unevenly, and that the only sensible, the only genuinely Christian, course of action begins with the clear recognition of what gifts one has and what gifts one has not.

"Quod Deus non dat, Salamanca non praestat," said a medieval proverb: What God has not given, no university can provide. If God has not granted an individual the gift of sexual abstinence, then the Church not only cannot supply it by dint of strict discipline and cold showers, but cannot demand it of such an individual. If you cannot live without sex, then get married; and "each man should have his own wife and each woman her own husband" (1 Cor 7:2). There are excellent reasons for remaining unmarried; self-discipline is definitely not one of them:

> To the unmarried and the widows I say that it is well for them to remain single as I do. But if they cannot exercise self-control, they should marry. For it is better to marry than to be aflame with passion (1 Cor 7:8–9).

B. The Married

Having dealt with the unmarried and with whether or not it is good for them to marry or remain single, Paul turns to the married. Once more, Paul carefully—and admirably—distinguishes between a teaching of the Lord and his own personal opinion ("I say, not the Lord" in 1 Cor 7:12, 25, 6, 8, etc.). It is so easy to confuse the two, to mistake one for the other. The temptation is so great to regard one's own opinion, however right and well-founded, as God's own revealed truth. From "opinion" to "dogma" is but a step, and "dogma" comes from the Greek "to have an opinion." But Paul is careful to keep distinct "my opinion" and "the command of the Lord" (1 Cor 7:25, 40; 2 Cor 8:10; see 1 Cor 7:10; 9:14; 11:23; 14:37; 15:3). In other words, he is aware of what is "dogma" (in our current sense of the term) and what is technically called a "theologoumenon," a theological opinion:

> To the married I give charge, *not I but the Lord,* that the wife should not separate from her husband (but if she does, let her remain single or else be reconciled to her husband)—and that the husband should not divorce his wife (1 Cor 7:10–11; see Mk 10:11–12; Mt 5:32; 19:3–9; Lk 16:18).

Since Paul very rarely quotes any "word of the Lord" (1 Cor 7:10–11; 9:14; 11:23; 14:37; 1 Thess 4:15), his recourse to it in the question of divorce and remarriage must underline not merely the importance of the question, but the need for unquestionable authority to back up its unusual—both for Jews and Gentiles—and unpalatable answer. The reference to "the Lord" underlines, of course, the authority of the risen Jesus, the exalted Lord, behind the teaching of the earthly Jesus (Mk 10:11–12 and parallels). It is a teaching that restores the Genesis 2:24 "the two shall become one flesh" bond which remains intact until death (Mk 10:2–9; Mt 19:3–9):

> A wife is bound to her husband as long as he lives. If the husband dies, she is free to be married to whom she wishes, only in the Lord (1 Cor 7:39; see Rom 7:2–3).

Thus, the teaching of the Lord on marriage "in the Lord," a teaching so thoroughly alien to the prevalent opinion in the world to which it was proclaimed, is stated by Paul in such a way as to put it beyond all casuistry and cavil. The nicety of the distinction between a wife "separating" from her husband and a husband "divorcing" his wife is turned around, and so is the order of "wife-husband" and "husband-wife" in 1 Cor 7:12–16. This might well be "an indication of the equality of the sexes" (H. Conzelmann, *1 Corinthians*, p. 120). But the absolute prohibition of divorce and remarriage applies to both partners equally and without distinction.

C. Remarriage

Another question put to Paul by the Corinthians had to do with a different situation: a case where one of the partners in a marriage was a believer and the other was not. Before proceeding any further, it is of the utmost importance to keep in mind that the marriage itself is every bit as solid and binding as any. No question whatsoever can be raised about its "validity." Now as long as the unbelieving partner "consents to live" with the believer, then there is no question or possibility of divorce (1 Cor 7:12,13).

> But if the unbelieving partner desires to separate, let it be so; in such a case the brother or sister is not bound (1 Cor 7:15).

That is, the believing partner is now free to marry.

No amount of sophisticated exegesis or casuistry can get around the fact that Paul, having just stated unequivocally and insisted on what is clearly the command of the Lord (1 Cor 7:10–11), now allows an exception to it (7:12–15). Therefore, it is important to know exactly the reason why Paul takes this position, i.e., why he "permits a true divorce with the consequent right of remarriage" (J. Murphy-O'Connor, *1 Corinthians,* p. 66). Paul's reason for taking this bold step is the "law of freedom" (H. Conzelmann, *1 Corinthians,* p. 123), and this is precisely what he means when he adds:

> For God has called us to peace (1 Cor 7:15c).

This statement "can refer only to the Lord's saying, to which we are not bound like slaves in such cases" (W. Foerster, *"eirene," T.D.N.T.,* vol. II, p. 416). Even a clear "command of the Lord" is not meant to bind the believers in such a way as to deprive them of their freedom. Indeed, what the RSV translates as "the brother or sister is not bound" in 1 Corinthians 7:15 is literally "not enslaved." The "new law" is not meant to substitute a new slavery for the old.

The two people in question entered marriage because, as Paul would put it, they could not "exercise self-control" (1 Cor 7:9). They did not have the "special gift from God" (7:7) to live a celibate existence. Now such a person finds that the unbelieving partner "desires to separate" (7:15); and, of course, the unbeliever can go off and get married without any difficulty, legal or religious. It is Paul's opinion, in the face of the clear, absolute prohibition of the Lord, that the believing partner, who wanted and needed marriage in the first place, who had no "charism" of celibacy, is now free to remarry. "Paul's decision here . . . is in flat contradiction to Jesus' prohibition of divorce" (J. Murphy-O'Connor, *1 Corinthians,* p. 66). The Christian abandoned by the unbelieving partner is not to be condemned to a life for which he or she is not called and is not suited. Not even the clear command of the Lord could be made into an enslaving law that would deprive a Christian of the freedom for which Christ has set us free:

> For God has called us to peace (1 Cor 7:15c).

D. Celibacy

Now, what of those who are unmarried and face the alternative of remaining as they are or getting married? Here again Paul is perfectly frank right at the outset:

> Now concerning the unmarried [*parthenoi,* virgins of both sexes], I have no command of the Lord, but I give my opinion as one who by the Lord's mercy is trustworthy (1 Cor 7:25).

It is, of course, the opinion of one who has the special gift himself and has made the choice to remain unmarried. Naturally enough, he wishes "that all were as I myself am" (1 Cor 7:7). But he never for a moment doubts that "it is no sin" to marry (7:36).

> But if you marry, you do not sin, and if a girl marries she does not sin (1 Cor 7:28).

Whatever the reasons Paul gives for remaining celibate, this one fact has to be kept firmly in mind: it is not a sin to marry. Moreover, the principle he enunciated at the start of his discussion of this whole question must be seen as underlying whatever he says about celibacy:

> But each has his own special gift from God, one of one
> kind and one of another (1 Cor 7:7).

Thus, marriage itself is not sinful, and celibacy is a gift (*charisma*) from God which is not given to everyone. No amount of wishing could make it otherwise. Paul knew—as the Church, alas, chose not to know—that you cannot decree an ideal, certainly not a Christian ideal. Celibacy is not subject to fiat. "Da quod iubes et iube quod vis," prayed Saint Augustine for the gift of continence: "Give what you command, and command what you will" (*Confessions* X.29.40). Though its legislation chose to forget or ignore it, the Church has always been impotent to give what it commands.

To avoid any terminological misunderstanding, it is perhaps good to note at this juncture that when Paul speaks of the "unmarried" he means the chaste woman and man bound to total sexual abstinence, "chastity." This is not the sense in which the terms "celibacy" and "chastity" are commonly used today, largely because we have grown accustomed to regard chastity in terms of sin and not in terms of gift. Thus, today there are many celibate who are not chaste, and many chaste who are not celibate.

Having given his very realistic reason for getting married, namely, "the temptation to immorality (*porneia*)," the "lack of self-control (*akrasia*)" (1 Cor 7:2, 5b), Paul expresses the quite understandable wish that "all were as I myself am" (7:7a). Thus he really does not contradict the Corinthian "ascetic" tenet that "it is well for a man not to touch a woman" (7:1b), but he is careful to add to it an indispensable qualification:

> Each has his own special gift (*charisma*) from God, one of one kind and one of another (1 Cor 7:7b).

> Only, let everyone lead the life which the Lord has assigned to him, and in which God has called him. This is my rule in all the churches (1 Cor 7:17).

Those who have this charism, this God-given gift to live a celibate life of "self-control" and resistance to the "temptation to immorality," and who "refrain from marriage," will, in Paul's opinion, "do better" (1 Cor 7:38) and "be happier" (7:40).

E. Reasons for Celibacy

Now, apart from Paul's understandable *parti pris,* what reasons does he advance for this clear preference of celibacy over marriage for a Christian? Or, to put it another way: Knowing full well that sexual abstinence is a gift from God, what reason has the Christian who has this gift to assume the demanding and lifelong burden of the total sexual abstinence it entails? The gift of total sexual abstinence, like all divine gifts, is a heavy burden which makes costly demands and requires vigilant responsibility. So what reason is there for the actual exercise of such a gift within the Christian community? This is the question at issue here.

For Paul, the exercise of sex is confined to marriage: "Each man should have his own wife and each woman her own husband" (1 Cor 7:2; see 7:38). As we have already seen, those who are married can, under certain specified conditions, abstain from sexual intercourse for a specified, limited period (7:5). But all Christians, married and unmarried alike, had to "lead a life worthy of God" (1 Thess 2:12), to let their "manner of life be worthy of the gospel of Christ" (Phil 1:27), and to conduct themselves "becomingly as in the day, not in reveling and drunkenness, not in debauchery and licentiousness, not in quarreling and jealousy" (Rom 13:13, which—by the way—was the famous "tolle, lege" [take up and read] text of Augustine's conversion; see *Confessions* VIII.12.29).

What Paul is talking about in 1 Corinthians 7 is the gift that some, and by no means all, Christians have to live a life of total abstinence from sex. That they have the gift does not, of course, mean that they no longer have to struggle against "Satan's temptation" (see 1 Cor 7:5), or that they are not "aflame with passion" (7:36), or that what passions they have are not "strong" (7:36). It does not mean that they do not have a lifelong struggle to maintain their "desire under control" (7:37). So the question is: Why should they?

In responding to this question and urging his case, Paul is extremely careful to insist that he is putting forth, not a command of the Lord, but his own personal opinion:

> Now concerning the unmarried, I have no command of the Lord, but I give my opinion as one who by the Lord's mercy is trustworthy (1 Cor 7:25).

The first reason Paul gives for the unmarried (1 Cor 7:25 where *parthenos* applies to virgins, both men and women as in, e.g., Rev 14:4) to remain unmarried is "in view of the present [impending] distress" (1 Cor 7:26), i.e., the imminence of the return of the Lord. The time of the parousia is short, and Paul thinks that, consequently, "it is well for a person to remain as he is" (7:26). Nevertheless, despite his belief in the "impending (eschatological) distress," Paul keeps his wits about him:

> Are you bound to a wife? Do not seek to be free. Are you free from a wife? Do not seek marriage. But if you marry, you do not sin, and if a girl marries she does not sin (1 Cor 7:27–28a).

So, even under the pressure of an imminent—as Paul thought—parousia, marriage is not a sin. Unfortunately, this is something Christians forgot even long after the coming of the Lord had receded into a less urgent hope.

The second reason Paul gives for his opinion is another example of his realism.:

> Yet those who marry will have worldly troubles, and I would spare you that (1 Cor 7:28b).

Marriage, at any time, is a heavy burden, but when, as Paul thought, "the appointed time has grown very short" (1 Cor 7:29), when "the form of this world is passing away" (7:31), then it becomes advisable even for the married to live "as though" they were not married (1 Cor 7:29b; see Mk 13:17 and parallels).

The third—and most enduring—of Paul's reasons is "to

promote good order and to secure your undivided devotion
to the Lord" (1 Cor 7:35), whether the Lord's coming is near
or far, imminent or retarded indefinitely. Such undivided devotion requires freedom from "anxieties," from "anxious
care" (7:32 NEB). It requires undivided interest (7:34), and
freedom from solicitude "about worldly affairs" (7:34):

> I want you to be free from anxieties. The unmarried man
> is anxious about the affairs of the Lord, how to please the
> Lord; but the married man is anxious about worldly af-
> fairs, how to please his wife, and his interests are divided.
> And the unmarried woman or girl is anxious about the
> affairs of the Lord, how to be holy in body and spirit; but
> the married woman is anxious about worldly affairs, how
> to please her husband (1 Cor 7:32–34).

All this desire to be free of care and anxiety is not, and
cannot be, from a motive of self-interest, from a general dis-
affection with marriage, or from a blighting cynicism about
human relationships. This counsel of Paul is, of course, not
for those whose celibacy is forced upon them by an accident
of nature or of society; nor is it meant for the sardonic mis-
anthropes who never loved and never lost. Nor can such a
counsel be meant for those who, from a perverse spirituality,
and on the pretext of "undivided devotion to the Lord," turn
their backs on this world and their neighbor.

Put very simply, this third reason given by Paul can be
termed "apostolic." If it is embraced in order to dedicate oneself more fully to the "affairs of the Lord" (1 Cor 7:32), celibacy and—to Paul's view of things—the consequent life of
total sexual abstinence makes sense in a world where marriage is the rule and its opposite the surprising exception.
But, evidently, this is a gift not given to everyone; and Paul is
eager to insist yet again that it is not a sin to marry:

> If anyone thinks that he is not behaving properly toward
> his betrothed, if his passions are strong, and it has to be,
> let him do as he wishes: let them marry—it is no sin (1 Cor
> 7:36).

Yet, for one who is "firmly established in his heart, *being under no necessity* but having his desire under control" (7:37), it is better to refrain from marriage:

> so that he who marries his betrothed does well; and he who refrains from marriage will do better (1 Cor 7:38).

Furthermore, despite his own clearly expressed preference, Paul insists on the freedom even of widows to remarry:

> A wife is bound to her husband as long as he lives. If the husband dies, she is free to be married to whom she wishes, only in the Lord. But in my judgment she is happier if she remains as she is (1 Cor 7:39–40a).

None of these counsels of Paul is an invitation to embrace an ascetic ideal for its own sake:

> I say this for your own benefit, not to lay any restraint upon you, but to promote good order and to secure your undivided devotion to the Lord (1 Cor 7:35).

Paul was not victim to that later mentality which became so widespread in Christianity: the conviction that the harder the thing, the better and the more Christian it is. "Non ideo quia durum aliquid, ideo rectum, aut quia stupidum, ideo sanum," remarked Saint Augustine (*De Civitate Dei* XIV.9.6): Just because something is difficult does not make it good, any more than something is salutary just because it is stupid. People ought not to judge the unmarried state as the loftier, or nobler, or more a reason for boasting. For such as have the gift from God to remain unmarried and who freely ("under no necessity"—1 Cor 7:37) choose to exercise it, the unmarried state is better simply because it enables them to give their "undivided devotion to the Lord" (7:35). They are under no "restraint" (7:35) to choose to exercise a gift given them by God. They should be aware of the enormous and lifelong struggle such an exercise requires. But if they embrace this way of life, they do so, not out of a motive of vainglory, nor to strain after some difficult and lofty ideal, but simply to put to use a divine gift by dedicating themselves wholly and undividedly to the service of the Lord and their neighbor.

Are the first two reasons given by Paul for remaining unmarried—"the impending distress" (1 Cor 7:26) and the belief that the "appointed time has grown short" (7:29)—to be judged therefore wholly worthless in considering this question? No! I believe—with so many others—that this choice to remain unmarried in total abstinence from sex has always served as an eschatological sign in the Church. It is a constant reminder to the Christian community that the final age, the advent of the kingdom of God, has broken in upon us. It keeps alive in the Christian community precisely that eschatological dimension of its hope which the passage of centuries obtunds. Those who remain unmarried and lead a life of total sexual abstinence in order to dedicate themselves to the service of the Lord and their neighbor, "anxious about the affairs of the Lord, how to please the Lord" (7:32), are—or at least ought to be—witnesses to the community that "the form of this world is passing away" (7:31), that, no matter how long the "master is delayed in coming," the master will come on a day we do not expect and at an hour we do not know (see 1 Thess 5:2–6; 2 Thess 2:1–2; Lk 12:45–46).

Lest it be overlooked, a final remark about Paul's way of expressing his opinions and exercising his considerable authority is necessary at this point. His attitude to the Corinthians, as to the other churches, is best summed up in these words:

> I say this for your own benefit, not to lay any restraint upon you, but to promote good order and to secure your undivided devotion to the Lord (1 Cor 7:35).

Even, as in the case of the incestuous member of the community (1 Cor 5:1–5), when the enormity of the deed brooked no delay, Paul did not resolve issues by decreed fiats, even though he himself was in no doubt whatsoever about what had to be done (1 Cor 5:3; see 10:15). This was simply not his idea of how authority in the Church should be exercised. His reason for this attitude is put very succinctly in his letter to Philemon:

> Though I am bold enough in Christ to command you to do what is required, yet for love's sake I prefer to appeal to you . . . . I preferred to do nothing without your consent in order that your goodness might not be by compulsion but of your own free will (Phlm 8–9,14).

This was his rationale in dealing, not only with an individual such as Philemon, but with all the churches. Having set down his view, he adds, "I speak as to sensible men; judge for yourself what I say" (1 Cor 10:15). "In no case does [Paul] solve a problem by telling them what to do, because he did not believe that authority in the church should function that way. . . . Authenticity is achieved only through personal decision and so he is by turns rational, emotional, persuasive, and passionate. The subtlety of his forthright personality is nowhere more evident" (J. Murphy-O'Connor, *1 Corinthians*, p. 58).

In this too, the Church has chosen—by and large—to praise Paul but to ignore him. He has not had many followers.

27. The Church and the Lord's Supper

Basic to Paul's understanding of the Church is his understanding of the Lord's Supper, and indispensable for properly viewing either is his understanding of baptism. Paul's views on the Lord's Supper take up considerable space in 1 Corinthians. But before examining these views it is helpful first to see where Paul situates the sacrament of baptism in Christian life. To this end, his assertion in this epistle provides us with a primary consideration:

> Christ did not send me to baptize but to preach the gospel (1 Cor 1:17).

Sacraments and the sacramental ministry are to Paul—as they ought to be to any church in possession of its theological wits—secondary to preaching the gospel. Indeed, it could be said of any sacrament what Paul says of the Lord's Supper:

> For as often as you eat this bread and drink the cup, you
> proclaim the Lord's death until he comes (1 Cor 11:26).

Sacraments are one way of proclaiming the Lord's death, but they are not the only way, nor the principal way.

In other words, sacraments are—at least for Paul—strictly subordinate to the "priestly service of the gospel of God" (Rom 15:16). This particular point needs making if only because Christians belonging to the more sacramentally-minded churches tend to overlook it. It was (perhaps still is?) a not uncommon caricature to use "preaching" and "sacraments" as the distinguishing marks of Protestant and Catholic ministry respectively.

Although Paul affirmed that he was not sent "to baptize but to preach the gospel" (1 Cor 1:17), he did in fact baptize "Crispus and Gaius . . . also the household of Stephanas" (1 Cor 1:14, 16). He did not share with today's instant religious reformers the misconception that whatever is not of primary importance is unimportant, that a candle is not worth lighting just because it is not the sun. Paul was not dismissing baptism out of hand but establishing an order of priority in the work of the ministry. Of course, he himself was baptized, and, the account of Acts 9:18 notwithstanding, Paul regarded his baptism not so much "a personal experience of conversion" as "inclusion into the community of the elect" (H. Koester, *Introduction,* vol. 2, p. 100):

> For by one Spirit we were all baptized into one body—
> Jews or Greeks, slaves or free—and all were made to drink
> of one spirit (1 Cor 12:13).

> Do you not know that all of us who have been baptized
> into Christ Jesus were baptized into his death? We were
> buried therefore with him by baptism into death, so that
> as Christ was raised from the dead by the glory of the Fa-
> ther, we too might walk in newness of life (Rom 6:3–4).

Thus, Paul knew well where baptism fitted into the order of things, and viewed his ministerial practice accordingly.

What then did Paul understand by the action of baptizing

Crispus, or Gaius, or the household of Stephanas? What he says about baptism is fundamental to what he has to say about the Lord's Supper, which "repeats under different imagery one of the central motifs of baptism" (W.A. Meeks, *The First Urban Christians*, p. 158). For if Paul was grateful that he did not baptize many of the Corinthians himself, it was because of his deep concern for the unity of Christ and of the community, a unity which he had reason to believe was severely threatened by the formation of cliques and factions in Corinth:

> Each one of you says, "I belong to Paul," or "I belong to Apollos," or "I belong to Cephas," or "I belong to Christ." Is Christ divided? Was Paul crucified for you? Or were you baptized in the name of Paul? I am thankful that I baptized none of you except Crispus and Gaius (1 Cor 1:12–14).

Baptism, then, has to do with the unity of Christ, with the unity of the Christians in Christ, and with their belonging to Christ and to no one else, because Christ and no one else was crucified for them.

Paul admirably sums up all this by having recourse to the image of the body—an image which, despite all the current theological preference to it of almost every other image of the Church, remains fundamental and irreplaceable:

> For just as the body is one and has many members, and all the members of the body, though many, are one body, so it is with Christ. For by one Spirit we were all baptized into one body (1 Cor 12:12–13; see 6:11).

> For as many of you as were baptized into Christ have put on Christ. There is neither Jew nor Greek, there is neither slave nor free, there is neither male nor female; for you are all one in Christ Jesus (Gal 3:27–28).

"Equality in Practice"

First of all, these verses of Galatians are not a program for world citizenship, or else what would Paul mean by:

We ourselves, who are Jews by birth and not Gentile sinners: (Gal 2:15)?

Nor are they an emancipation declaration, or else why would Paul say:

Were you a slave when called? Never mind (1 Cor 7:21; see Phlm 16; Eph 6:5–9; 1 Tim 6:1–2)?

Nor are they a manifesto for "women's liberation," or else what reason would he have for insisting:

The head of a woman is her husband (1 Cor 11:3; see 14:34; Eph 5:22–24; 1 Tim 2:11–12)?

What such verses as 1 Corinthians 12:12–13 and Galatians 3:27–28 and Colossians 3:11 say is infinitely more profound and—if the social reformers would but listen—far more socially relevant than the abolition of racial distinctions, social strata, or sexual differences. What such verses, as well as their ostensible opposites in Galatians 2:15; 1 Corinthians 7:21; 11:3, etc., say is that, as far as the attaining of salvation, the belonging to and the being united with Christ, as far as membership in his body is concerned, these classifications, distinctions, and stratifications in society make not one bit of difference. What you are, who you are, and where you happen to be contribute not one iota toward your being in Christ, toward your being a member of his body. Factors like race, social status or sex contribute as much to the individual's justification as "the works of the law" do: exactly nothing.

That this fact has had so little effect on the actual social life of Christians and the conduct of their communities is no reason either to deny its truth or, worse still, to pretend that Paul is saying something else and to refashion that something else into a sociological ideology. What Paul really says in 1 Corinthians 12:12–13 and Galatians 3:27–28 has been superbly captured in a vignette by the great Dominican classical scholar, A.-J. Festugière:

One can readily see what the gospel brought the poor, the slaves, the little ones. They had nothing. A slave is called in Greek *soma,* a body. Many an inscription lists slaves in the plural as *somata,* after the cattle *ktemata.* Such neuter plurals express a category of objects, a property that one possesses. In Rome the slave is a *res:* something bought and sold. For the peasant Cato, a slave out of service is worth less than an old cow: one can at least eat the cow. Reporting the massacre of all the servants of one family, Tacitus adds, "Vile damnum" [small loss]. To these dis-inherited individuals the Good News gave everything: a sense of dignity, a sense of their human person. A God has loved them and died for them. He has assured them the finest places in his Kingdom. The patricians enjoyed no advantage here. In the Christian assembly they min-gled with this unwashed crowd, whose breath reeked of garlic and cheap wine, who belonged to another race, whom they could by a single word of command have had beaten to death. Yet these lowly beings were their own brothers. Let no one say that this was normal progress in the customs of the time, or the outcome of Stoic instruc-tion. Seneca's beautiful preaching never brought about such changes. Having carefully penned his Letter XLVII to Lucilius, Seneca would never have dined with his own slaves. There would have been at least two separate tables set up. Real equality in practice began only with the Lord's Supper. This is one of the greatest miracles of the Chris-tian religion (A.-J. Festugière, *L'Enfant d'Agrigente,* pp. 104–105).

It is at the table of the Lord that this "equality in practice" receives its constant affirmation. Here, as nowhere else, nei-ther race, nor gender, nor social position, nor worldly pos-sessions, nor ecclesiastical dignity makes any difference whatsoever—all the popular opinions to the contrary and all the evident past and present abuses notwithstanding. Should this principle of "the transformation of a multiplicity of in-dividuals into a unity" (W.A. Meeks, *The First Urban Christians,* p. 159) be in any way violated, then, as Paul is bold enough to assert, and we ourselves are far too slow to believe:

> When you meet together, it is *not* the Lord's Supper that
> you eat (1 Cor 11:20).

Paul affirms this, not because the Corinthians did not have a
"properly ordained minister," nor because of any defect—as
moralists and canonists are wont to say—"of sacramental matter or form," but simply because:

> In eating, each one goes ahead with his own meal, and one
> is hungry and another is drunk. What! Do you not have
> houses to eat and drink in? Or do you despise the church
> of God and humiliate those who have nothing? (1 Cor
> 11:21–22).

In other words, the conduct of the Corinthians destroys the
very character of the Lord's Supper (H. Conzelmann, *1 Corinthians*, p. 194). Nowadays, to be sure, eating and drinking are
not the worst ways of humiliating others at the Lord's Supper,
nor are they the most destructive of its character. But there
are other, surer and more destructive ways to do so, and
Paul's harsh conclusion remains every bit as valid.

The Church

In 1 Corinthians Paul is talking of a situation where the
"Supper of the Lord" was not separated from the community
meal, the "agape." This is important to keep in mind because
the prevalent tendency among contemporary Christians is to
see Paul's words in 1 Corinthians 11:21–22 as a call to those
who have this world's goods to share them with those who
have not. But this is not what Paul is talking about here,
though he does elsewhere and often (2 Cor 8:1–5, 8, 12–15;
Gal 6:2; 2 Cor 9:6–15; Rom 12:13; 15:26–27; 1 Tim 6:17–
19). The harsh judgment which Paul pronounces on the Corinthians' celebration of the Lord's Supper is an indictment
of their unthinking behavior in the assembly itself, a behavior
which "humiliates those who have nothing" (1 Cor 11:22).
This self-centered disregard for the others is what offends
against the "church of God" (11:22), disrupts the community

("each one goes ahead with *his own* meal"—11:21), and renders the celebration of the Lord's Supper null and void:

> It is not the Lord's Supper that you eat (1 Cor 11:20).

Paul is addressing the Corinthian community as a church: "when you assemble *as a church*" (1 Cor 11:18). This community of believers assembled to confess Jesus as its Lord, and to worship him by the "remembrance" of his redeeming death and resurrection is what Paul calls the "church" (1 Cor 11:18; 14:23). The term itself, *ekklesia* (whence "ecclesiastic," etc.), is the Septuagint rendering of the *qahal Yahweh,* the assembly called by God, of which the Old Testament speaks (Ex 12:6; 16:3; 35:1; Num 20:12; Dt 4:10; 9:10; 18:16; 23:1–8; 31:30). The Greek term itself bears overtones of its use in the political life of the *demos* (people). But it is its use in the New Testament which gives *ekklesia* its specifically Christian significance as the community of those who believe and confess the Lordship of Jesus, worshiping him as Lord and Savior in their Eucharistic assemblies.

In the numerous instances of its usage in his letters, Paul speaks of "the church of the Thessalonians in God the Father and the Lord Jesus Christ" (1 Thess 1:1; see 2 Thess 1:1), as he does of the "church(es) of God in Christ Jesus," or merely "the church(es) of God" (1 Cor 1:2; 2 Cor 1:1; 1 Cor 10:32; 11:16, 22; Gal 1:13; 1 Tim 3:5), or "the church(es) of Christ" (Rom 16:16; Gal 1:22—"in Christ"), or "the churches of God in Christ Jesus" (1 Thess 2:14; compare 1:4).

This last appellation, "the churches of God in Christ Jesus," is perhaps the most compendious of all: the Church is called together (*ekklesia* comes from the Greek verb "to call," *kaleo*) by God in Christ Jesus, who by his death and resurrection is the Lord of the assembled community which confesses him as Lord "to the glory of God the Father" (Phil 2:11). This is why the author of 1 Timothy can speak of the Church as "the household of God" (1 Tim 3:15), and Ephesians can say that God made Christ "the head over all things for the church, which is his body" (Eph 1:22–23; 5:23, 24; Col 1:18; but compare the fundamentally different metaphor in 1 Cor 12:27), that Christ himself "loved the church and gave himself up for her" (Eph 5:25), and that he "nourishes and cherishes" the Church (Eph 5:29).

These metaphors are but ways of making explicit the "profound mystery" of Christ and the Church (Eph 5:32). They are corollaries that underline the constitutive role of the Christ event for the Church. This saving event is what has to be kept in mind, whether we speak of the "churches of Galatia" (Gal 1:2; 1 Cor 16:1, 19), or "of Macedonia" (2 Cor 8:1), or "at Corinth" (1 Cor 1:2; 2 Cor 1:1), whether we speak of the Church which is at the house of Aquila and Prisca (1 Cor 16:19; see Rom 16:5; Phlm 2; Col 4:15), or whether we speak of all these churches as "the Church" (1 Cor 6:4; 10:32; 14:4, 5, 12; 15:9; Gal 1:13; Phil 3:6; Eph 3:10).

But it would make no sense to speak of the Church as a diffuse and undefined mass of unrelated but well-meaning people, any more than it makes sense to call "Church" a closely knit group that neither believes, nor confesses, nor worships Christ as Lord. This is the reason why Paul's Eucharistic instruction is addressed to the Corinthians "when you assemble as a church" (1 Cor 11:18). On the other hand, you cannot very well withhold the appellation "Church" from a community of believers which does assemble to confess and worship Jesus as Lord—a simple fact that Vatican II, however belatedly, had to acknowledge.

For, however wide the divergences and unresolved the disputes on the nature and structure of such assemblies of believers (or, to use the current sociological jargon, the "models" of such churches), there can be no mistaking the essential elements which, when present, make any such assembly "the Church of God in Christ Jesus," rather than some office of propaganda, a help and aid organization, or a crisis-oriented club for the emotionally effete.

Thus, Paul's admonitions to the Corinthians are addressed to them as "the church of God which is at Corinth" (1 Cor 1:2), and not merely as some "voluntary association" or a "cultic society" (W.A. Meeks, *The First Urban Christians*, pp. 158 and 168). The community that comes together to celebrate the Lord's Supper (the "Eucharist," as it soon thereafter came to be called) celebrates it as the body of Christ, and, in celebrating it, becomes itself the body of Christ, since the church is in fact "not 'like' a body, but *is* the body of Christ" (H. Conzelmann, *1 Corinthians,* p. 172).

The Eucharistic Celebration

This is the reason why in Chapter 10 of 1 Corinthians Paul needed to invert the customary order of the eucharistic celebration, mentioning first the cup and then the bread (1 Cor 10:14–22). For it is the traditional bread formula which furnishes him with his key argument there:

> The cup of blessing which we bless, is it not a participation (*koinonia,* communion) in the blood of Christ? The bread which we break, is it not a participation (communion) in the body of Christ? Because there is *one bread,* we who are many are *one body,* for we all partake of the *one bread* (1 Cor 10:16–17).

Paul used the bread-body formula in these verses in order to explain to the Corinthians the nature and the unity of their community. It is therefore easy to see how, in Paul's view, anything that fragments the unity of such a community, anything that sets one member of the body against another, anything that "humiliates" the other, renders the celebration "not the Lord's Supper" (1 Cor 11:20).

It was Paul's "anxiety for all the churches" (2 Cor 11:28) that prompted him to recall the Corinthians to their senses by citing the tradition of the Lord's Supper:

> For I received from the Lord what I also delivered to you, that the Lord Jesus on the night when he was betrayed took bread, and when he had given thanks (*eucharistesas*), he broke it, and said, "This is my body which is for you. Do this in remembrance of me." In the same way also the cup, after supper, saying, "This cup is the new covenant in my blood. Do this, as often as you drink it, in remembrance of me." For as often as you eat this bread and drink the cup, you proclaim the Lord's death until he comes (1 Cor 11:23–26).

(a) "For I received from the Lord" is, evidently, not a reference to any private communication of the Lord on the road to Damascus. Paul is using a consecrated formula for the Christian tradition: receiving and handing on (compare 1 Cor 15:3—"I delivered . . . what I also received") the gospel of salvation in Jesus Christ. Behind this uninterrupted and uninterruptible process of the community of believers stands "not only the historical but also the risen Lord" (G. Bornkamm, "Lord's Supper . . . ," p. 131) both as the "originator" of the tradition and as its ultimate guarantor. Therefore, to the familiar catechism question on whether Jesus Christ "instituted" the Eucharist, Paul's answer would be, "I received *from the Lord*. . . ." "The mediated word," Bornkamm goes on to comment on this account in 1 Corinthians 11, "is the word of the Living One. . . . The tradition not only passes on the Lord's word from the past . . . but as this tradition it is his word" ("Lord's Supper . . . ," p. 131).

(b) "On the night when he was betrayed" anchors the institution of the Lord's Supper securely and firmly within history: a specifically datable event having links and connections with antecedent and subsequent events. The reference to the betrayal leaves no doubt about the link of the Supper with the passion that was to follow shortly thereafter—a link made explicit in 1 Corinthians 11:26: "you proclaim the Lord's death."

There is, it is to be noted, no reference here to the Supper as a Passover meal. Paul, of course, knows and uses the paschal theme elsewhere ("Christ, our paschal lamb, has been sacrificed"—1 Cor 5:7), but not in connection with the Eucharist. The reason this particular point is important to make is that "the accounts of the institution themselves do not receive their meaning from the Passover at all, nor are they to be interpreted in the light of the Passover" (G. Bornkamm, "Lord's Supper . . . ," p. 133). A misguided zeal in current ecumenism has nothing to gain by overlooking this point. "Important though the Passover-motif may otherwise be in the christological ideas of early Christianity, for the words of institution it contributes nothing" (G. Bornkamm, "Lord's Supper . . . ," p. 134).

(c) "Do this in remembrance of me." It is fashionable to refer to these words as a "rubric," a liturgical notation like some red-letter instructions to be noted in the missal but not recited. This would explain their omission by the other New Testament authors who handed on the tradition of the institution (Mk 14:22–24; Mt 26:26–28; Lk 22:15–20, where verses 19b–20 are, on the basis of the conflicting evidence of our manuscripts, not altogether certain as belonging to the original text of Luke's Gospel).

Nevertheless, the command of repetition to "Do this in remembrance of me" is theologically meaningful and, in view of its biblical background (see Ex 12:14; Dt 16:3), significant. Paul's understanding of the Lord's Supper is in terms of the "participation," the *koinonia*, the "communion" he elaborated in 1 Corinthians 10:16:

> The cup of blessing which we bless, is it not a participation
> in the blood of Christ? The bread which we break, is it not
> a participation in the body of Christ?

Thus, the "remembrance" is closely linked to the death of Christ on the cross, and those who celebrate the Lord's Supper have a "share in the saving significance of his death" (G. Bornkamm, "Lord's Supper . . . ," p. 140). The "remembrance" not only gives the individual believer a share in the saving event of the cross, but also brings all the believers together into the unity of the community of the redeemed:

> Because there is one bread, we who are many are one
> body, for we all partake of the one bread (1 Cor 10:17).

No, the injunction to "Do this in remembrance of me" not only assures the perpetuation of the rite, but also interprets its meanings: "*anamnesis,* 'remembrance,' is more than mere commemoration; it means a sacramental presence" (H. Conzelmann, *1 Corinthians*, p. 198). Thus it is that those who celebrate the Lord's Supper share in his saving death. Therefore, the better to grasp the meaning of "Do this in remembrance of me," we have to look at Paul's concluding statement of the account of the Lord's Supper.

(d) "For as often as you eat this bread and drink the cup, you proclaim the Lord's death until he comes." The eating of the bread and the drinking of the cup not only give "the celebrants a share in the saving significance of his death," but also, at one and the same time, proclaim the "saving significance of this death" (G. Bornkamm, "Lord's Supper . . . ," p. 140). The accent, as is all too evident from the text, falls on the act of eating and drinking, not on the elements of bread and cup as such. Every sacramental gesture is in its own way an act of proclamation of the saving significance of the death of Christ; the Eucharist, i.e., the eating of the bread and the drinking of the cup, is that proclamation *par excellence*.

Herein lies Paul's genius in interpreting both the community and the Eucharist by means of the "body of Christ" metaphor. But "metaphor" here is misleading. For Paul the Eucharist *is* the body of Christ, and the Church too *is* the body of Christ. It is not only that the death of Christ gathered the believers into a Church, into a community of believers, but that this Church's act of worship proclaims Christ's saving death and, in so doing, manifests its own unity as a body:

> As this broken bread was scattered upon the mountains, but was brought together and became one, so let thy Church be gathered together from the ends of the earth into thy kingdom (*Didache* IX.4).

So prays the *Didache*, a work dating from the late first or early second century, in its account of the "Eucharist." It is precisely in this work, by the way, that we find one of the first instances of the term "Eucharist" coming to replace the "Lord's Supper" as a technical term.

(e) "This is my body which is [broken] for you. . . . This cup is the new covenant in my blood." Paul is not only a hander-on of the tradition but its first interpreter. He uses the traditional words of institution to interpret for the Corinthian Christians the meaning and the implications of their celebration of the Lord's Supper.

The first thing to keep in mind here is that "body and blood" do not form a pair. "Body and soul" (1 Thess 5:23; Mt

10:28) do; "flesh and blood" (1 Cor 15:50; Mt 16:17) do; but not "body and blood." Therefore, one has to consider each entity in itself: "my body" and "this cup . . . the new covenant in my blood." Paul had already had recourse to the traditional formula of "blood" and "body" in the tradition of the Lord's Supper (1 Cor 10:16–17) in order to elaborate his theological view of the Church as the body of Christ. "Paul is aiming at an interpretation of the community by means of the Lord's Supper. . . . This link between the Lord's Supper and the concept of the church is the new element which he introduces into the understanding of the sacrament" (H. Conzelmann, *1 Corinthians,* p. 172). Thus it is that "participation in the body of Jesus makes us into the Body of Christ" (E. Käsemann, "Pauline Doctrine . . . ," p. 109). Or, as Bornkamm put it, in the sacrament "we receive the body of Christ and, by receiving it, are and show ourselves to be the body of Christ" (G. Bornkamm, "Lord's Supper . . . ," p. 144).

The "particular and penetrating relation that exists for Paul between the Lord's Supper and the church" (G. Bornkamm, p. 138) is further stressed by the cup formula (1 Cor 11:25). Here again, what Paul said in 1 Corinthians 10 has to be kept in mind:

> The cup of blessing which we bless, is it not a participation (*koinonia,* communion) in the blood of Christ (1 Cor 10:16)?

This "participation" in the blood is a sharing in the saving death of Christ, in Christ himself, a "participation in the body of Christ."

But this cup is also "the new covenant in my blood" (1 Cor 11:25), i.e., it is the final, the eschatological order of salvation, which ushers in the definitive reign of God on earth. With an unfailingly accurate instinct, the Church prays "Thy kingdom come" before it partakes of the body and blood of the Lord in the Eucharist. That is precisely why the celebration of the Lord's Supper is a proclamation of his Lordship "until he comes" (1 Cor 11:25). It is the one and the same Lord who was crucified, who gives himself in the Eucharist, and who shall come: the "crucified Lord of glory" (see 1 Cor 2:8). The community of believers gathered in his name to commemorate and participate in the saving event of his death is his Church, the body of Christ.

28. "Concerning Spiritual Gifts"

It is hard to avoid the impression that the Corinthian Church encountered practically every problem which could arise in any Christian community anywhere. Thus, another question put to Paul by the Corinthians had to do with *pneumatika,* spiritual gifts. In responding to their various questions, but especially to this one about the spiritual gifts, Paul gives us in 1 Corinthians 12–14 "a richer insight into community life than in any other passage in the New Testament, and especially into the busy life of divine worship in Corinth" (H. Conzelmann, *1 Corinthians,* p. 204). When you add to these three chapters the previous two (1 Cor 10–11), with their rich insight into the Lord's Supper and its celebration in Corinth, you have almost a theological compendium of community, community worship and practice—almost a miniature ecclesiology.

"Theological" is of course the right description for this compendium, since Paul is consistent in applying basic, elementary principles of the Christian gospel to the examination and the discussion of each of the questions put to him. This is what has rightly been called "the thoroughgoing uniformity of the theological criticism of Paul" (Conzelmann, p. 204). The principle underlying this theological criticism is, of course, the eschatological event of the death and resurrection of Jesus Christ.

Now, Paul's comprehensive name for that event as a saving event is simply "grace" (*charis*), just as John's comprehensive term for it is "eternal life," and the Synoptists' is "the kingdom." Thus Paul speaks variously of "the grace of God which was given you in Christ Jesus" (1 Cor 1:4), "the grace of our Lord Jesus Christ" (2 Cor 8:9), and "the grace of God and the free gift in the grace of that one man Jesus Christ" (Rom 5:15). Ephesians, which is practically a cento, almost a patchwork, of verses culled from the Pauline epistles, sums up this concept admirably when it speaks of

> his glorious grace which he freely bestowed on us in the Beloved. In him we have redemption through his blood, the forgiveness of our trespasses, according to the riches of his grace which he lavished upon us (Eph 1:6–8; see Rom 3:24; 5:2).

Needless to say, this grace is a gift ("the grace of God and the free gift in the grace of that one man Jesus Christ"—Rom 5:15). It is a gift that is freely given, as any true gift has to be. Indeed, when Paul speaks of grace or gift, we have to keep in back of our minds three conditions which must be simultaneously fulfilled for any act of giving to be genuinely so designated:

(a) A gift has to be freely and willingly given, "freely bestowed" (Eph 1:6; Rom 3:24). Its giver has to give it spontaneously and gratuitously, i.e., be under no obligation whatsoever, either to return a good for another good, or to pay a justly earned wage, or to reward a deserving deed, or to compensate a rendered service:

> Now to one who works, his wages are not reckoned as a gift but as his due (Rom 4:4; see 1 Cor 3:8).

The utter and total gratuity of the gift is of its very essence.

(b) A gift has to be freely accepted. Unless someone receives what I freely and willingly give, my act of giving remains only an empty gesture. The thing given is not a gift unless someone accepts it. In other words, "grace as a gift" implies a relationship between two free persons, the giver and the receiver, both of whom have to be there somehow for the gift to be a gift, else it would be "in vain" (2 Cor 6:1; 1 Cor 15:10).

(c) A gift not only has to be freely given and freely accepted, it has to be recognized in the very act of its acceptance as free, as gratuitous, as unearned and entirely unmerited (Rom 4:4; see 1 Cor 3:8). This is what constitutes gratitude, thanksgiving, which in Greek is *eucharistein*. Indeed, the Greek root *char* is the one whence derive *chara* (joy), *charis* (grace), and *charisma* (gift), as well as *eucharistein/eucharistia* (giving thanks/eucharist). So, even a philological reflection on the Greek root and its derivatives will make clear the conditions that ordinary everyday experience stipulates for any donation to become a gift.

To have recourse to the medieval Scholastic idiom for just a brief moment: grace is not a "substance," not a thing, but a "relation." You can speak of a substance in and by itself, but you always need two terms related to one another in order to be able to speak of a "relation." In other words, to speak of a gift, you need to have both a giver and a receiver. In the particular instance of grace, all of the three relational conditions listed above have to exist at one and the same time before we can speak of "grace." This is why—at least in Paul's understanding of it—grace is not susceptible of increment or diminution. You cannot have "more" grace or "less" grace. It is not something that can exist independently of its acceptance and its acknowledgement as a freely given, unearned, and—in the case of the Christ event—uniquely unearnable gift.

To be sure, that Christ died and was raised from the dead is, if you wish, a fact which exists independently of me. But unless I accept that death and resurrection as "for me" (see Gal 2:20), unless I acknowledge it as the free gift of God in Jesus Christ, then it is not, and cannot be "grace." Of course, the third constitutive element of grace, the acknowledgement by the receiver of its utter gratuity, can be spoken of as being greater or less: my acknowledgement of a gift, my recognition of its being freely given, my realization of my own unworthiness and inability to earn such a gift—all are susceptible of increase as well as decrease.

This is what Paul means when he says, for example, that "where sin increased, grace abounded all the more" (Rom 5:20). The significance of these words is not lost on the saints. That is why they have such—to us at least—an exaggerated sense of their sinfulness. It is not scrupulosity, let alone masochism, on their part, but simply the outcome of grace recognized increasingly as unearned and undeserved. Any person who has ever awakened to the realization of being genuinely loved by another has a fair notion of what the saints are talking about. Recognition of being loved begets in us the only true humility we are ever to know. Growth in the recognition of the gratuity of the gift of grace in Christ is thus the only path to true Christian holiness.

But what is of more immediate concern for the Corinthians' question about the "spiritual gifts" is the understanding of "charism" (*charisma,* whose plural is *charismata*). Put very succinctly and briefly, a "charism" is an individuated gift, a personalized grace (*charis*). The grace of Jesus Christ is that he died for all. Each individual believer accepts this gift and appropriates this event, makes it his or her own, in a unique, individual way. This grace thus individually appropriated is technically called a "charism." Thus, every Christian has his own or her own individual charism, insofar as each Christian accepts and appropriates the gift of salvation in a unique way, which depends on the individual's background, talents, temperament, and constitutional makeup:

> Each one has his own special gift (*charisma*) from God, one of one kind and one of another (1 Cor 7:7b).

It should be noted here that it is precisely this infinite and limitless variety of charisms that constitutes a community:

> If all were a single organ, where would the body be? As it is, there are many parts, yet one body. The eye cannot say to the hand, "I have no need of you," nor again the head to the feet, "I have no need of you" (1 Cor 12:19–21).

Such diversity is, of course, essential to any society. Clones do not a community make.

But not only the multiplicity and the diversity, but also the hierarchy of the charisms is essential for the constitution of a community. It is of course almost inevitable that all these charisms, these individuated and personalized appropriations of the one and the same gift, should be rated differently by the individuals who possess them more for their éclat and their display value than for their usefulness. It is almost equally inevitable that those who have one specific charism tend to rate it the one absolutely necessary and uniquely desirable, the *sine qua non* for salvation. This is what caused the problem in Corinth.

In a nascent community, moreover, there always seems to be, and often is, a great abundance of what Max Weber called "the charism of leadership." Although, by its very definition, such a charism is not everybody's, its necessary exercise in the community almost inevitably gives rise to factions and divisions. In a religious community with a special message to proclaim and a distinctive life of fidelity to that message to be lived, the exercise of this gift of leadership often runs into conflict with the various demands and claims of those who possess the more "enthusiastic" and spectacular charisms.

However inadequate and sketchy the above two paragraphs, they only seek to provide some glimpse into the evidently confused situation in Corinth. Whether Paul himself grasped fully the nature of the phenomena exhibited in that city or not, his dealing with the resulting problems is forthright and clear:

> Now concerning spiritual gifts, brethren, I do not want you to be uninformed (1 Cor 12:1).

Since it is through the "Spirit of Christ" that the grace of the salvation event is present in the community, its appropriation by the individual believers is, necessarily, the work of the Spirit. Hence, Paul calls the charism a "spiritual gift." For him, "spiritual gifts" (*pneumatika*) and "charisms" (*charismata*) are generally interchangeable expressions (compare 1 Cor 12:1 with 12:31a), and he deals with them by setting down three commonsensical principles.

A. The Principle of "Orthodoxy"

Thus, for example, one of the most common phenomena of enthusiasm is some form of "ecstasy"—literally, being outside oneself. Paul does not discuss the nature of the phenomenon itself. But since the Corinthians have been misled ("led astray . . . moved"—1 Cor 12:2) about the proper function of this spectacular phenomenon within the Christian assembly, Paul sets a criterion for its use:

> Therefore I want you to understand that no one speaking by the Spirit of God ever says "Jesus be cursed (*anathema*)!" and no one can say "Jesus is Lord (*kyrios*)" except by the Holy Spirit (1 Cor 12:3).

This clear criterion of fidelity to the truth of the gospel is, of course, valid for all the spiritual gifts. "Jesus is Lord" is the acclamation of the Christian community at worship. It is a function of the Holy Spirit in that community: "No one can say 'Jesus is Lord' except by the Holy Spirit." One might therefore say that the first principle set down by Paul for judging the extraordinary phenomena in the community is the principle of "orthodoxy," of dogmatic soundness. What the ecstatic says has to be judged, not by its novelty and power of attraction, nor by its abstruseness and outlandishness, but by its fidelity to the gospel message.

B. The Principle of Unity

The second principle set down by Paul is that of the fundamental unity of all the gifts:

> Now there are varieties of gifts, but the same Spirit; and there are varieties of service, but the same Lord; and there are varieties of working, but it is the same God who inspires them all in everyone (1 Cor 12:4–6).

If the first principle provided the criterion for judging the quirkiness of the enthusiasts, the second offers the antidote to that perennial conflict which has aptly been described as the conflict between "charism and institution." All the charisms, the humblest and the most exalted, the flashiest and most conspicuous as well as the hidden and most unremarkable, have their origin in the one and the same "Spirit, Lord, and God." It is because of their unity of origin that all the charisms can and should work together for the same end.

C. The Principle of the "Common Good"

The third, and most important, principle regards the purpose of these charisms:

> To each is given the manifestation of the Spirit for the common good (1 Cor 12:7).

All the diversity of personal charisms in the community is there, not for any individual member's complacence, but for the "common good." Every gift in the Christian community brings with it the concomitant obligation to serve the community. The end of every gift is the "common good" (*sympheron*), which is whatever builds up the community, "so that the church may be edified" (1 Cor 14:5, 3, 12). This "common good" is what K. Weiss calls the "basic rule for the charismata granted to the whole community" (K. Weiss, *T.D.N.T.*, vol. IX, p. 77). "*Sympheron* is that which edifies the community. The profit of the individual is far less important than this. This ranks first for Paul himself and his apostolic ministry" (K. Weiss, p. 76):

> not seeking my own advantage, but that of many, that they may be saved (1 Cor 10:33).

The author of Ephesians sums up the finality of the charismata admirably when he writes:

> And his gifts were that some should be apostles, some prophets, some evangelists, some pastors and teachers, to equip the saints for the work of ministry, for building up the body of Christ (Eph 4:11–12; see 1 Cor 14:26).

So no matter what the charism happens to be, whether apostleship, or prophecy, or teaching, or healing, or helping, or administering, or speaking in tongues (1 Cor 12:27–30; 12:8–10; 14:26):

> All these are inspired by one and the same Spirit who apportions to each one individually as he wills (1 Cor 12:11).

But they are all "inspired" to the one and the same end: "the common good" (1 Cor 12:7), "so that the church may be edified" (14:5), for "building up the church" (14:12). No gift in the Church is given for the personal gratification and glory of the individual believer, and certainly none is there to enable its possessor to lord it over the "less fortunate" others:

> What have you that you did not receive? If then you received it, why do you boast as if it were not a gift? (1 Cor 4:7).

Nevertheless, people do boast of what they have, envy others for what they have not, and never cease comparing the one with the other. So Paul goes on to use the metaphor of the body and its members to remind the Corinthians in their divisive enthusiasm of the inevitable hierarchy of their gifts, of the need to properly rank and subordinate them, and of the necessary mutuality of dependence and harmonious sympathy between the possessors of these highly diversified gifts:

> that there may be no discord in the body, but that the members may have the same care for one another. If one member suffers, all suffer together; if one member is honored, all rejoice together (1 Cor 12:25–26).

Paul never denies the very evident difference in value of the individual gifts to the whole body, nor does he seek to eliminate the varying degrees of honor accorded to the individual members (12:21–25). But he is careful to remind the Corinthians of the reverse scale of values that maintains within the Christian community:

> But God has so composed the body, giving the greater honor to the inferior part, that there may be no discord in the body, but that the members may have the same care for one another (1 Cor 12:24–25).

Unfortunately, however, what is true in the eye of God, and ought to be true in the eyes of the believers, is seldom, if ever, true in the eyes of mortals.

Those who take up so readily nowadays the slogans of "charism" against the "institution" would do well to reflect long on Chapter 12 of 1 Corinthians. It should be noted there that Paul goes even so far as to hierarchize the charisms without any care to distinguish—had such distinction occurred to him—those usually associated with the "institution" from those that are the boast of the self-styled "charismatics." He knows what these are inclined to forget, that all Christians are in the strictest sense of the term "charismatics":

> Now you are the body of Christ and individually members of it. And God has appointed in the church first apostles, second prophets, third teachers, then workers of miracles, then healers, helpers, administrators, speakers in various kinds of tongues. Are all apostles? Are all prophets? Are all teachers? Do all work miracles? Do all possess gifts of healing? Do all speak with tongues? Do all interpret? (1 Cor 12:27–30; see Eph 4:11–12; 1 Cor 12:8–10; Rom 12:6–8).

But, when all is said and done, there is in the Christian community one reigning principle of order, one gift estimable beyond all others, and one that must be possessed by every single member, if any of the gifts is to have any value whatsoever: and that is love. Not all have the same gifts, nor do they all have them in the same way or to the same degree: "having gifts that differ according to the grace given to us" (Rom 12:6). It is quite understandable that some seek to acquire what they have not got, or to increase what they imagine not to possess in sufficient quantity; for, as the poet Martial said, "Many have too much; but none has enough." Yet, as Christians, as members of the same body, all ought to have one single aim, one object of all their striving:

> Make love your aim (1 Cor 14:1).

This is the "still more excellent way" (1 Cor 12:31b), which 1 Corinthians 13 describes so lyrically and yet so realistically. For there is no escaping the fact that love is hard work, no matter how dithyrambic poets may wax in describing the beauty and the splendors of its antecedents, its concomitants and consequences.

What negative criticism there is of the gifts, the *charismata* (1 Cor 12:31a) in Chapters 12 and 14 of 1 Corinthians is not directed against the gifts as such but against the Corinthians' understanding and use—or, rather misunderstanding and misuse—of them. But if these spiritual gifts are to be truly for the upbuilding of the community and not the cause of its fragmentation and undoing, if the charismata are given for the common good and not as personal ornaments, if their variety and diversity is a reflection of the various and diverse needs of the community, and not of the carefully graded prizes in a contest of personal accomplishments, then the only way to harness them for the good of the community and the service of the Lord is by subjecting all of them without exception to a love that is not jealous or boastful, not arrogant and rude, not insistent on its own way, not irritable or resentful or gloating at another's wrong, but a love that is patient and kind, rejoicing in the right, bearing all things, believing all things, hoping all things, enduring all things. This love, and this love alone, "never ends":

> As for prophecies, they will pass away; as for tongues, they will cease; as for knowledge, it will pass away (1 Cor 13:8).

This then is the "more excellent way" (RSV), the "still higher path" (Moffatt), "the best way of all" (NEB), which ought to be the constant aim of every Christian: "Make love your aim" (1 Cor 14:1). This is, in the final analysis, the one, sole "command of the Lord" (see 1 Cor 14:37; Rom 13:9–10; 1 Tim 1:5), which alone can guarantee that, in the community, "all things . . . be done decently and in order" (1 Cor 14:40). In such a community, love and not personal boasting or glory is the true aim of the believers, the unique criterion of all their actions, and the only available and genuine test of their service.

29. The Resurrection

> If Christ has not been raised, then our preaching is in vain and your faith is in vain (1 Cor 15:14).

This is the heart and essence of the gospel preached by Paul, and not by him only but by any other true apostle of Christ (Gal 1:8). This is the gospel than which there is no other (Gal 1:6). This is what underlies everything Paul had to say to the Corinthians, the basis of his considered answers to their questions, the ultimate reason for his counsels, his advice, his exhortations:

> Now I would remind you, brethren, in what terms I preached to you the gospel, which you received, in which you stand, by which you are saved, if you hold it fast—unless you believed in vain (1 Cor 15:1–2).

The gospel proclaimed by the apostle and the corresponding faith professed by the believers ("so we preach and so you believed"—1 Cor 15:11) have a definite dogmatic content. The faith, in other words, can be enunciated in propositions. The (vague?) rumors reaching Paul from Corinth required a reminder of precisely the terms in which the gospel had been preached to them. So, using the standard formula of tradition ("I delivered . . . what I also received"—1 Cor 15:3) which he had already employed in the account of the Lord's Supper (11:23), Paul sets forth what is of "first importance" (15:3) in what he preached and what the Corinthians believed (15:11):

> That Christ *died for our sins* in accordance with the scriptures, that he was buried,
> that he *was raised* on the third day in accordance with the scriptures, and that he *appeared* to Cephas . . . (1 Cor 15:3–8).

Evidently, this traditional formula antedates Paul's letter to Corinth, and antedates even his first mission there. Indeed, it might well be the oldest credal formula we possess in the New Testament, perhaps rivaling in antiquity even that found in Romans 1:3–4 (see above, No. 19). But, before coming to consider the essential components of the formula in 1 Corinthians, a few preliminary observations are necessary.

(a) The "in accordance with the scriptures" in the first part of the formula modifies, not the "for our sins," but the death of Jesus, i.e., Jesus died according to what the author of Acts calls "the definite plan and foreknowledge of God" (Acts 2:23; see Eph 1:9–10; 3:9). This, of course, is the plan which was prophesied and revealed in the Scriptures.

(b) So too does the second "in accordance with the scriptures" modify the "on the third day" (see Hosea 6:2) rather than the "he was raised."

(c) Moreover, lest it prove the inevitable distraction to the main issue that it can be, and has often been, the statement that "he was buried" is a confirmation of "he died" rather than a proof of "he was raised." It is not, in other words, intended to propose the empty tomb as an argument to prove the truth of the resurrection. In and of itself, the empty tomb is ambivalent. It requires an interpretation, such as that provided, for example, by Mark 16:6:

> Do not be amazed; you seek Jesus of Nazareth, who was crucified. He has risen, he is not here; see the place where they laid him.

By itself, the formula "he was buried" admits of more than one explanation (as, for example, "His disciples came by night and stole him away while we were asleep" in Matthew 28:13). In 1 Corinthians 15, the "he was buried" serves to confirm the reality of the death of Christ, underlining his being like us "in every respect" (Heb 2:17; see Rom 8:3).

(d) The list of appearances might and might not have belonged to the traditional formula handed down. This is a question that continues to be discussed by scholars. But, notwithstanding the provenance of the list, some of its particulars call for attention.

Cephas leads the list as he does elsewhere in other lists of the apostles (e.g., Mk 3:16; Mt 10:2; Lk 6:14; Acts 1:13). The use of Cephas rather than the Greco-Roman Peter in the formula could well be an index of its Aramaic origin and, hence, of the antiquity of the tradition enshrined in it. So too Luke's narrative of the resurrection appearances reflects, in all likelihood, an adjustment in the account of the two disciples on the road to Emmaus in order to accommodate this ancient tradition of the appearance to Peter first: "The Lord has risen indeed, and has appeared to Simon!" (Lk 24:34).

A second point which deserves attention is that the list of appearances distinguishes, and does not confuse, "the twelve" and "all the apostles." The former, "the twelve," were destined to disappear from the scene with the disappearance of the "apostolic age." Their significance was principally eschatological. It is evident in the care that the author of Luke-Acts takes to replace Judas (Acts 1:20–21) before the momentous event of Pentecost. "The twelve" are eschatologically important because they represent the Israel of the last days, the Church, which—at least in the view of Luke-Acts—comes to be on the day of Pentecost. Later on, when James, one of "the twelve," dies, he is not replaced (Acts 12:2).

Third, the omission of any resurrection appearance to the women, such as that narrated in Matthew 28:1–10 or in John 20:11–18, is simply due to the fact that the list is citing "witnesses," and women did not fulfill that role in Judaism (see Lk 24:10–11, 22–24). This peculiarity of the list could be a further index of its antiquity, or at least of its Palestinian origin.

Finally, whatever may be said about the antecedents of the list in the tradition underlying 1 Corinthians, the "last of all, as to one untimely born, he appeared to me" (1 Cor 15:8) is clearly Paul's own addition. Its purpose is more apologetic than anything else; for Paul puts himself on a par with the other apostles and "official witnesses" of the resurrection. The appearance to Paul could well have been the last in the series and the conclusion of the appearances of the risen

162 PAUL: HIS LETTERS AND HIS THEOLOGY

Lord. But, to Luke, such an appearance was not, and could not have been, on a par with the appearances to the "apostles," which were definitively concluded with the ascension ("he parted from them, and was carried up into heaven"—Lk 24:51).

So, in this sense at least, since to be an "apostle" one had to have been an eyewitness to the risen Jesus (see Acts 1:21–22), Paul could not be regarded by Luke as one of the "apostles." Luke, of course, is the one who limits the category of "apostle" to that of "the twelve." Paul's sensitivity about this point, on whether he was to be counted as an apostle or not, is especially evident in his polemics in both Galatians and 2 Corinthians. It was not just a question of nomenclature. On the evidence of Luke, the question remained alive long after Paul was dead.

But in discussing the question of the resurrection, the identity of the person who appeared is of far greater import. For, in Luke's accounts, the Jesus who appears to "the apostles" prior to the ascension appears in personal intimacy ("Have you anything here to eat?"—Lk 24:41; Acts 1:2–3), but he who appeared to Paul on the road to Damascus is the already exalted and glorified Lord (see, e.g., Acts 9:3–6). Perhaps it will make the distinction between the appearances a bit clearer to say that, while for Luke the appearances of the risen Jesus to the apostles are a closed series of unique events, the appearance to Paul could not have been—to Luke's way of thinking at least—very different from the appearance of Jesus, say, to some mystic like Catherine of Siena.

The Credal Formula

Having made these preliminary remarks, we can concentrate our attention on the core of the credal formula in 1 Corinthians 15:3–4:

that Christ died	for our sins
that he was raised	that he appeared.

The first thing to keep in mind here is the need to distinguish—not to separate, but to keep distinct—the historical, verifiable fact from the faith interpretation of that fact, an interpretation that is not subject to, nor susceptible of, verification. Thus, that "Christ died" is an historical and historically verifiable fact. As such it differs hardly at all from statements like "Alexander the Great died" or "Cyrus died." But the "for our sins" is an interpretation of Jesus' death—an interpretation moreover that only faith can make. What it says is that this death is unique in the history of the world, because its significance for sinful humanity is unique. Jesus was not the only one to die ignominiously on a cross, but his death was the only one to have saving significance for those who believe in the need for redemption and in the possibility of a Redeemer.

It is precisely at this juncture that "in accordance with the scriptures" (1 Cor 15:3) comes to illuminate that death with all the light that "the law and the prophets" can shed: from the sacrifice of Isaac (Gen 22) down to the suffering servant (Is 53) and the plangent accents of Psalm 22.

The two elements of the second part of the formula, however, "he was raised . . . he appeared," are in just the reverse order: the "he appeared" is the fact, while the "he was raised" is its faith interpretation. For, however fantastic and incredible it might seem, certain people said that they "saw" Jesus of Nazareth, or affirmed that Jesus had "appeared" to them. That they had this experience, extraordinary though it be, need not be called into question. We might find the experience itself incomprehensible, since we know nothing comparable to it in our lives, but we do not have to dismiss it as untrue for all that.

The list of witnesses in 1 Corinthians 15:5–8 provides the evidence necessary to overcome the reluctance of believers, but an infinitely longer list or even a personal encounter with the risen Lord would leave an unbeliever unconvinced ("Neither will they be convinced if someone should rise from the dead"—Lk 16:31). Some of the witnesses, as Paul says, were "still alive." The fact that "he appeared to more than five hundred brethren at one time" (1 Cor 15:6) should dispel most reasonable doubt, etc. These and similar arguments are employed regularly to establish the reliability of the resurrection *witnesses*.

Nevertheless, to conclude from the fact that "he appeared" to the affirmation that "he was raised" is to interpret an event through the eyes of faith. This faith has to believe at least that God could raise the dead to life. If that be not so, then to hear the disciples' claim to have seen Jesus of Nazareth after his death would lead one to conclude that they were either drunk, or the victims of a hoax (see Mt 28:11–15), or individuals who were psychologically disturbed (recall the arch remark of Ernest Renan that any perceptive person could have told you on Holy Saturday that Jesus was going to rise on Easter Sunday), or any number of like explanations. In other words, to say "he was raised" from the dead is not the only possible explanation of the "he appeared," nor is it the first that comes to mind. But it is the explanation that is possible to faith alone, and to a faith informed by "the scriptures":

> And beginning with Moses and all the prophets, he interpreted to them in all the scriptures the things concerning himself (Lk 24:27).

One further point. The disciples who "saw" the risen Jesus, or to whom the risen Jesus "appeared," claimed to have seen far, far more than Jesus of Nazareth. They said that they saw "the Lord" (Jn 20:18, 25), or that "the Lord" appeared to them (Lk 24:34). Now, "the Lord" is by definition an eschatological reality belonging to a world which "no one has ever seen" (Jn 1:18a). Whether or not such a reality can be visible and the way in which such a reality can become visible are questions to which I myself have no answer, nor do I possess the wherewithal to hypothesize one. A Christian's faith does not and cannot rest on the verifiability of the testimony of eyewitnesses. Put very simply, a Christian does not believe in the resurrection *because* Cephas, or the Twelve, or James, or Paul said he or they saw him.

As has been remarked above, even the appearance of the

risen Jesus itself needs an interpretation. Consider, for instance, the superb account in Luke 24:13–31, which could well be as close as anyone shall ever come to understanding the genesis of the Easter faith, i.e., how faith in the resurrection of Jesus was born. In the Lucan narrative, it was born out of an interpretation of "all the scriptures . . . concerning himself" (Luke 24:27).

In his polemic against those in Corinth who denied the "resurrection of the dead" (1 Cor 15:12), Paul too sheds some light on the genesis of the Easter faith by establishing the right order of belief:

> If there is no resurrection of the dead, then Christ has not been raised (1 Cor 15:13).

Faith in the eschatological reality of the resurrection of the dead has to precede faith in the resurrection of Christ. Yet Paul adds:

> But in fact Christ has been raised from the dead, the *first fruits* of those who have fallen asleep (1 Cor 15:20).

In other words, it is the resurrection of Christ that now founds, provides the basis for, the Christian's faith in the resurrection of the dead:

> For if the dead are not raised, then Christ has not been raised. If Christ has not been raised, your faith is futile and you are still in your sins. Then those also who have fallen asleep in Christ have perished. If for this life only we have hoped in Christ, we are of all men most to be pitied (1 Cor 15:16–19).

If this sounds like a circuitous argument, it is. The disciples first came to believe in the resurrection of Jesus because they already believed in the resurrection of the dead. Christians believe in the resurrection of the dead because Christ himself is risen from the dead. Deny any single item in this circular argument and the whole argument collapses: "Your faith is futile" (1 Cor 15:17).

What lies behind this puzzling mode of argument is the fact—all too often forgotten by Christians brought up to regard every item of their faith as provable as a euclidean theorem and as demonstrable as the sphericity of the earth—that faith is not susceptible either of proof or of demonstration. We are so prone to forget that the "Christ was raised" was a divinely revealed truth, a revealed truth that is proclaimed as good news: "Christ is preached as raised from the dead" (1 Cor 15:12). As a divinely revealed truth, there are only three possible reactions to it: total acceptance, total rejection, or utter indifference.

The Resurrection of the Dead

At this point we rejoin Paul's own argument in 1 Corinthians:

> Now if Christ is preached as raised from the dead, how can some of you say that there is no resurrection of the dead? But if there is no resurrection of the dead, then Christ has not been raised; if Christ has not been raised, then our preaching is in vain and your faith is in vain. We are even found to be misrepresenting God, because we testified of God that he raised Christ, whom he did not raise if it is true that the dead are not raised (1 Cor 15:12–15).

That Christ is preached as raised from the dead means that there is a resurrection of the dead. It means that I, the believer, will one day be raised from the dead. But it means a bit more than just a statement about my final destiny. It says something also about my present reality as a believer:

> For if the dead are not raised, then Christ has not been raised. If Christ has not been raised, your faith is futile and you are still in your sins (1 Cor 15:16–17).

The proclamation of the good news is, of course, the proclamation of the good news of our salvation. The message of the resurrection says something, not only about those who "have fallen asleep" (1 Cor 15:6), but also about the believers living here and now. We have had occasion to mention above (No. 19) the triple aspect of the gospel message: the soteriological, the eschatological, and the apocalyptic (see 1 Thess 1:9–10 and No. 21 above). In 1 Corinthians, Paul expresses the connections and the interrelations that bind these three aspects together when he goes on to explain:

> But in fact Christ has been raised from the dead, the first fruits of those who have fallen asleep. For as by a man came death, by a man has come also the resurrection of the dead. For as in Adam all die, so also in Christ shall all be made alive. But each in his own order: Christ the first fruits, then at his coming (*parousia*) those who belong to Christ. Then comes the end, when he delivers the kingdom to God the Father (1 Cor 15:20–24).

It is the God who raised Christ from the dead who will also raise us "who belong to Christ." It is to God the Father, who raised Jesus from the dead and who will raise "those who belong to Christ" that Christ will "deliver the kingdom."

Since death itself is linked to sin, and sin (see below, No. 31) to the law, then for any redemption to be genuine, it has to set us free from all three:

> The sting of death is sin, and the power of sin is the law. But thanks be to God, who gives us the victory through our Lord Jesus Christ (1 Cor 15:56–57).

To proclaim the resurrection of Christ from the dead then is to proclaim what is but the first act in what Paul calls the "new creation" (2 Cor 5:17). Christ is "the first fruits" (1 Cor 15:23). The proclamation of his resurrection is the proclamation of his definitive victory over death, his own and ours:

> "Death is swallowed up in victory." "O death, where is thy victory? O death, where is thy sting?" (1 Cor 15:54–55).

Christ's victory over death means the end of the reign of sin as well as the end of the law:

For Christ is the end of the law (Rom 10:4).

This, as Galatians shows (see above, Nos. 23 and 24) and as Romans insists, is what the Christian gospel of freedom really means.

Moreover, conscious of the kind of audience he was addressing in 1 Corinthians, Paul raises the inevitable question that arises out of the proclamation of this gospel:

But someone will ask, "How are the dead raised? With what kind of body do they come?" (1 Cor 15:35).

He takes up the rest of chapter 15 to formulate some sort of answer to this question. Yet, despite all the varied imagery he calls forth from botany ("kernel" in v. 37), biology (the various kinds of flesh in v. 39), astronomy (the celestial bodies in vv. 40–41), and philosophy (the perishable and the imperishable in v. 42, the physical and the spiritual in v. 44), Paul really has no answer to give whatsoever. He simply does not know how the dead are raised. His very prolixity is avowal enough of his ignorance.

The real mystery in all this is, of course, why theologians persist in trying to "eff the ineffable," to do what evidently cannot be done. If Paul, who claimed to have seen the risen Lord ("Have I not seen Jesus our Lord?"—1 Cor 9:1), could not come up with anything like an intelligible explanation, if someone who claimed to have seen a risen body cannot tell us anything about how the dead are raised, then why the dogged persistence in trying to invent an answer where none can be found? Agnosticism about how the dead are raised is not skepticism about the resurrection, and to confess ignorance is not an act of disbelief.

Faith in the resurrection of Christ, and hence in our own resurrection, and therefore in our liberation from death and sin and the law, cannot be demonstrated by any argument, nor established by any proof. The only available and acceptable argument for the resurrection, the only genuine proof of its validity is the life the believer lives here and now:

Therefore, my beloved brethren, be steadfast, immovable, always abounding in the work of the Lord, knowing that in the Lord your labor is not in vain (1 Cor 15:58).

This life which is lived for others, which seeks not its own good but the good of the other (1 Cor 10:24), this life therefore which brings real life to the other, is the only available, indeed the only necessary, proof that the believer really believes that Christ is raised from the dead, "the first fruits of those who have fallen asleep" (1 Cor 15:20).

SEVEN

The Correspondence in 2 Corinthians

30. The Testing of the Apostle

The collection of letters or fragments of letters which make up 2 Corinthians is hard to determine with accuracy, harder to date with precision, and hardest to analyze and structure into any definable aggregate of themes. This collected correspondence represents perhaps the saddest interlude in Paul's life as an apostle—his "wilderness years," as it were. He knew humiliating failure, suffered crushing setbacks, and underwent the harshest assault on his person, his methods of evangelizing, and his gospel. It would indeed be tempting to say that he kept his head, weathered the storm, and came out "smelling roses." But these would be only the clichés they surely are. The temptation to employ them, moreover, is more than resistible to anyone who knows the "bitterness, the wormwood and the gall" of failure, frustration and humiliation. Whoever was responsible for the gathering together of these epistolary fragments into one letter must have been aware of the extent of Paul's sufferings when he prefaced the letter with the customary thanksgiving formula:

> Blessed be the God and the Father of our Lord Jesus Christ, the Father of mercies and God of all comfort, who comforts us in all our affliction, with the comfort with which we ourselves are comforted by God. For as we share abundantly in Christ's sufferings, so through Christ we share abundantly in comfort too (2 Cor 1:3–5).

170

Paul had plans to visit Corinth "soon" (1 Cor 4:19; 16:5–7; 11:34), but the plans fell through (2 Cor 1:15–16; compare 13:1; 12:14), and that disappointed and angered the Corinthians to such an extent that they accused Paul of vacillating and acting in a worldly manner:

> Was I vacillating when I wanted to [visit you]? Do I make my plans like a worldly man, ready to say Yes and No at once? As surely as God is faithful, our word to you has not been Yes and No (2 Cor 1:17–18; see 1:15).

Perhaps the troubled situation in Corinth was what caused Paul to defer his planned visit. Judging by the vehemence of the Corinthians' reaction, that was a bad decision. What Paul could not perhaps foresee was that the situation in Corinth had deteriorated to such an extent that even an innocent change in his plans to visit the city would suffice as an excuse to mount an attack on his integrity. The Corinthians were a bit too eager to accuse Paul of lying (2 Cor 1:18).

What, then, was responsible for this alarming change of attitude of mutual civility and affection which prevailed throughout 1 Corinthians? The answer has to be pieced out of the letters or fragments that make up 2 Corinthians. But this is a delicate task, complicated first of all by the difficulty of determining the precise limits of the individual components, and, secondly, by the even more difficult problem of dating them, or at least of setting them in some chronological sequence.

One convincing way of identifying the various fragments in 2 Corinthians is to see one letter in 2:14—6:13 and 7:2–4. The verses that are in between 6:14 and 7:1, having long been a subject of dispute, are best regarded as a "non-Pauline interpolation" (J.A. Fitzmyer, *CBQ* 23 [1961] 280). There is part of another letter preserved in Chapters 10—13. There are two, almost duplicate, letters about the "offering for the saints" (9:1) in Chapters 8 and 9 respectively. Finally, there is the letter, or the fragment of a letter, preserved in 1:1—2:13 and 7:5–16 (see H. Koester, *Introduction*, vol. II, p. 130). Yet all of these letters and fragments do not allow us to determine with any exactitude "the reason for the turbidity of the relation between Paul and the congregation" (W.G. Kümmel, *Introduction*, p. 208).

As far as one can determine, other missionaries, whose identity and whose teachings are perhaps the thorniest problem of all, had come to Corinth and managed to win the Corinthian community to their way of thinking. Their doctrines were, evidently, so opposed to Paul's that they succeeded in generating hatred, not just of his teaching, but of his very person. There is little doubt that they were Jewish-Christian missionaries who were proud of their Jewishness:

> Are they Hebrews? So am I. Are they Israelites? So am I.
> Are they descendants of Abraham? So am I (2 Cor 11:22).

But they were not the same kind of Jewish-Christians as those we encountered in Galatians. They do not seem to have been advocating circumcision and the observance of the Law.

The success of these Jewish-Christian missionaries raised many uncertainties about the gospel Paul had preached in Corinth, about the methods he employed in his evangelization, and about his dealing with the Corinthian congregation. So Paul wrote a letter (perhaps that preserved in 2 Corinthians 2:14—6:13 and 7:2–4) to try to call the Corinthians to their senses and to win them back to the true gospel. But the letter fell far short of its purpose, and Paul decided to visit Corinth in person. The visit must have been, in Professor Koester's words, "a catastrophe" (H. Koester, p. 129). Humiliated and anguished, Paul returned to Ephesus and wrote from there the letter which we have (partially?) preserved in 2 Corinthians 10—13. This might well have been the letter he wrote "out of much affliction and anguish of heart and with many tears, not to cause you pain but to let you know the abundant love that I have for you" (2 Cor 2:4; see 2:9 and 7:8–10).

Some time must surely have elapsed before the situation calmed down and good relations were restored. This was in no small part due to the mediations of Titus and his "ministry of reconciliation":

> But God, who comforts the downcast, comforted us by the coming of Titus, and not only by his coming but also by the comfort with which he was comforted in you, as he told us of your longing, your mourning, your zeal for me, so that I rejoiced still more (2 Cor 7:6–7).

The restored amicable relations between the Corinthian community and its apostle find further echoes in the two letters preserved in chapters 8 and 9 respectively. The principal concern of these letters is the collection, "the relief of the saints" (2 Cor 8:4). In them Paul urges the Corinthians to "give proof, before the churches, of your love and of our boasting about you to these men" (2 Cor 8:24). He even speaks of the "surpassing grace of God in you," and concluded with:

> Thanks be to God for his inexpressible gift (2 Cor 9:14–15).

Thus ended that crisis-ridden period of Paul's life, leaving us fragments of four or five letters which, in their lack of unity and in the very "contradictory impression" they convey (W.G. Kümmel, p. 206), still manage to leave us a wealth of profound, and profoundly disturbing, instructions on the true meaning of the Christian life, the proper conduct of the Christian apostle, the genuinely appropriate tools for the ministry of the gospel, and above all the basic difficulty of trying to compete with those who peddle Christian salvation at a discount.

The Opponents

These instructions emerge out of the lengthy series of charges and counter-charges (see W.G. Kümmel, pp. 208–209) which crisscross 2 Corinthians like so many streaks of lightning in a menacing sky. The tempest, however, did leave in its wake some of the most memorable moments in Paul's epistolary apostolate. We can try, therefore, through an examination of the heated polemic and the impassioned apologetic of these letters, to understand something about the mind of Paul's opponents, those "false apostles, deceitful

workmen, disguising themselves as apostles of Christ" (2 Cor
11:13). But, above all, we can try to understand the true apostle's real strength in weakness, "for when I am weak, then I
am strong" (2 Cor 12:10b):

> We are treated as impostors, and yet are true; as un-
> known, and yet well known; as dying, and behold we live;
> as punished, and yet not killed; as sorrowful, yet always
> rejoicing; as poor, yet making many rich; as having noth-
> ing, and yet possessing everything (2 Cor 6:8b–10).

We have already seen that the Corinthians charged Paul
with inconstancy and worldliness. He had planned to visit
them, not once, but twice. But, for reasons that to him at least
seemed good and honorable, he had to delay his visit. The
Corinthians' reaction was not merely one of expected disappointment but of something closer to rage and outright
hatred. Their invective and their exaggerated reaction provide a hint of the extent to which their minds had been poi-
soned against him. They seemed on the lookout for any
excuse at all to declare their hostility. Paul, like so many accused innocents, could only state the facts of the case:

> I wanted to visit you on my way to Macedonia and have
> you send me on my way to Judea. Was I vacillating when
> I wanted to do this? Do I make my plans like a worldly
> man, ready to say Yes and No at once? (2 Cor 1:16–17;
> see 10:2).

Paul's assurance throughout the bitter exchanges did not
rest on worldly weapons or the knowledge of worldly tactics:

> For, though we live in the world, we are not carrying on
> a worldly war (2 Cor 10:3–4).

It rested rather on his awareness of his commission, and on
his conviction of the divine origin of his vocation and ministry:

> But it is God who establishes us with you in Christ, and has commissioned us; he has put his seal upon us and given us his Spirit in our hearts as a guarantee (2 Cor 1:21–22).

One test of a genuine charism is the ability of its possessor to stand alone, to withstand the argument of the majority, and to refuse to succumb to the blackmail of popularity. Paul knows what gifts he has, what gifts he has not, and where all his gifts come from. This knowledge gives him the courage to face his opponents' charges:

> But I call God to witness against me—it was to spare you that I refrained from coming to Corinth. Not that we lord it over your faith; we work with you for your joy (2 Cor 1:23–24).

The Message

Another charge of the Corinthians against Paul, and a more serious one for a preacher of the gospel, was the obscurity of his message, the lack of clarity in his epistles. This is not the same thing as the complaint made, quite justly, by an author two or three generations later that there are in Paul's letters "some things . . . hard to understand" (2 Pet 3:16). The Corinthians' accusation was more closely akin to that petulant and stubborn refusal to understand which marks children of all ages. It sprang not so much from an honest failure to comprehend what Paul had said as from a perverse unwillingness to listen to what he had to say:

> For we write you nothing but what you can read and understand (2 Cor 1:13).

Someone had come along and offered the Corinthians one of those short-cuts to religious success, a deceptively simple solution to the difficulites they encounter, a ready panacea for the ills that beset them. By comparison with this, Paul's gospel is of course very hard to understand, and Paul puts his finger at the real evil: their willful blindness, their refusal to see:

And even if our gospel is veiled, it is veiled only to those who are perishing. In their case the god of this world has blinded the minds of the unbelievers, to keep them from seeing the light of the gospel of the glory of Christ, who is the likeness of God (2 Cor 4:3–4; see Mt 13:13–15; Is 6:9–10).

"Peddlers of God's word" (2 Cor 2:17) had come to Corinth and, in "disgraceful, underhanded ways," practiced their cunning and tampered with the gospel message (4:2). They found a ready market at Corinth. They offered redemption at a discount: a simplistic faith with verifiable credentials, provable tenets and immediately sensed results, but without the need to strain after the mystery. It was a message tailored for its audience. Success was its aim, and personal popularity its criterion. All that Paul could say against this was the helpless statement of fact:

> For what we preach is not ourselves, but Jesus Christ as Lord, with ourselves as your servants [slaves] for Jesus' sake (2 Cor 4:4–5).

The missionaries in Corinth, moreover, had come armed with "letters of recommendation" (2 Cor 3:1–3). That perennial variety of preachers is a hardy breed and difficult to eradicate. They mistake the duly attested and sealed credentials for the reality they ought to proclaim and the faith out of which they ought to proclaim it. Paul had to remind the Corinthians that the only genuine "letter of recommendation" which has any validity at all is the community which is served and built up by the preaching:

> You yourselves are our letter of recommendation, written on your hearts, to be known and read by all men; and you show that you are a letter from Christ delivered by us, written not with ink but with the Spirit of the living God, not on tablets of stone but on tablets of human hearts (2 Cor 3:2–3).

For Paul, any other recommendation is spurious and, ultimately, harmful, because such a recommendation would always be ready to "tamper with God's word" in order to make it fit the attested and certified dossier of the preacher.

It would be invidious—though relatively easy—to illustrate the continuing existence of this problem in the Church. But anyone with any reflective experience in seminaries and schools of divinity or theology will readily apprehend the grave temptation besetting such institutions to tamper cunningly with the word of God in order to accommodate its exigent demands to the requirements of the accrediting agencies, employment bureaus, or some business-minded corporate Maecenas. Yet all that any genuine minister of the word can do in the face of all this is to reiterate Paul's assurance:

> Therefore, having this ministry by the mercy of God, we do not lose heart. We renounce disgraceful, underhanded ways; we refuse to practice cunning or to tamper with God's word, but by the open statement of the truth we can commend ourselves to every man's conscience in the sight of God (2 Cor 4:1–2).

The true Christian minister simply has no other way, no real alternative.

"Superlative Apostles"

But there is no limit to the fertility of an ill-disposed imagination. The Corinthians manage to find fault even with the way Paul talks and with the way he walks:

> For they say, "His letters are weighty and strong, but his bodily presence is weak, and his speech is of no account" (2 Cor 10:10; see 11:6).

They find his conduct reprehensible, even scandalous (6:3). They suspect him of "acting in a worldly fashion" (10:2), of wronging them, corrupting them, and taking advantage of them (7:2; 12:17). Even his unwillingness to accept pay from them for his ministry is turned against him:

> Did I commit a sin in abasing myself so that you might be
> exalted, because I preached God's gospel without cost to
> you. I robbed other churches by accepting support from
> them in order to serve you. And when I was with you and
> was in want, I did not burden anyone, for my needs were
> supplied by the brethren who came from Macedonia. So
> I refrained and will refrain from burdening you in any
> way (2 Cor 11:7–9; see 12:13).

> But granting that I myself did not burden you, I was
> crafty, you say, and got the better of you by guile (12:16).

Now that the Corinthians have seen the "superlative
apostles" (2 Cor 11:5; 12:11b), skilled in speaking (11:6),
charging respectable fees for their services (11:7), flashing
their diplomas and letters of recommendation (3:1; 4:2), and
dazzling the crowd with their show of "signs and wonders and
mighty works" (12:12)—is it any wonder they found Paul and
his gospel not up to par? Like so many Christian communities
down the centuries, they thought they deserved the best, not
for any love of excellence, but from a sense of self-flattery. Of
course, the best, the super apostles, provided them with what
they liked: the simplified truth, the readily demonstrable
mystery, the immediately perceptible results of faith, and
above all the sensed, the felt warmth of religious "experience." This is the kind of ornament the Corinthians could display, boast of, and compare with one another. The believers
in their wonder-working Christ and in the tangibility of divine power were themselves wonder-workers, whose prayers
were guaranteed efficacious, whose faith rested on irrefuta-
ble proof and the irrefragable testimony of eye-witnesses, and
whose religious sensibility was never long without the pleasant and reassuring warmth of religious consolation.

Judged by these preferences, Paul was found by the Corinthians to be not only inferior to the super apostles, but no
apostle at all. The Corinthians were sure he was not a "true
apostle" (2 Cor 12:12), nor did he belong to Christ (10:7), nor
did Christ speak in him (13:3). Such a devastating assessment
of Paul, his gospel and his "legitimacy" as an apostle is by itself

sufficient proof of the success of the missionaries in Corinth and, consequently, of Paul's failure there.

Those missionaries, as indicated above, were not just ordinary Jewish Christians; for they boasted of being "Hebrews . . . Israelites . . . descendants of Abraham . . . servants of Christ" (2 Cor 11:22–23) in some superlative way. Unlike the Judaizers encountered in Galatians (see Nos. 22 and 23 above), their principal concern was not circumcision or the observance of the law. Their views could well have been those of Jewish converts who saw in Christianity the "renewal of the true Jewish religion" with all the pristine splendor of its mighty deeds and wonders (2 Cor 12:11–12), its mystical ascent of the mountain of God (12:1–4), its "spiritual exegesis" of the law of Moses and its new "theology of the covenant" (3:4–18) (H. Koester, *Introduction*, vol. 2, pp. 127–128).

Nevertheless, the general outline of Paul's opponents in Corinth remains hazy. The disparate elements of their teachings are variously obscured by the vehemence of their invective and by their sworn opposition to Paul and to everything he stood for. Paul's own impassioned defense of his personal conduct and his teachings is less valuable for the uncertain light it casts on the identity of those opponents in Corinth than for the outline of Christian life and the Christian ministry it allows to emerge. The whole affair in Corinth forced Paul to do what he was resolved not to do: to speak of his own spiritual experiences and to boast of his own credentials, even if "there is nothing to be gained by it" (2 Cor 12:1).

Paul's opponents in Corinth were in fact only a minority (see 2 Cor 2:6; 10:2: "*some* who suspect us"). Therefore, it is a tribute to their ingenuity or, better still, to the inherent attractiveness of their teachings, that the damage they caused the Corinthian community was so extensive and so difficult to repair. They were able, for instance, to use the money they made by their preaching as an argument against Paul's legitimacy as an apostle precisely because he "preached God's gospel without cost" (2 Cor 11:7; 12:13). But Paul was not slow to grasp the real motive behind their zeal: greed. They were "peddlers of God's word" (2:17), who "preyed" on and "took advantage" of the Corinthians (11:20). Of course, in order to carry out this evangelical swindle successfully (see 11:19–20), they had to con their listeners with their "letters of recommendation" (3:1b). They had, in today's PR jargon, "to sell themselves." They "commend themselves," says Paul, and they "measure themselves by one another, and compare themselves with one another" (10:12; see Jer 17:5).

Readers of 2 Corinthians can recognize in the tactics of Paul's opponents the methods and techniques of modern advertising. Yet today, as frequently in the history of Christianity, there are still those who advocate the adoption of precisely such methods and techniques by the Christian ministry. They would do well to reflect on Paul's—admittedly rather impotent-looking—statement:

> "Let him who boasts, boast of the Lord." For it is not the man who commends himself that is accepted, but the man whom the Lord commends (2 Cor 10:17–18; see Jer 9:23–24).

How differently the quotation from Jeremiah sounds here from its ringing assurance in 1 Corinthians 1:31!

It was essential for the opponents in Corinth to "pride themselves on a man's position" (2 Cor 5:12), to boast and make claims to do not only what other preachers do but to do it better (11:12), to boast of "worldly things" (11:18). Their approach required such an attitude as part of the necessary means to sell God's word like some luxury good on an already glutted market. The religious market of the day was already crammed with some exquisite items of (mostly Oriental) imports. The newcomers to Corinth did not delay in showing off their own variety of extraordinary religious phenomena: their ecstasies (2 Cor 5:13), their visions and the abundance of their revelations (12:1, 7), and—perhaps the most delectable morsel of all—their strange and exotic elements in prayer. Those "super apostles" (12:11; 11:5) could also perform "signs and wonders and mighty works" (12:12). As Jews, of course, they could not resist the comparison with Moses, and as Christians they could not avoid the claim of surpassing him (3:4–18).

As "super apostles" of this new religion, the missionaries used all their impressive credentials and their spectacular religious experiences and spiritual powers to insist that they alone, and not Paul and his ilk, knew Christ and belonged to him as his true servants (2 Cor 11:23; see 5:16; 10:7). This knowledge is what legitimated their claim to apostleship (11:5; 12:11), to being "apostles of Christ" (11:13). Of course, the Christ they proclaimed was a product of their theological preferences, a Christ to the measure of their own religious values (5:16). The miracle-working, spectacularly triumphant leader of a victorious army of followers is the Christ they preached, and preached—as is usually the case—very successfully:

> For if someone comes and preaches another Jesus than the one we preached, or if you receive a different spirit from the one you received, or if you accept a different gospel from the one you accepted, you submit to it readily enough (2 Cor 11:4).

And here is the real problem. It is all of a piece. You preach the Christ that best suits your aims, meets your aspirations, fulfills your expectations: "The Vision of Christ that thou dost see/Is my vision's greatest enemy." But such a view of Christ is always contrary to the one true gospel of the crucified Lord. Such a view can only engender a "Christ from a human point of view":

> From now on, therefore, we regard no one from a human point of view (*kata sarka*, according to the flesh); even though we regarded Christ from a human point of view, we regard him thus no longer (2 Cor 5:16).

It is so difficult for believers to keep always clearly in mind:

> All this is from God, who through Christ reconciled us to himself . . . in Christ God was reconciling the world to himself. . . . For our sake he made him to be sin who knew no sin, so that in him we might become the righteousness of God (2 Cor 5:18, 19, 21).

The perversion of this gospel, whose "ambassador for Christ" he was (2 Cor 5:20), lay at the heart of Paul's concern for the Corinthian community, at the center of his impassioned polemic against the corrupters of its faith. But the struggle was not a theological debate, not an orderly discussion of the finer points of dogma between mutually respectful partners in an apostolic enterprise. If the methods of Paul's missionary opponents were to succeed, then Paul himself had to be personally discredited, his methods seriously questioned, his motives doubted, and his Christ and his gospel rejected (see 2 Cor 11:3–6).

It was, therefore, a rather unequal battle. But then the preaching of the gospel of Christ leaves you few options, deprives you of all the seemingly indispensable tools of propaganda, and more often than not leaves you without anything to show for your toils, bereft of any demonstrable signs of success. Thus it has always been. Those who fight for the true gospel often fight alone, the "new creation" in Christ (2 Cor 5:17) being highly refractory to advertising and marketing techniques.

The True Apostle

This uncongenial fact is admirably documented in 2 Corinthians. For, against his inclination, against his better judgment, Paul is drawn into this contest of credentials, achievements, boasting and ostentation. But in the end Paul's attempt did not work, and its very failure is the lesson on preaching the gospel which 2 Corinthians has preserved for us. For the inescapable fact of the matter is:

> Though we live in the world we are not carrying on a worldly war, for the weapons of our warfare are not worldly (2 Cor 10:3–4).

Even when Paul is forced to meet his enemies on their own terms, he knows all too well that to measure oneself by another and to compare oneself with the other is to be "without understanding" (10:12). He knows that to boast is to speak "like a fool," "like a madman" (11:21b, 23). Yet, when he finally does boast, he is forced to stand the whole system of values on its head:

> But whatever anyone dares to boast of—I am speaking as a fool—I also dare to boast of that. Are they Hebrews? So am I. Are they Israelites? So am I. Are they descendants of Abraham? So am I. Are they servants of Christ? I am a better one—I am talking like a madman—with far greater labors, far more imprisonments, with countless beatings, and often near death. Five times I have received at the hands of the Jews the forty lashes less one. Three times I have been beaten with rods; once I was stoned. Three times I have been shipwrecked; a night and a day I have been adrift at sea; on frequent journeys, in danger from rivers, danger from robbers, danger from my own people, danger from Gentiles, danger in the city, danger in the wilderness, danger at sea, danger from false brethren; in toil and hardship, through many a sleepless night, in hunger and thirst, often without food, in cold and exposure. And apart from other things, there is the daily pressure upon me of my anxiety for all the churches (2 Cor 11:21–28).

Thus, in the midst of this unsavory contest, in the midst of all the passion and bitterness, Paul finds the one single incontrovertible truth of the Christian apostolate:

> If I must boast, I will boast of the things that show my weakness (2 Cor 11:30).

Paul does not deny the "visions and revelations of the Lord," however reluctant he is to put them on display (2 Cor 12:1). They were not granted for this purpose. They never are. Yet even here, in the midst of this flood of divine favors, the validating sign is not wanting:

> And to keep me from being too elated by the abundance of revelations, a thorn was given me in the flesh, a messenger of Satan, to harass me, to keep me from being too elated. Three times I besought the Lord about this, that

it should leave me; but he said to me, "My grace is sufficient for you, for my power is made perfect in weakness"
(2 Cor 12:7–9a).

Prayers, even Paul's prayers, are not always answered;
and there is no particular method or technique to get them
answered, all the claims and pretensions of the missionaries
in Corinth and their successors throughout history notwithstanding. Extraordinary favors in prayer, moreover, are not
the stuff of Christian boasting. They are not ornaments for
display. What really matters in the apostle's life is precisely
what the Corinthians found most congenial to sidestep, and
what their unsurprisingly successful missionaries rejected out
of hand:

> I will all the more gladly boast of my weaknesses, that the
> power of Christ may rest upon me. For the sake of Christ,
> then, I am content with weakness, insults, hardships, per-
> secutions, and calamities; for when I am weak, then I am
> strong (2 Cor 12:9b–10).

This is the real challenge of the Christian apostle: to
know oneself to be nothing and yet not to feel "inferior" (2
Cor 12:11b). When his opponents demanded "proof that
Christ is speaking in" him (13:3), Paul had only one real proof
to offer: the gospel of the Christ who was "crucified in weakness, but lives by the power of God" (13:4).

Paul had to fight hard to bring the Corinthians back to
their senses:

> Examine yourselves, to see whether you are holding to
> your faith. Test yourselves. Do you not realize that Jesus
> Christ is in you?—unless indeed you fail to meet the test!
> I hope you will find out that we have not failed (2 Cor
> 13:5–6).

He had to resort to all kinds of tactics in his dealings with
them, and in the controversies with his opponents among
them. But he knew—and in that knowledge lay his strength—
that the authority which the Lord had given him was "for

building up and not for tearing down" (13:10). Above all, he never forgot that, as far as the gospel of Christ is concerned:

> We cannot do anything against the truth, but only for the truth (2 Cor 13:8),

all indications, statistics, proofs and documentary evidence to the contrary notwithstanding.

The world of the Christian is a topsy-turvy world where the humble is not inferior, the weak is not the loser, the helpless is not defeated, and the Christ who was crucified now lives in glory.

EIGHT

The Correspondence in Philippians

31. Christ Proclaimed

The discussion of Paul's Christology, i.e., of Paul's understanding of who Jesus is, of his relation to God, his meaning for and his relation to the Christian, could be said to be a major theme in any epistle that bears the apostle's name. To take up this theme under the Epistle to the Philippians is simply a matter of choice, but a choice motivated by the presence in the epistle of a "Christological hymn" which is as compendious a statement of who Jesus is in relation to God and to the believers as any found elsewhere in the Pauline corpus.

The "Christological hymn" in Philippians 2:6–11 is, of course, not unique in the New Testament. Other examples can be found in Colossians 1:15–20, 1 Timothy 3:16 and perhaps also 2:5–6, 1 Peter 3:18, and, of course, in the Prologue to the Gospel of John. However one may wish to decide their hymnic nature, these compositions are essentially acts of praise, of acclamation and worship. Hence, the liturgy of the community is where they found their principal—though by no means exclusive—use, and their inclusion in the writings of the New Testament bears the marks of their provenance.

Early in the second century, Pliny the Younger, the governor of a Roman province in Asia Minor, wrote to the Emperor Trajan about a problem he had encountered in the ordinary discharge of his duties. Having carried out an investigation of a new religion that had come under suspicion, Pliny reported:

> [The Christians] affirmed . . . that they were in the habit
> of meeting on a certain fixed day before it was light, when
> they sang in alternate verses [antiphonally] a hymn to
> Christ, as to a god (*carmenque Christo quasi deo dicere secum
> invicem*) (*Letters* X.96).

After careful examination of the evidence against the Christians, whose religion had recently been banned by an imperial edict, and after torturing two women ministers (*ex duabus ancillis, quae ministrae dicebantur*) to get at the truth about that proscribed religion, Pliny concluded that the whole thing was nothing more than a mindless and insignificant superstition (*superstitio prava, immodica*). Prescience was evidently not among the Younger Pliny's charisms!

The brief remark in Pliny's letter about the hymn sung by the Christians is, however, instructive. For a genuine Christology always issues in an act of worship, not in a formula or a committee statement. So it is not at all surprising that Paul and other authors of the New Testament should take up such hymns from Christian worship and use them to instruct the believers in a Christology, as well as to exhort and advise them to live out its implications. Such exhortation and advice is what is technically referred to as "paraenesis."

It is quite understandable, then, that the hymn in Philippians is not only Christological but also, as is amply evident from its context, paraenetic:

> So if there is any encouragement in Christ, any incentive
> of love, any participation in the Spirit, any affection and
> sympathy, complete my joy by being of the same mind. Do
> nothing from selfishness or conceit, but in humility count
> others better than yourselves. Let each of you look not
> only to his own interests, but also to the interests of others.
> Have this in mind among yourselves, which is yours in
> Christ Jesus . . . (Phil 2:1–5).

The Christological hymn follows immediately after this paraenesis. At the end of the hymn, Paul takes up the paraenesis with "Therefore, my beloved, as you have always obeyed, so now . . ." (Phil 2:12). Thus, this whole section in Philippians is an admirable illustration of what is axiomatic in the Christian religion: as we pray, so we believe, and as we believe, so must we live.

Christology

Before we come to examine the specific Christology expressed in the hymn in Philippians, a few prefatory remarks are needed about "Christology" in general and Paul's in particular. The New Testament in fact contains not one but several Christologies, the loftiest of which is still only a partial confession of the inexhaustible mystery of Jesus Christ.

To begin with, there is Jesus of Nazareth, "born of a woman" (Gal 4:4), a descendant of David (Rom 1:3; 2 Tim 2:8), who gathered disciples around him and went about "preaching the gospel of God and saying, 'The time is fulfilled, and the kingdom of God is at hand' " (Mk 1:14–15; Mt 4:17). Some of his own contemporaries wondered: Is he the one "who is to come"? (Mt 11:3; Lk 7:19), i.e., Is he the long-awaited Messiah promised by the prophets?

The followers of Jesus of Nazareth saw in him a great teacher possessed of unusual authority (Mk 1:22; 6:2; Mt 7:29; Lk 4:32). They came to believe that he was indeed the Messiah, the anointed one (see Lk 4:18), the *christos* in Greek: "You are the Christ" (Mk 8:29). Of course, it is from *christos* that the term "Christology" derives.

Thus, as has already been remarked, a Christology is a convenient shorthand for any answer one gives to the question put by Jesus to the disciples at Caesarea Philippi: "Who do you say that I am?" (Mk 8:29). To respond, as Peter did, "You are the Christ (*christos*)" (Mk 8:29), is, of course, a Christology, but so also is the recognition that he is "the Son of David" (Mk 10:47; Mt 1:1; see Mt 22:42), or "Teacher" (Mt 8:19), or "Master (Rabbi)" (Mk 9:5), or even "Son of God" (in its biblical sense of someone who enjoys God's special protection, as in Mt 3:17—see Ps 2:7 and compare Mt 5:9, 45).

Under the governorship of Pontius Pilate, Jesus of Nazareth—like so many messianic pretenders and figures of his day—was crucified (see Mt 27:11 and parallels; Jn 18:36; 1

Tim 6:13). It was only after his resurrection that his disciples recognized him as "Lord." We often tend to forget that this Christological title of "Lord" (*kyrios*) is the specifically paschal title of Jesus. The good news of the Easter event was proclaimed precisely as "The Lord is risen" (Lk 24:34); "I have seen the Lord" (Jn 20:18, 20); "We have seen the Lord" (Jn 20:25). A whole list of titles (the last Adam, the image of God, the radiance of divine glory, the power and wisdom of God, the Word, etc.) came to be employed in order to describe the risen Jesus, to express what his death and resurrection meant for the community of those who believed in him.

But of greater importance than this proliferation of Easter titles was the fact that even those titles used of him in his lifetime assumed a hitherto unexpected significance: the Messiah, the Christ, the King of Israel, the Son of Man, the Savior (Acts 5:31), "the one to redeem Israel" (Lk 24:21), etc. What happened of course was that someone had the insight, was inspired, received a divine revelation—or however you may choose to describe that momentous act—to see that all that the Scriptures had spoken of through the prophets, all God's promises to Israel, all his covenants with his people had finally found their ultimate and definitive realization, fulfillment and culmination in this one man Jesus Christ. From then on there was practically no end to the titles applied to him in order to explain what he meant to those who believed in him.

That it was Jesus himself who initiated that tendency to interpret his own person by means of the Old Testament prophecies is clearly an idea we find in Luke's Gospel (Lk 24:27). What is of utmost importance, however, is the fact that such a connection had to be grasped, such a link had to be made, between Jesus and the Old Testament before any real Christology could be said to have taken place.

Another—and perhaps no less important phenomenon—was that the multifarious titles applied to him were not limited in their use to the risen Jesus. They were readily retrojected into his earthly life and applied to his earthly ministry. The Gospels furnish examples of this on practically every page, as when they have Jesus of Nazareth addressed as "Lord" (e.g., Mt 8:2, 6, 8, etc.). As might be expected, this phenomenon of retrojecting the titles of the risen Jesus onto the Jesus of Nazareth was not confined to his public ministry, but reached farther back into the narrative of his infancy and birth, as witness the first two chapters of both Matthew and Luke.

This retrojection of the titles of glory of the risen Jesus into his public life and even into the accounts of his birth and infancy constituted, in a way, a *second* stage in the development of the early Church's Christology: a further development in the gradual awakening of the believers' awareness of the true meaning of Jesus of Nazareth. Thus, the titles conferred on the risen Jesus by the Easter community might well be seen to constitute the *first* stage of New Testament Christology.

It seems hardly necessary to add an obvious warning here: To speak of a first and a second stage in Christology could be misleading; so too could speaking of a "development," without further qualification. In fact there is no hard and fast rule for detecting and sorting out which title belongs to what stage. Yet one clear exception has to be made for the title "Lord" (*kyrios*), which could not conceivably have been used by any Jew to address another Jew, simply because it belonged exclusively to "Yahweh." This is one very clearly paschal title which the evangelists retrojected into their account of the public ministry of Jesus. Moreover, to speak of a "development," one has to be mindful that it was neither monolinear nor unidirectional. Several lines of Christology were developing concurrently and in different directions. The Christologies do not all say the same thing about Jesus of Nazareth, nor are they reducible to one uniform Christology.

Thus, for example, in Palestine itself, within any Jewish community, within the traditions of the Old Testament and the apocalyptic literature of later Judaism, the titles that were applied to Jesus—that is to say, the Christologies—followed along lines that were both comprehensible and relevant to Jewish Christians: e.g., Son of David, Messiah, Son of Man, the Servant of the Lord, Son of God, the eschatological Prophet, etc. In Gentile territories, on the other hand, the titles— understandably enough—followed a different pattern: Christ, Lord (*kyrios*), Savior (*soter*), Wisdom, etc.

But, of course, overlapping and crisscrossing between one type of Christology and another were more the rule than the exception. Judaism and Hellenism were not sealed off and compartmentalized segments of the ancient world. Such lines of demarcation as existed between them—could they be traced—did not constitute barriers or unbridgeable chasms.

The Christologies

Having made these necessary qualifications, we can proceed to examine, by means of concrete examples, some of the emergent Christologies. As the titles of the risen Jesus came to be retrojected from Easter into the public ministry and farther back into the infancy, the birth, and the very conception of the child who was set "for the fall and rising of many in Israel" (Lk 2:34), it was almost inevitable that the trend should seek to climb higher still. Thus, to call the risen Jesus "Lord" is but the logical first step to calling him "Lord" before his crucifixion, and indeed to calling him "Lord" from the very first moment of his conception (see Lk 1:43).

Conversely, calling Jesus "Son of God" during his public ministry (see, e.g., Mt 8:29) came to acquire a far profounder meaning after Easter, as when Paul speaks of "the gospel concerning his Son, who was . . . designated Son of God in power . . . by his resurrection from the dead" (Rom 1:3–4; see Mk 1:1). This more profound meaning of the title was, of course, eventually retrojected into the public ministry (as, e.g., in Mt 26:63).

The amazing thing about all this—a thing almost more incredible than some of the titles applied to Jesus—is the astonishing rapidity with which much of the process took place. One has only to think of such a credal formula as that in Romans 1:3–4 as already current in some early Christian community barely twenty years after the crucifixion. So, when we say, for instance, that this so-called *third* stage in the Christology took a little more time to emerge, we are only speaking relatively.

The "third stage" marks the application of Christological

titles to Jesus Christ as the pre-existent one, i.e., prior to his conception and birth. Such pre-existence Christology was already in evidence before the end of the first century. The believers who believed him Lord in his resurrection from the dead, and therefore Lord and Son of God during his public ministry and even from the very moment of his conception, were almost bound eventually to speak of Jesus as Lord and Son of God even *before* his conception, indeed from all eternity. This is the stage that is commonly referred to as "pre-existence." It regards this Jesus of Nazareth not only as the risen Lord, but also as the Son of God from all eternity.

To be sure, a great deal had to happen before this step could be taken. To confess Jesus as the Son of God from all eternity was not the kind of credal affirmation that a Jewish Christian, for instance, would readily or even willingly make. Nor was it the kind of creed that a Gentile Christian could easily reconcile with a professed and uncompromising monotheism. But, of course, a great deal did happen, and that in a surprisingly brief span of time. But whether that time was as short as, say, the thirty or so years that separated the death of Jesus from that of Paul, remains, I believe, a moot question. I am only speaking here of that stage at which Christology had advanced enough to enable Christians to speak of the pre-existent Christ—to speak for instance as does the Prologue of John's Gospel:

> In the beginning was the Word, and the Word was with God, and the Word was God (Jn 1:1).

Such a statement is quite different from Paul's address in Romans:

> The gospel concerning his Son, who was descended from David according to the flesh, and designated Son of God in power according to the Spirit of holiness by his resurrection from the dead, Jesus Christ our Lord (Rom 1:3–4).

Moreover, this "third stage" in Christology had to be reached long before anything like a doctrine of the Trinity could even begin to emerge. For, as Bishop Stephen Neill once remarked, the Trinity is not a doctrine about God but about Christ. It is Christology that is about God. This, I believe, is what the hymn in Philippians illustrates admirably. In other words, the doctrine of the Trinity says how Christ could be God without injury to the unity of the "one God, the Father, from whom are all things and for whom we exist" (1 Cor 8:6). Christology, on the other hand, says how "God has done what the law . . . could not do: sending his own Son in the likeness of sinful flesh and for sin" (Rom 8:3), how God "did not spare his own Son but gave him up for us all" (Rom 8:32).

None of these preliminary observations need alarm or disturb anyone possessed of even a nodding acquaintance with the history of Christianity. Needless to add, not everything a Christian believes is found in the New Testament— no one but a die-hard fundamentalist would wish to maintain that. The Christian faith, for all the solidly dogmatic content of its creed (see, e.g., 1 Cor 15:3–4), is not a congealed lump in cryogenic stasis; nor is the New Testament—for all its unique importance and the singular value of its writings—just another code of law whose immutable words Christians mouth in uniform and stereotyped confessions of their faith. It is not only in morals but, to a far greater extent than one can imagine, in dogma that "the written code kills" (2 Cor 3:6).

The process of formation of the Christian gospel, moreover, is quite the reverse of that to which our own confession of faith has accustomed us: God the Father and Creator, God the Son and Redeemer, God the Holy Spirit and Sanctifier. In the New Testament and in the development consequent upon the diffusion of the Christian message, there is discernible an "ascending" line: from Jesus of Nazareth, to the risen Lord, to the pre-existent Son of God, culminating ultimately in the Trinitarian confessions of the early centuries. Of course, all this is in a manner of speaking. The motion was not uninterrupted, nor was its culmination an end. The history of Christology, as Karl Rahner has remarked, does not come to an end just because some theologians have nothing more to say. For us, brought up on the formulas of the creed and the catechism:

> What we call the beginning is often the end
> And to make an end is to make a beginning.
> The end is where we start from (T.S. Eliot, "Little Gidding").

We are accustomed to begin with the Trinity, with God the Father sending his eternally-begotten Son into the world, and the Son taking flesh and becoming man, being crucified and rising from the dead. This, so to speak, "descending" order of exposition makes for a compact clarity that is desirable in a credal formula but could prove misleading when we try to understand the meaning of that formula. There should be nothing surprising in all this. We know from ordinary experience that any succession of causally-linked events is the reverse of that in which we discover them. Think, for instance, of a detective story where the detective, by logically sequential steps, argues from the discovered corpse back to the weapon, back to the murderer, and ultimately to the motives that precipitated the crime.

Theology
All the previous remarks are by way of underlining the fact that the Christology we encounter in Paul is one that is still in the process of development. This is important to keep in mind in order to guard against introducing into the discussion elements extraneous to, and meaningless within, the context of the Pauline epistles. For you can—and indeed Paul himself does—elaborate a Christology without reference, say, to the miracles of Jesus, or to his claims, or to his teachings. Therefore, we should not put to Paul questions that trespass beyond the data provided by his epistles—questions like: Did Paul believe in the virgin birth? What does Paul say about Jesus' "self-awareness"? and so forth.

Nevertheless, there are questions which, though not always asked in this context, are indispensable for the proper understanding of Pauline Christology. The most fundamental of these is, of course, the question about God; for, as has already been remarked, Christology is really about God. Of course, most of what Paul has to say about God is but part of his Jewish patrimony. He holds this in common with all the authors of the New Testament, for all of whom the credal affirmations about God are axiomatic:

"There is no God but one" (1 Cor 8:4; Rom 3:30; 1 Tim 1:17; 2:5);

—the Creator (Rom 1:25; Col 3:10), "who created all things" (Eph 3:9; 1 Tim 4:4);

—"the Father, from whom are all things and for whom we exist" (1 Cor 8:6; 11:12; Rom 11:36);

—"who gives life to the dead and calls into existence the things that do not exist" (Rom 4:17; 1 Tim 6:13);

—"the Lord Almighty," whose power is eternal (2 Cor 6:18; Rom 1:20; 4:21; 9:17; Eph 1:19; 3:20; 1 Tim 1:17).

He is the "living and true God" (1 Thess 1:9; 2 Cor 6:16; 1 Tim 3:15; 4:10), "immortal" and "eternal" (Rom 1:23; 16:26; 1 Tim 1:17).

The "only wise God" (Rom 16:27; Eph 3:10), whose judgments are unsearchable and "inscrutable his ways" (Rom 11:33), is the God who is "faithful" to his word and his promises (1 Cor 1:9; 10:13; 2 Cor 1:18; Rom 3:3–4; 15:8; 1 Thess 5:24; 2 Tim 2:13).

He is "the God of peace" (1 Thess 5:23; Rom 15:33; 16:20; 1 Cor 14:33; 2 Cor 13:11; Phil 4:7, 9), of "kindness" (Rom 2:4; 11:22), of "mercies . . . and of all comfort" (2 Cor 1:3; Rom 9:15–16; Eph 2:4).

He is "the God of love" (2 Cor 13:11; Rom 5:5, 8; Eph 1:5; 2:4; Titus 3:4).

This litany should be kept in mind whenever one comes to examine what Paul has to say about Jesus Christ and his

death on the cross, about sin and redemption, about resurrection and the new creation. The God in whom we believe is
he "who gives life to the dead and calls into existence the
things that do not exist" (Rom 4:17), the God "who raises the
dead" (2 Cor 1:9), who "raised the Lord and will also raise us
up by his power" (1 Cor 6:14; 2 Cor 13:4; Eph 1:20; Col 2:12).
The God of the New Testament is eminently the God who
"raised from the dead Jesus our Lord" (Rom 4:24; see 1 Pet
1:21). Therefore, the characteristically Christian attribute of
God in the New Testament is that he is "the God and Father
of our Lord Jesus Christ" (2 Cor 1:3; 11:31; Rom 15:6; Eph
1:3; see Phil 2:11). Moreover, it is only because God is "the
God and Father of the Lord Jesus" (2 Cor 11:31) that he is
also "our God and Father" (1 Thess 1:3; 3:11, 13; 2 Thess 1:1;
2:16; 1 Cor 1:3; 2 Cor 1:2; Gal 1:4; Rom 1:7b; Phil 1:2; 4:20;
Col 1:2b; Eph 1:2; Phlm 3; and see 2 Cor 6:18).

Christology

The Jesus whom Paul proclaims is he "who was de-
scended from David according to the flesh" (Rom 1:3; see
9:5; 2 Tim 2:8) and who "died for our sins in accordance with
the scriptures" (1 Cor 15:3; Rom 8:32), is the "Christ crucified" who is forever a "stumbling block to Jews and folly to
Gentiles" (1 Cor 1:23; Gal 5:11):

> For I decided to know nothing among you except Jesus
> Christ and him crucified (1 Cor 2:2; Phil 2:6–8).

But God the Father "raised him from the dead" (Gal 1:1; 1
Thess 1:10; 1 Cor 6:14; 15:15; Rom 4:24–25; 6:4; 8:11; 10:9)
and designated him "Son of God in power" (Rom 1:4; Phil
2:9–11). This Christ Jesus "who died . . . who was raised from
the dead, who is at the right hand of God" (Rom 8:34; Col
3:1; Eph 1:20; 2:6) is he whom "every tongue confesses" as
Lord (*kyrios*) (Phil 2:11; Rom 1:4). He is the one whom every
believer awaits as the "Son from heaven, whom [God] raised
from the dead, Jesus who delivers us from the wrath to
come"(1 Thess 1:10; Phil 3:20–21). It is on that awaited day
that "God judges the secrets of men by Christ Jesus" (Rom
2:16; 1 Cor 4:4–5; 11:32; 2 Cor 5:10), who then:

delivers the kingdom to God the Father. . . ." For God has put all things in subjection under his feet." . . . When all things are subjected to him, then the Son himself will also be subjected to him who put all things under him, that God may be everything to everyone (1 Cor 15:24, 27, 28; Phil 3:21; Col 1:13–14).

Pneumatology

This, in brief, is Paul's Christology. But it does not stop here. For Paul goes on to add, "Now the Lord is the Spirit" (2 Cor 3:17); and it is God himself who has "sent the Spirit of his Son into our hearts, crying, 'Abba! Father!' " (Gal 4:6; Rom 8:11, 14–17; Eph 2:17–18). Without this Spirit (*pneuma*), without pneumatology, Christology remains incomplete; for this Spirit is the abiding power of the risen Jesus in the community of the believers:

> If the Spirit of him who raised Jesus from the dead dwells in you, he who raised Christ Jesus from the dead will give life to your mortal bodies also through his Spirit which dwells in you (Rom 8:11; 1 Cor 6:14; 15:45).

But the work of creation and redemption by the "God and Father of our Lord Jesus Christ" (Rom 15:6; 2 Cor 1:3; 11:31; Eph 1:3; Col 1:3) in "sending his own Son in the likeness of sinful flesh" (Rom 8:3; Gal 4:4; Phil 2:7), as also in sending "the Spirit of his Son into our hearts" (Gal 4:6), is one and the same work. Yet, as is evident, Paul speaks of it as the work done by the Father, by the Son, and by the Spirit. He even speaks of all three in the same context and, sometimes, even in one and the same formula:

> The grace of the Lord Jesus Christ and the love of God and the fellowship of (*koinonia*, participation in) the Holy Spirit be with you all (2 Cor 13:14; 1 Cor 12:4–6 see 8:6; Eph 4:4–6; 1 Thess 1:3–5; 1 Cor 2:1–4; Gal 4:4–6; Rom 1:1–4; 5:1–5).

It would however be premature to call such Pauline formulae and expressions "Trinitarian." It would be more accurate to speak of them as "triadic" formulae, just as we might speak of numerous other formulae as "dyadic":

> Yet for us there is one God, the Father, from whom are all things and for whom we exist, and one Lord, Jesus Christ, through whom are all things and through whom we exist (1 Cor 8:6; see Phil 2:1; 1 Thess 1:9–10; Rom 5:11, etc.).

But, however useful such triadic and dyadic formulae will prove to be for the future Trinitarian debates and doctrines and definitions, the important thing to keep in mind here is that the work of our redemption in Christ Jesus is the work of God in the power of the Spirit. It is one, unfragmented and unfragmentable work, even if we find it necessary—for the purpose of clarity in our search for a better understanding—to speak now in terms of God the Father, now in terms of Jesus Christ, and now in terms of the Holy Spirit. Throughout, it is God who is and remains the Creator of all things and the Redeemer of all sinful humanity and the Sanctifier of all who believe.

Paul's Christology, however, did not have its starting point in abstract concepts. Its point of departure was the fact that, in the death of that "one man Jesus Christ" (Rom 5:15), God "reconciled us to himself" (2 Cor 5:18; Rom 8:1), and "sent the Spirit of his Son into our hearts" (Gal 4:6). Paul's conversion had finally brought him to see with the eyes of faith that:

> God has done what the law, weakened by the flesh, could not do: sending his own Son in the likeness of sinful flesh and for sin, he condemned sin in the flesh (Rom 8:3).

> Therefore, if anyone is in Christ, he is a new creation; the old has passed away, behold, the new has come (2 Cor 5:17).

It is then quite understandable why Paul came to regard this Christ as "the last Adam" (1 Cor 15:45; see 15:22). While the Old Testament and Jewish tradition saw to it that the story of man's first disobedience and the fruit of that forbidden tree was part of Paul's theological background, the good news of our redemption in Jesus Christ made him—as it were—rethink the whole plan of the history of salvation. Consequently, Paul's Christology cannot be divorced from his soteriology, from his understanding of Christ's work of redemption within God's plan of salvation.

The Hymn in Philippians

This is precisely why the hymn in Philippians 2:6–11 can serve as such a good, compendious statement of Paul's Christology. It is, above all, a hymn to God the Father. Though it escaped Pliny the Younger's power of theological observation, this subtle fact ought not to escape the attention of the Christian exegete. The whole, beautifully symmetrical, literary composition moves with faultless logic toward its conclusion: "to the glory of God the Father" (Phil 2:11). In this sense, all true Christology is about God. Everything that Jesus Christ is and everything he does is to that one end: "the glory of God the Father." But the hymn is also unmistakably soteriological, the "death on a cross" (2:8) forming its center and turning point.

Now, though this hymn in Philippians is usually regarded as tripartite, outlining—so to speak—the three stages of the Son's existence, there is, I believe, a more compelling reason for seeing it as bipartite. For in the more common division of the hymn into three parts:
(a) The first statement:

> Who, though he was in the form of God, did not count
> · equality with God a thing to be grasped (Phil 2:6),

is taken to be a reference to the pre-existence of Christ in—as John would put it—"the bosom of the Father" (Jn 1:18).
(b) The second part in the next two verses:

> But emptied himself, taking the form of a servant (*doulos*, slave), being born in the likeness of men. And being found in human form he humbled himself and became obedient unto death, even death on a cross (Phil 2:7–8),

is then taken to refer to the incarnation of the Son, his *kenosis* (his emptying himself), and his ultimate abasement in the death on the cross.

(c) Then, of course, the third part would refer to his resurrection and exaltation:

> Therefore God has highly exalted him and bestowed on him the name which is above every name, that at the name of Jesus every knee should bow, in heaven and on earth and under the earth, and every tongue confess that Jesus Christ is Lord, to the glory of God the Father (Phil 2:9–11).

Nevertheless, given the fact that the hymn is firmly embedded within a paraenetic context, i.e., within a context which exhorts the Christians:

> Do nothing from selfishness or conceit, but in *humility* count others better than yourselves. Let each of you look not only to his own interests, but also to the interests of others. Have this mind among yourselves, which is yours in Christ Jesus, who . . . (Phil 2:3–5),

and given the fact that the hymn itself (verses 6–11) is followed by another exhortation:

> Therefore, my beloved, as you have always *obeyed,* so now . . . Do all things without grumbling or questioning . . . (Phil 2:12, 14–16),

it is very difficult to see how a tripartite division could really make sense. In such a tripartite division it would be hard to see what Paul's exhortation to "have this mind among yourselves, which is yours in Christ Jesus" could be all about. Even if a Christian could be called upon to follow the Lord in his lowliness and abasement, and even if this Christian entertains the real hope of being raised up one day as Christ was raised, what is there in the first stage that any Christian could possibly follow, aspire to, or imitate?

Within its present paraenetic context, it is more convincing to see the hymn in two parts, the "therefore" in verse 9 acting as its hinge. Paul, first of all, does not elaborate a Christology just for the sake of erecting a theological system. Any Christology in Paul has for its purpose the life in faith of the Christian believers. Secondly, if Paul could be said to have resurrected the figure of Adam from the Genesis account of the creation and the fall, then he did so in order to better describe the redemptive work of Christ, and not to gloss a Christology of pre-existence.

Now, it was Adam who, though he was made in the "image and likeness" of God (Gen 1:26; 5:1b), "grasped" for equality with God: "You will be like God" (Gen 3:5; see Phil 2:6; compare 2 Cor 4:4 and Col 1:15). Moreover, the contrast between the "first Adam" and the "last Adam" (1 Cor 15:45, 22; Rom 5:12–21) is recognizably Pauline. For Paul sees in Adam "a type of the one who was to come" (Rom 5:14). So, unlike the first Adam, who through his disobedience grasped for equality with God and brought sin and death into the world, the second Adam reversed that mortal gesture and "emptied himself." As a man, he was in the image and the likeness of God; but even that he gave up, becoming "a worm, and no man," in the words of that most quoted of Psalms in the passion narrative (Ps 22:6). He became the lowest of men: a slave; and the most despised of slaves: a criminal condemned to the most ignominious death in the annals of cruelty. "Therefore God has highly exalted him and bestowed on him the name which is above every name . . ." (Phil 2:9–11).

Thus, Paul's Christology is indissolubly linked to his soteriology. He understands who Jesus is by understanding what Jesus did for us, what God the Father did for us through him, through his obedience and death on the cross, and through his resurrection and exaltation. The two parts of the hymn in Philippians are inseparable, either part remaining incomplete without the other. The *kenosis,* the self-emptying, of Jesus is not merely a prelude to, but a condition of, his Lordship. "Was it not *necessary* that the Christ should suffer these things and enter into his glory?" (Lk 24:26). The abasement is meaningless without the exaltation, just as the Lordship remains incomprehensible without the "even death on a cross" (Phil 2:8). Both make sense only as the creative and redemptive work of God. Both are, therefore, "to the glory of God the Father" (Phil 2:11).

This way of understanding the hymn in Philippians makes the paraenetic context more comprehensible. For there is a way a Christian can attain to "mature manhood" (Eph 4:13), and "be renewed in the spirit of your minds, and put on the new nature, created after the likeness of God in true righteousness and holiness" (Eph 4:23–24). This way is by putting off "your old nature which belongs to your former manner of life" (Eph 4:22); by not "grasping" for what is already yours; by not scrambling up some ladder of perfection; by doing "nothing from selfishness, but in humility count others better than yourselves" (Phil 2:3); by "emptying" oneself, and becoming obedient like him who "humbled himself and became obedient unto death, even death on a cross":

> Therefore, my beloved, as you have always obeyed, so now . . . work out your own salvation with fear and trembling; for God is at work in you, both to will and to work for his good pleasure" (Phil 2:12–13).

The new order of redemption is the topsy-turvy world of the last being first and the first last (Mk 9:35; Mt 20:27; see Mt 19:30; 20:16; Mk 10:31; Lk 13:30). This order reverses the whole order of priorities of the first Adam. It enables the Christian to possess that genuine freedom which could "in humility count others better than yourselves" (Phil 2:3), which could serve others and be a slave to others and do "nothing from selfishness or conceit" (Phil 2:3). Surely, these are but the indispensable conditions for the selfless and loving service of the neighbor. The redemptive Christology in the hymn in Philippians is the surest foundation of Paul's exhortation to Christian life. A Christology, after all, is elaborated in order to teach us how to live, not how to devise theories and propound dogmatic systems.

One has only to compare this hymn in Philippians 2 with that in Colossians:

> He is the image of the invisible God, the first-born of all creation; for in him all things were created . . . all things were created through him and for him. He is before all things, and in him all things hold together. He is the head of the body, the church; he is the beginning, the first-born from the dead, that in everything he might be pre-eminent. For in him all the fullness of God was pleased to dwell, and through him to reconcile to himself all things, whether on earth or in heaven, making peace by the blood of his cross (Col 1:15–20).

This hymn too is linked to a soteriological context which offers thanks to the Father who

> has delivered us from the dominion of darkness and transferred us to the kingdom of his beloved Son, in whom we have redemption, the forgiveness of sins (Col 1:13–14).

It also has a paraenesis appended to it: "that you continue in the faith, stable and steadfast" (Col 1:23). But the hymn in Colossians clearly speaks a less familiar language than that in Philippians. Just as clearly, its verses imply a pre-existence of Christ. Thus, when it says that he is "the first-born of all creation" (Col 1:15), the point "is not temporal advantage but rather the superiority which is due to him as the agent of creation who is before all creation. As the first-born he stands over against creation as Lord" (E. Lohse, *Colossians,* p. 49). So, too, when the hymn affirms that "he is before all things," it proclaims the fact that "as the pre-existent one he is Lord over the universe" (Lohse, p. 52).

Nevertheless, one cannot but be aware that the Christology here has veered in a different direction from that which we see in Philippians. The hymn in Colossians is addressing a changed situation in a markedly different language from that encountered in the other Pauline epistles. Even the concept of Lordship has undergone a perceptible shift in meaning, its horizons having been further extended. For not only is Christ given the name "which is above every name" (Phil 2:9) in his resurrection and exaltation, but that very title of

Lordship is his from the very beginning, when he presided at the creation of the universe.

To point out these characteristics in the hymn in Colossians is neither to discount nor to put an undue value on pre-existence in Christology. It is not the purpose of this exposition to deny that Christ is the pre-existent Son of God. But it is its purpose to caution against a common attitude in theology which presupposes that more is better, that the "higher" the Christology the more orthodox the Christianity. Pauline Christology ought to show us how false and misleading this attitude can be.

Having affirmed, as the hymn in Philippians does, that "God has highly exalted him . . ." (Phil 2:9–11), it is hard to imagine what more could be said. The important thing is that, if Jesus is truly Lord, then that Lordship must be evident where it really matters: in the life of the individual Christian, in the Christian's obedience to the illogic of the cross, and in the unqualified acceptance of that Lordship in and through the cross:

> For I decided to know nothing among you except Jesus Christ and him crucified (1 Cor 2:2).

In Paul's Christology, Christ is clearly the Son of God. This is in evidence from the First Epistle to the Thessalonians (1:10) down to Romans (1:3–4, 9; 5:10; 8:3, 29; see 1 Cor 1:9; 15:28; 2 Cor 1:19; Gal 1:16; 2:20; 4:4–6). But Christ is also "the power of God and the wisdom of God" (1 Cor 1:24), whom God "made our wisdom, our righteousness and sanctification and redemption" (1 Cor 1:30). This Christ, moreover, is he who reveals the love of God (Rom 5:5–8; 8:39; Eph 2:4–6; see 3:14–19; Tit 3:4–6) and the grace of God (1 Cor 1:4; Rom 3:24; 5:2, 17, 21; Eph 2:7–10; Tit 2:11). He is the fulfillment of all the divine promises, the ultimate witness to God's fidelity to his word:

> For the Son of God, Jesus Christ, whom we preached among you . . . was not Yes and No; but in him it is always Yes. For all the promises of God find their Yes in him.

That is why we utter the Amen through him, to the glory
of God (2 Cor 1:19–20).

But perhaps the best summary statement of Paul's Christology is:

If you confess with your lips that Jesus is Lord and believe
in your heart that God raised him from the dead, you will
be saved (Rom 10:9; see Phil 2:9–11; 1 Cor 12:3; 8:6).

For, in the last analysis, the confession of the Lordship of Jesus Christ is an act of praise and thanksgiving by those who have been saved by his death on the cross and his resurrection from the dead. It is a confession which recognizes in the person of Jesus, in his life, death and resurrection, not only the fulfillment of all the divine promises and the realization of all that vast germination of hope which is our Old Testament, but also the new creation of God in Christ, "who is God over all, blessed for ever. Amen" (Rom 9:5).

NINE

The Epistle to the Romans

32. The Redemption in Christ Jesus

It was from his prison in Ephesus that Paul wrote to the Philippians and to Philemon ("Paul, a prisoner for Christ Jesus . . . during my imprisonment for the gospel . . ." Phlm 1 and 13). This Ephesian imprisonment must have ended around the "beginning of the year 55" (H. Koester, *Introduction,* vol. 2, p. 136), when the collection for the Church in Jerusalem, which must have been seriously interrupted by the crisis in Corinth, could again occupy Paul's attention. For, once the reconciliation with the Corinthians took place, he was eager to bring the collection project to its completion, not so much out of a sense of philanthropy, as out of a realization of what such an act of intercommunal charity might mean for the unity of the Church in the one gospel:

> For the rendering of this service not only supplies the wants of the saints but also overflows in many thanksgivings to God. Under the test of this service, you will glorify God by your obedience in acknowledging the gospel of Christ, and by the generosity of your contribution for them and for all others (2 Cor 9:12–13).

The restored atmosphere of calm brought Paul back to Corinth "during the winter of 55–56" for what turned out to be his last visit there. Then, when the collection was finally ready, Paul decided to take it to Jerusalem himself, as he explained in a letter he wrote from Corinth "to all God's beloved in Rome" (Rom 1:7):

206

> But now, since I no longer have any room for work in these regions, and since I have longed for many years to come to you, I hope to see you in passing as I go to Spain, and to be sped on my journey there by you, once I have enjoyed your company for a little. At present, however, I am going to Jerusalem with aid for the saints . . . for the poor among the saints at Jerusalem (Rom 15:23–26).

So, thanks to that brief interval between the end of Paul's mission in the eastern part of the Mediterranean world and his setting out to travel west to the "ends of the earth," we have that great—perhaps that greatest—of his epistles, the Epistle to the Romans. It is the last letter we possess from him. For, as things turned out, the Jerusalem visit ended with another imprisonment, from which Paul was eventually escorted under guard to Rome "for the decision of the emperor" (Acts 25:21). There, in all likelihood, he remained under house arrest (Acts 28:16) until his death around the year 60.

The Epistle to the Romans is a letter written in amicable placidity, far from the "madding crowd's ignoble strife." It is a self-introduction of both the apostle and his gospel, recollecting in relative tranquillity the major themes of God's grace in Jesus Christ: the gift of freedom that is our redemption in Christ Jesus (see No. 24); the Christian's faith in the Lordship of Christ (see No. 31); the relation of this faith in Jesus Christ to the law (see No. 23); then, consequently, the relation of Gentile Christianity to Jewish Christianity (see Nos. 3–5); and, ultimately, the relation of Jewish and Gentile Christians to the Jews who are, as Paul never forgets,

> Israelites, and to them belong the sonship, the glory, the covenants, the giving of the law, the worship, and the promises; to them belong the patriarchs, and of their race, according to the flesh, is the Christ (Rom 9:4–5; see 3:1–4).

Thus, the advantage of the Jews is "much in every way" (Rom 3:1–2). For, "to begin with, the Jews are entrusted with the oracles of God" (Rom 3:2). A comprehension and an ap-

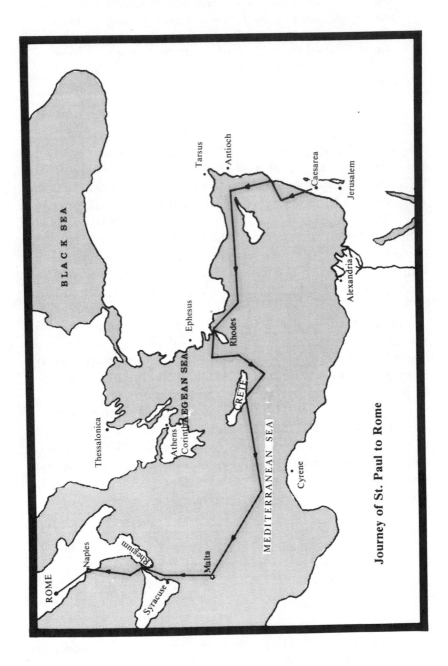

Journey of St. Paul to Rome

preciation of this fundamental fact of our redemption is indispensable for any understanding of the gospel of Paul:

> Since all have sinned and fall short of the glory of God, they are justified by his grace as a gift, through the redemption which is in Christ Jesus, whom God put forward as an expiation by his blood, to be received by faith (Rom 3:23–25).

Because, while Paul understands this "redemption" as our liberation from death, sin and the law, and while he opposed vehemently any attitude that took this law as in any way a means of salvation, Paul never for a moment tries to make Jesus Christ comprehensible independently of that law. In other words, Paul sees in "the law and the prophets" our principal and only way to understanding what we mean when we confess our faith in the "gospel concerning his Son" (Rom 1:3). The "in accordance with the scriptures" in the credal formula of 1 Corinthians 15 is not confined to Christ's death and resurrection, but underlies and founds everything Paul has to say about the appearance of the grace of God "for the salvation of all men" (Tit 2:11).

So, in order to explain God's grace in Jesus Christ, which is—as we have seen above (No. 28)—his way of referring to the whole salvation event, Paul has recourse to the figure of the first Adam (No. 31). This is a bit unusual, for, after the initial story of the creation and the fall in the opening chapters of Genesis, there is hardly any mention of Adam in the Old Testament (see Gen 3:17, 21; 4:1, 25; 5:1, 3, 4, 5; 1 Chr 1:1). But in the apocryphal literature—as part of the vast body of literature that proliferated in the period between the two Testaments is usually referred to—the figure of Adam emerges anew (see, e.g., Tob 8:6; Sir 49:16; perhaps also Wis 10:1).

The figure of Adam, moreover, occupies an even more noteworthy place in that other part of "intertestamental literature" which is commonly called the "pseudepigrapha" of the Old Testament, especially in works like the *Book of Jubilees* and the *Apocalypse of Baruch*. In this latter work, not only is our death linked to the sin of Adam (23:4; 54:15), but the whole doctrine of the fall is neatly summed up in:

> Each of us has been the Adam of his own soul (*Apocalypse of Baruch* 54:19).

Sin

Paul, therefore, was not so much rediscovering the figure of Adam as putting it to a new use. We have already had occasion to refer (see above, No. 30) to one possible use in the contrast that the hymn in Philippians makes between the disobedience of "the first man Adam" and the obedience unto death of the one whom Paul calls "the last Adam" (1 Cor 15:45). Let us now turn to a more explicitly drawn parallel between the two Adams:

> Therefore as sin came into the world through one man and death through sin, and so death spread to all men because all men sinned . . . Yet death reigned from Adam to Moses, even over those whose sins were not like the transgression of Adam, who was a type of the one who was to come (Rom 5:12, 14).

That sin came into the world "through one man" was but a commonplace in Paul's Jewish background (but see Sir 25:24). Yet, though the account in the Book of Genesis links death to sin ("lest you die"—Gen 3:3, 19), it does not explicitly list death as one of the prime consequences of that sin. Such a link between death and sin is made explicit by Paul:

> Sin came into the world through one man and death through sin (Rom 5:12).

Death, then, is a punishment for sin: "For the wages of sin is death" (Rom 6:23). Yet Paul does not base this statement on the tradition common to the Jewish circles of his day. He is, as we shall see, arguing rather in reverse order: from the present situation back to a primeval cause. As the author of 1 Timothy puts it: "The saying is sure and worthy of full acceptance, that Christ Jesus came into the world to save sinners" (1 Tim 1:15). Everyone born into the world lives under the reign of death. So, Paul argues, "death spread to all men because all men sinned" (Rom 5:12).

But this statement is itself reversible: because all die, all sin. In other words, "to sin" for Paul is a good deal more than the Hebrew term for "to miss the mark," more than disobedience to a divine command. It is a loss of life in the very attempt to secure it and to circumvent death. Every sin committed by a creature is a sin ultimately because, rather than accept God's gift of life ("See, I have set before you this day life and good, death and evil . . . therefore choose life"— Dt 30:15,19; see Jer 21:8), rather than acknowledge the Giver as the sole Lord of life ("For with thee is the fountain of life"— Ps 36:9), the creature presumes to find life, to hold on to it, to seek guarantees against its loss—all on his own.

Seen in this light, sin is the creature's attempt to deny his creaturehood, grasping for and taking hold of some imagined secure grip on life:

> His trust was with the Eternal to be deemed
> Equal in strength, and rather than be less
> Cared not to be at all (Milton, *Paradise Lost*).

Sin thus manifests a radical disobedience to the Creator, who alone gives life (Dt 32:39). It is in this rebellion against the status of a mortal creature that the relationship with the Creator is damaged. Every sin is in its own way the creature's clumsy attempt to avoid, evade or forestall the inevitable fact of death. A moment's reflection will show how this is true in every sin.

Paul argues from the present situation back to the link of sin with death. He starts, not with the datum of Adam in the Genesis account, but with the gospel of Jesus Christ, "through whom we have received our reconciliation" (Rom 5:11). The good news proclaims the grace which reigns "through righteousness to eternal life through Jesus Christ our Lord" (Rom 5:21). From that proclamation Paul knows that "we are reconciled to God by the death of his Son" (Rom 5:10), and that through this Son "we have now received our reconciliation"

(5:11; Eph 2:16; Col 1:20–22), and "have peace with God" (Rom 5:1):

> All this is from God, who through Christ reconciled us to himself and gave us the ministry of reconciliation; that is, in Christ God was reconciling the world to himself, not counting their trespasses against them, and entrusting to us the message of reconciliation (2 Cor 5:18–19).

From this "reconciliation," "righteousness," and "peace," Paul argues back to an original transgression, offense, and enmity with God (Rom 5:14).

Justification

Thus, the restoration of the proper relationship between the creature and God, the righting of the situation between the creature and the Creator, is what Paul commonly refers to as "justification" or "righteousness." Alas, neither of these terms renders satisfactorily what Paul means by words like *dikaioma* and *dikaiosyne,* which are not so much juridical terms as salvific:

> And the free gift is not like the effect of that one man's sin. For the judgment following one trespass brought condemnation, but the free gift following many trespasses brings justification (*dikaioma*) (Rom 5:16).

Now such reconciliation, justification, and righteousness are, and can only be, the free gift of God:

> the grace of God and the free gift in the grace of that one man Jesus Christ (Rom 5:15).

They constitute the saving effect of the good news which proclaims that God has "raised from the dead Jesus our Lord, who was put to death for our trespasses and raised for our justification" (Rom 4:25). Thus it is that God is the source of your life in Christ Jesus, whom God made our wisdom, our righteousness (*dikaiosyne*) and sanctification and redemption (1 Cor 1:30).

From this reconciliation, this setting aright the relationship between us and God, which has been made possible by the death and resurrection of Jesus Christ, Paul argues back to the one whose trespass disrupted the primeval relationship, upset the established order, and was responsible for the enmity between the creature and the Creator. From Christ's humility and obedience unto death, "even death on a cross" (Phil 2:8), Paul argues back to the pride and disobedience of the first Adam, "who was a type of the one who was to come" (Rom 5:14).

Similarly, from the good news that "God raised him from the dead" (Rom 10:9; 4:24; 1 Cor 15:4), Paul argues, not only backward to the "through one man . . . death through sin" (Rom 5:12), but also forward to:

> For as in Adam all die, so also in Christ shall all be made alive (1 Cor 15:22).

> He who raised the Lord Jesus will raise us also with Jesus (2 Cor 4:14; 1 Cor 6:14; 15:12–28).

In other words, as it was Christ's death and resurrection that destroyed "the last enemy, death" (1 Cor 15:26) and brought us "the free gift of God" which is "eternal life in Christ Jesus our Lord" (Rom 6:23), so also, Paul argues, it was "because of one man's trespass" that "death reigned through that one man" (Rom 5:17):

> For as by a man came death, by a man has come also the resurrection of the dead. For as in Adam all die, so also in Christ shall all be made alive (1 Cor 15:21–22).

Thus it is that a great deal of the difficulty usually encountered in trying to grasp what Paul understands by the grace of our redemption in Christ Jesus can be avoided. Unlike many who theologize on sin and redemption, Paul starts with the given of the gospel, not with the story of Genesis. For him Christ is the absolute starting point of all soteriology. What Christ did for us reveals what had to be done, and this in turn shows what had initially been undone. From Christ's obedience unto death "even death on a cross" (Phil 2:8), we grasp not only "man's first disobedience" but also what it was that brought death and sin into the world.

The Conquest of Death

In Christ's conquest of death (1 Cor 15:54–55) we are set free from the reign of death (Rom 5:17, 14) as well as from sin, which "reigned in death" (Rom 5:21), and from the law:

> When the commandment came, sin revived and I died;
> the very commandment which promised life proved to be
> death to me (Rom 7:9–10).

The victory of the resurrection, then, was over the interconnected and mutually dependent reigns of death, sin and the law:

> The sting of death is sin, and the power of sin is the law
> (1 Cor 15:56).

This triple liberation, this setting free from the triple bondage of death and sin and the law, is what Paul understands by the grace of redemption: the free and gratuitous gift of God in Christ Jesus seen in its comprehensive effect on and in those who believe the gospel proclamation of the event of his death and resurrection.

The resurrection, therefore, cannot but be at the very core of Paul's theology. He means what he says literally when he reminds the Corinthians:

> If Christ has not been raised, then our preaching is in vain and your faith is in vain. . . . If Christ has not been raised, your faith is futile and you are still in your sins (1 Cor 15:14, 17).

Thus the resurrection is every bit as intimately linked to the remission of sin as is Christ's death "for our sins" (1 Cor 15:3). No amount of insistence on the centrality of the cross of Christ in Paul's theology could afford to overlook this for a moment. Here again, as in the discussion of "Paul's gospel" (see No. 19 above), it is not a matter of either/or. The so-called *theologia crucis* (theology of the cross) cannot be contrasted with or set in opposition to the *theologia gloriae* (theology of glory). If these phrases are used to describe Protestant and Catholic theologies respectively, then it is not for the sake of valuing one over the other, but of pointing to a falsifying defect in both one and the other.

The crucifixion by itself would be an impotent symbol; the resurrection by itself would remain a pleasing myth. The "last enemy," death, had to be overthrown, not only by the actual death on the cross of its victor, but also by his resurrection from the dead. As the Easter Sequence put it, "Mors et vita duello conflixere mirando . . ." (death and life were locked in an awesome struggle). They had to be, in order that death might be defeated once and for all, and life triumph eternally. This is the good news which Paul proclaims and which Pauline theology tries to make both intelligible and coherent:

> And he died for all, that those who live might live no longer for themselves but for him who for their sake died and was raised (2 Cor 5:15).

It is axiomatic for Paul that "sin came into the world through one man and death through sin, and so death spread to all men because all men sinned" (Rom 5:12). But this is not a theorem in modern anthropology, Darwinian or otherwise. Paul's concern is not with evolution, monogenism, polygenism, or what have you; nor could his words be used for any such purpose. His use of the figure of Adam is principally— almost exclusively—as a foil to that of Christ. So it would be utterly idle to put to Paul questions that come not within his ken. He sees death as a consequence of sin, he knows that the death of one man has set us free from the slavery of both sin and death, and, from the final (*eschato*logical) act of this one

man, he argues back to that primal (*proto*logical) act of the first
Adam:

> Then as one man's trespass led to condemnation for all
> men, one man's act of righteousness led to acquittal and
> life for all men (Rom 5:18).

The order of these two phrases should not mislead us. The
concrete given with which Paul starts is that *"all* die":

> What man can live and never see death? (Ps 89:48).

The gospel Paul proclaims is that Christ died for all and rose
again from the dead so that all might live. Therefore, he argues:

> For as by a man came death, by a man has come also the
> resurrection of the dead. For as in Adam all die, so also in
> Christ shall all be made alive (1 Cor 15:21–22; Rom 5:15).

Newness of Life

Any religion that proclaims salvation has to deal, in one
way or another, with the fact that "all die." The Christian religion deals with it by saying that Jesus Christ died on the cross
and was raised from the dead by God never to die again;
"death no longer has dominion over him" (Rom 6:9). But,
being more than just a system of beliefs, the Christian religion
sees a permanent link between sin and death. So the gospel it
proclaims is a gospel of salvation from both death and sin,
through the death and resurrection of Christ "for us," "for
our sins." It is therefore not at all surprising that the rite of
initiation into this religion should take care to make this amply clear:

> Do you not know that all of us who have been baptized
> into Christ Jesus were baptized into his death? We were
> buried therefore with him by baptism into death, so that
> as Christ was raised from the dead by the glory of the Fa-
> ther, we too might walk in newness of life (Rom 6:3–4).

Walking "in newness of life" is made possible by the Christian's belief:

> If we have been united with him in a death like his, we shall certainly be united with him in a resurrection like his. . . . For he who has died is freed from sin. But if we have died with Christ, we believe that we shall also live with him. For we know that Christ being raised from the dead will never die again; death no longer has dominion over him (Rom 6:5, 7–9).

The logic of the argument is thus inescapable. Christ "died to sin, once for all," and so "the life he lives he lives to God" (Rom 6:10). Christ's death to sin, therefore, brings the only available and definitive ("once for all") reconciliation of the sinful creature with God. It brings it as a totally gratuitous and free gift. Yet the conclusion to be drawn from this overwhelming grace of salvation is not license to "continue in sin that grace may abound" (Rom 6:1), but rather a fundamental premise of faith which henceforth affects the life of every Christian believer here and now: a life that puts to death all "fornication, impurity, passion, evil desire, and covetousness, which is idolatry . . . anger, wrath, malice, slander, and foul talk . . ." and puts on "compassion, kindness, lowliness, meekness, and patience, forbearing one another . . . forgive one another. . . . And above all these put on love, which binds everything together in perfect harmony" (Col 3:5–14).

In other words, as Paul puts it, "How can we who died to sin still live in it?" (Rom 6:2). The life of the Christian is a life freed from the finality of death. It is a life lived in the freedom which only a genuine gift (see No. 28) can confer:

> So you also must consider yourselves dead to sin and alive to God in Christ Jesus. Let not sin therefore reign in your mortal bodies. . . . Do not yield your members to sin . . . but yield yourselves to God as men who have been brought from death to life. . . . For sin will have no dominion over you, since you are not under law but under grace (Rom 6:11–14).

Redemption

How did all this come about? The gospel message reiter-
ates the simple statement of the answer in many different
ways, which might compendiously be put thus:

> [God] raised from the dead Jesus our Lord, who was put
> to death for our trespasses and raised for our justification
> (Rom 4:24–25).

Paul, like the other authors of the New Testament, tries to
explain how this was accomplished: how Christ was "put to
death *for our trespasses*" (Rom 4:25), how he "died *for our sins*"
(1 Cor 15:3), and how it is that "one man's act of righteousness
leads to acquittal and life for all men" (Rom 5:18).

Various terms are employed to describe what took place.
Of course, they are all used figuratively and not literally.
Thus, for example, the death of Christ is spoken of as a "ransom (*lytron*) for many" (Mk 10:45). He "gave himself for us to
redeem us" (Tit 2:14; see Lk 24:21; 1:68; 2:38; Heb 9:12). This
is the vocabulary of slaves and hostages, of their manumission
and ransom. It says that Christ set us free from our slavery,
delivered us from our bondage. But it would be idle—indeed,
misleading—to translate the terms into a scale of currency
equivalents, or to ask who exacted the price, or to whom the
"ransom" was paid. These and similar questions have led into
more blind alleys in theology than generations of theologians
could possibly extricate us from.

Such questions often resulted in an image of God the
Father that was hardly more flattering than that of the ad-
versary. The traditional interpretation, whether implicit or
explicit, which is common to both Protestants and Catholics,
holds that the death of Jesus was a punishment he underwent
on our behalf (or in our place) in order to appease the anger
of God and to offer God a satisfaction that would then enable
him to exercise his mercy toward sinners, as though hitherto
prevented from doing so for lack of a sufficiently bloody sacrifice of expiation. This interpretation is the commonly so-
called theory of "vicarious satisfaction."

But Paul's own attempts to describe what happened led

him to employ, not one term, but a whole range of terms in his effort to keep the various elements of the mystery in some equilibrium. Thus, Jesus himself, while not called the "Redeemer" (*lytrotes*, which is used only once in the New Testament, and that with reference to Moses in Acts 7:35), is frequently called "Savior" (*soter*) (Phil 3:20; Eph 5:23; 2 Tim 1:10; Tit 1:4; Lk 2:11; 2 Pet 1:1, 11), and his work is often described as "salvation" (*soteria,* whence "soteriology") (Rom 1:16; 11:11; 13:11; 1 Thess 5:9), or "reconciliation" (Rom 5:10–11; 11:15; 2 Cor 5:18–19), or "purchase" (1 Cor 6:20; 7:23), or "expiation" (Rom 3:25; see 1 Jn 2:2; 4:10), or "justification" (*dikaioma*) (Rom 5:16; see 4:25), or as the cancellation of "the bond which stood against us" (Col 2:14). Christ's death on the cross is referred to either as his "blood" (Rom 5:9; 3:25; 1 Cor 10:16; 11:27; Eph 1:7; Heb 9:12, 14; 12:24; 13:12), or as his "offering and sacrifice" (Eph 5:2; Heb 7:27; 10:5–7).

The imagery is varied, but, despite the variation, elements of the marketplace, the law courts and temple worship do stand out. One can easily miss the point in trying to allegorize these evident tropes, seeking to determine precisely who the seller is and who the buyer; who the judge and who the accuser; why this victim for sacrifice and why such a mode of immolation, etc. But what is most important to keep in mind amidst these varied attempts at describing the death of Christ on the cross and its meaning for us is the fact stated by Paul so cogently in Romans:

> While we were still weak, at the right time Christ died for the ungodly. Why, one will hardly die for a righteous man—though perhaps for a good man one will dare even to die. But God shows his love for us in that while we were yet sinners Christ died for us. Since, therefore, we are now justified by his blood, much more shall we be saved by him from the wrath of God. For if while we were enemies we were reconciled to God by the death of his Son, much more, now that we are reconciled, shall we be saved by his life. Not only so, but we also rejoice in God through our Lord Jesus Christ, through whom we have now received our reconciliation (Rom 5:6–11).

Therefore, the death of Christ on the cross for us is, first and foremost, a grace of God. In his mercy and in his love for us, God gave us this grace while we were weak and could not earn it, while we were sinners and possessed no means of meriting it, and while we were ungodly enemies and had no reason to expect it. God's saving act in Jesus Christ is gratuitous and unilateral. By one definitive deed, it does away with all the requirements, conditions, and means of salvation. It is a wholly new covenant marked, not by the pretended reciprocity of partners in a court of law, but by the incomprehensible disparity between the sinner and the Redeemer. "O felix culpa, quae talem ac tantum meruit habere Redemptorem" (O happy fault, that deserved such and so great a Redeemer), chants the *Exultet*, the Easter Proclamation.

Nevertheless, so perverse is human ingenuity, so deep-rooted is the human desire to grasp for some equality with the divinity, that even the just and holy law of God is conscripted, not so much to obey God, but to manipulate him. After the long history of cyclic infidelities and repentance, of broken covenants and unrealized promises, God—so to speak—abandoned the attempt and did what neither law nor covenants could do, or were ever allowed to do. A wholly new start, a "new creation" (2 Cor 5:17), was needed. This is precisely what, centuries previously, Israel's prophets foresaw had to be done. They spoke of a new covenant (Jer 31:31), a new heart and a new spirit (Ez 18:31; see 11:19), and even "new heavens and a new earth" (Is 65:17). Nothing short of this newness could rid the creature of his pretexts, nothing else could set him so totally free from the servitude of his pretenses. In the very gratuity of the gift, even the possibility of a *quid pro quo*, of earned merit and requited efforts, is done away with.

The death of Christ on the cross was an obedience to God which abolished, once and for all, the state of enmity between the creature and the Creator. The reconciliation was permanent and irrevocable. The access to God was not only open but made unhindered and, henceforth, unhinderable. Even the "holy and just and good" law (see Rom 7:12) saw its definitive end in Christ (Rom 10:4). Thus it came about that our endless capacity for self-deception, wherein sin found such ready opportunity (7:11, 8), was rendered futile:

> For the law of the Spirit of life in Christ Jesus has set me free from the law of sin and death (Rom 8:2).

If, to many Christians, all this sounds incredible and far-fetched, it is not because it is unreasonable or untrue, but simply because we have managed—so to speak—to outwit even this liberating act of a gracious God. Our ingenuity to "submit again to the yoke of slavery" (Gal 5:1) has proved too much even for divine generosity. We have managed, somehow, to subject ourselves to a slavery more enthralling because it is willingly embraced and freely assumed. If it is not our restless quest to keep the law perfectly, then it is our unending anxiety to avoid violating it, avoiding sin being our preferred means of attaining salvation. We are so prompt to forget Paul's insistence:

> If justification were through the law, then Christ died to no purpose (Gal 2:21).

But here again we have been anticipated by the thoroughness of the divine mercy in Jesus Christ. A fundamental article of our creed is:

> Christ died for our sins (1 Cor 15:3).

Paul underscores the grace character of this redemptive act by insisting that God did it, not only without any help from us, but despite our own unrighteousness, despite our sinfulness and enmity (Rom 5:6, 8, 10). Through no possible or conceivable merit of our own, "while we were yet sinners," "while we were enemies," Christ died for us, reconciled us with God and saved us from sin and death (Rom 5:8, 10).

Paul, of course, is speaking of our own sins, all of them. He is not speaking of some privileged few among us, but of all of us, of each one of us. He insists that it is we who are the sinners so reconciled and saved and set free from sin and death and the law. The obedience of Christ unto death on the cross wiped out all our own sins, not just some unspecified titanic rebellion of a suppositious ancestor at the dawn of time. One might almost say that "sin" is no longer even a relevant category in the creature's relationship with God:

> Where there is no law there is no transgression (Rom 4:15b).

> For sin will have no dominion over you, since you are not under law but under grace (Rom 6:14).

> There is therefore now no condemnation for those who are in Christ Jesus. For the law of the Spirit of life in Christ Jesus has set me free from the law of sin and death (Rom 8:1–2).

It should be remarked here that "those who are in Christ Jesus," an extremely frequent phrase in Paul, is often the equivalent of the more familiar "Christians," which term had not as yet come into currency (see Acts 11:26). All Paul is saying, then, is: "There is therefore no condemnation for Christians," for those who believe in Jesus Christ. The reason for this is simply that those who believe in Christ Jesus, the author of their salvation, have been set free from sin, death, and the law.

Freedom from Death

Freedom from death however is not freedom from dying. "It is appointed for man to die once" (Heb 9:27). Christ took this upon him and died. But, in that very death, he altered radically its meaning, without abolishing the act of dying or, for that matter, diminishing its agony. This is why the death on the cross and the resurrection of Jesus cannot be separated. Christ is, to be sure, "the first fruits of those who have fallen asleep" (1 Cor 15:20). But faith in the resurrection neither abolishes death nor mitigates its terror (see Mk 15:34). As a matter of fact, resurrection presupposes death. Only the dead can rise to life. The "immortals," by definition, do not really die. This is why the death of Jesus and that of

Socrates have been so often, and so profitably, contrasted: the undignified horror of dereliction and abandonment as against the placid composure of leave-taking among disciples and loving friends. There is a world of difference between Socrates' last words, "Crito, we owe a cock to Aesculapius" (Plato, *Phaedo*, 118), and Jesus' crying out with a loud voice, "My God, my God, why hast thou forsaken me?" (Mk 15:34).

But the death and resurrection of Jesus gives the believer more than a future hope of eternal life, of being one day raised "to die no more." The saving event does more than alter the meaning of death from being the definitive severance of all relationships to becoming merely an interlude between life and eternal life. The death and resurrection of Jesus really saves us from death by granting us eternal life already now. The event of salvation grants us a life that is never under the dominion of death, even if it must be lived with the prospect of dying. This does not mean that we die no more but that, when we eventually die, we shall be raised from death to eternal life (see 1 Cor 15:36). Therefore, the message of the gospel is not immortality but resurrection:

> If, because of one man's trespass, death reigned through that one man, much more will those who receive the abundance of grace and the free gift of righteousness reign in life through the one man Jesus Christ (Rom 5:17).

The good news proclaims a wholly new life, because the relationship of this life to inevitable death has been radically altered:

> As Christ was raised from the dead by the glory of the Father, we too might walk in newness of life (Rom 6:4).

We do not sufficiently reflect, nor do theological writings usually help us to reflect, on the link that binds sin to death. Death is not merely the consequence of Adam's sin. It is, ultimately, the cause of all sin. The "first Adam" sinned because of his desire to be like God, immortal. Even in the Genesis account, "the fruit of that forbidden tree" was not only knowledge but life (see Gen 2:17; 3:3). Every subsequent sin, if we but reflect sufficiently on it, is the creature's attempt to grasp at or to try to seize life. But life is and remains exclusively the gift of the immortal Creator. Therein lies the element of rebellion in sin, its real evil. I, the creature, imagine that by my own action I could somehow lay hold—even if momentarily—on life itself, or at least on some assurance of it.

The centrality of the cross in the gospel message thus becomes all the more comprehensible. Christ's obedience unto death took the form of laying down his life. Rather than grasp for equality with the living God, he gave up his life, "so that, as sin reigned in death, grace also might reign through righteousness to eternal life through Jesus Christ our Lord" (Rom 5:21). For this reason:

> The death he died he died to sin, once for all, but the life he lives he lives to God. So you also must consider yourselves dead to sin and alive to God in Christ Jesus (Rom 6:10–11).

Therefore, the death that Christ died on the cross brought all of us "eternal life":

> But now that you have been set free from sin and have become slaves of God, the return you get is sanctification and its end, eternal life. For the wages of sin is death, but the free gift of God is eternal life in Christ Jesus our Lord (Rom 6:22–23).

Thus, Paul can speak of the whole salvation event as grace. The "redemption which is in Christ Jesus" (Rom 3:24) brings eternal life gratuitously and freely to sinners, to the enemies of God. Therefore, the opposite of "sin" is not, as we might imagine, "sinlessness." The opposite of "sin" is life, eternal life, life that is not under the dominion of death. This is why the grace of redemption in Christ is freedom. His death on the cross released us from the dominion of death. It set us free from the reign of death. Therefore, it set us free from the slavery of sin and from the servitude of the law.

Henceforth, our master is neither death, nor sin, nor the law. To have such a master is genuine slavery. The truly free Christian has only God as master, the God who "gives life to the dead and calls into existence the things that do not exist" (Rom 4:17), who alone could do and did what no one and nothing could: "raised from the dead Jesus our Lord" (Rom 4:24),

> so that what is mortal may be swallowed up by life (2 Cor 5:4).

Those who receive the gospel message need boast neither of their accomplishments, nor of their achievements, nor of their successes and attainments, whether in the religious or the secular sphere. Their only boast, if they genuinely accept the good news, "the word of life" (Phil 2:16), the gospel of the grace that is freely granted to every human being in Christ Jesus, is in God, who is

> the source of your life in Christ Jesus, whom God made our wisdom, our righteousness, and sanctification and redemption (1 Cor 1:30).

Herein lies genuine freedom, the only true freedom available to anyone willing to shoulder its obligations and assume its responsibilities. Only someone who knows this "glorious liberty of the children of God" (Rom 8:21) can truly say:

> If God is for us, who is against us? He who did not spare his own Son but gave him up for us all, will he not also give us all things with him? It is God who justifies; who is to condemn? . . . Who shall separate us from the love of Christ? Shall tribulation, or distress, or persecution, or famine, or nakedness, or peril, or sword? . . . No, in all these things we are more than conquerors through him who loved us. For I am sure that neither death, nor life, nor angels, nor principalities, nor things present, nor things to come, nor powers, nor height, nor depth, nor anything else in all creation, will be able to separate us from the love of God in Christ Jesus our Lord (Rom 8:31–39).

33. The Spirit of Holiness

The gospel of God proclaims that Jesus Christ was "designated Son of God in power according to the Spirit of holiness" (Rom 1:4). This Spirit of holiness is an essential component of the gospel in Paul's writings, which account for about thirty percent of the occurrences of *pneuma* (spirit) in the whole New Testament. Such a significant proportion of its use by Paul makes quite inevitable the multiplicity and variety of senses which *pneuma* expresses. The first thing to do, therefore, is to look at the different meanings the term has in Paul and in the New Testament.

Pneuma is the Greek term used most frequently to translate the Hebrew *ruah* of the Old Testament. Its spectrum of meaning there is broad and its uses are varied. *Ruah* is the breath "of his mouth" (Ps 33:6), "of his lips" (Is 11:4), or merely the breath of air:

> A spirit glided past my face; the hair of my flesh stood up (Job 4:15).

It is what gives life to human beings:

> All flesh in which is the breath of life (Gen 6:17; 7:15),

and is the seat of their emotions and of their intellectual powers:

> But it is the spirit in a man, the breath of the Almighty,
> that makes him understand (Job 32:8; Dt 34:9; Gen 41:8;
> 2 Kgs 19:7).

Because *ruah* is the "breath of the Almighty" that is the "spirit in man," the Lord is the "God of the spirits of all flesh" (Num 16:22; 27:16). He is the God "who gives breath to the people upon [the earth] and spirit to those who walk in it" (Is 42:5; see Ez 37:5). At death "the spirit returns to God who gave it" (Eccl 12:7).

The Spirit of the Lord, the *ruah Yahweh*, in the Old Testament is above all that which gives power: "the Spirit of the

Lord came mightily upon" Samson (Jgs 14:6, 19). It sets the prophet upon his feet (Ez 2:2; 3:24), induces ecstasy, and inspires prophecy:

> When the spirit rested upon them, they prophesied (Num 11:25, 29).

> Then the spirit of the Lord will come mightily upon you, and you shall prophesy with them and be turned into another man (1 Sam 10:6; 19:20; 2 Kgs 2:15).

> The Spirit lifted me up and took me away. . . . The Spirit lifted me up between earth and heaven, and brought me in visions of God to Jerusalem (Ez 3:14; 8:3).

This same Spirit speaks by the prophets:

> The Spirit of the Lord speaks by me, his word is upon my tongue (2 Sam 23:2).

> The Spirit of the Lord God is upon me, because the Lord has anointed me to bring good tidings to the afflicted (Is 61:1; see Lk 4:18).

It grants the leaders of Israel their "charism of leadership" and the required wisdom to go with it:

> The Spirit of the Lord came upon [Othniel] and he judged Israel (Jgs 3:10).

> I have filled [Bezalel the son of Uri] with the Spirit of God, with ability and intelligence, with knowledge and all craftsmanship (Ex 31:3; Dt 34:9).

But, of course, the Old Testament does not only speak of the spirit which is given by God; it also speaks of the spirit as God's own creative power and vivifying force:

> Come from the four winds, O *ruah* (breath, wind, spirit), and breathe upon these slain, that they may live (Ez 37:9–10, 12–14; see Gen 1:2; 2:7).

The *ruah Yahweh,* moreover, is the saving power of God, "his holy Spirit . . . who divided the waters before them . . . who led them through the depths" (Is 63:11–13); but it is also the power of his judgment, "a spirit of judgment and a spirit of burning" (Is 4:4; 30:27–28).

God himself is "spirit" and not "flesh" (see Is 31:3), a spirit that is present everywhere:

> Whither shall I go from thy Spirit?
> Or whither shall I flee from thy presence? (Ps 139:7).

In its unfathomable wisdom and power, the Spirit of the Lord created all things, and directs all things (Is 40:12–14):

> When thou sendest forth thy Spirit [breath], they are
>   created;
> and thou renewest the face of the ground (Ps 104:30; Is
>   32:15; 11:2).

This then is the Hebrew *ruah* which the Greek translators of the Old Testament rendered as *pneuma.* The Greek word itself already conveyed, even in its extrabiblical usage, many of the meanings found in the biblical *ruah. Pneuma* signified both breath and wind. It expressed power, whether the power of breath and life or the power which invisibly moves both animate things and inanimate. *Pneuma* is what breathes sweet life into a silent flute, inspires the poet, seizes in rapture the worshipers of the deity, and stirs the great oracle at Delphi into prophetic utterance. Because its actions are unpredictable, immediate and uncontrollable, *pneuma* was regarded as a divine power, as the way the gods demonstrated and exercised their might.

Pneuma is the term that the New Testament employs to express the dynamic power of the redemptive act, both in itself and in its permanence in the community of believers. Of course, the use of the term in the New Testament is not limited to this particular meaning. There are chiefly two other uses to which *pneuma* is put. It is used in a pejorative sense to refer to evil and malignant spirits, such as are frequently encountered in the Synoptic accounts of the exorcisms (Mk 1:23; 3:11, etc.). It is also used in its principal meaning of "breath" to denote life, the principle of life, the inner person, and similar senses constituting what is commonly called New Testament "anthropology," i.e., the New Testament's "philosophic" answer to the psalmist's "What is man?" (Ps 8:4).

New Testament Anthropology

The first thing that should be said about the answer Paul himself gives to this question is that it is not ours—certainly not that of our habitual way of thinking and speaking. We understand "man" to be made up of body and soul—one material and perishable, which is destined to return to the dust whence it came, and the other spiritual and immortal, which is what survives of us after death. Death for us is the separation of the soul from the body. The spiritual soul, we believe, receives its just recompense immediately after death and awaits the resurrection of its body at the resurrection of the dead on the last day.

Anything farther from Paul's response to "What is man?" is hard to imagine. For Paul, as for the biblical authors, when the *pneuma* leaves my body, then I, all of me, die. This, by the way, is how Jesus himself died: "he yielded up his spirit (*pneuma*)" (Mt 27:50), "he breathed his last" (Lk 23:46). We have to keep in mind that Paul's anthropology is, unlike ours, not so much a dichotomy of body and soul, as a trichotomy:

> May your spirit (*pneuma*) and soul (*psyche*) and body (*soma*)
> be kept sound and blameless (1 Thess 5:23).

The spirit-soul-body triad, however, does not exhaust Paul's anthropological terminology. For he refers to man as "flesh" (*sarx*):

> so that no human being (*sarx*) might boast in the presence
> of God (1 Cor 1:29; 2 Cor 4:11),

or as "flesh and blood" (Gal 1:16; 1 Cor 15:50). He speaks of the "renewal of your mind (*nous*)" (Rom 12:2), and of "the heart (*kardia*) of man" (1 Cor 2:9). This terminology forms part of the traditional biblical and Jewish anthropology:

> Try me; test my heart and my mind (Ps 26:2; 38:10).
>
> What can flesh do to me? (Ps 56:4).
>
> My flesh and my heart may fail (Ps 73:26).

When this mortal creature comes to the end of his days, then he dies—all of him, not just his body, nor only his flesh and blood, nor only his mind and his heart, but all of him: body and soul, flesh and spirit, heart and mind, what of him is visible and what is invisible—all die. The rich multiplicity of biblical terms, both technical and traditional, employed by Paul to describe this mortal creature, describes only aspects and facets of the individual. Thus, "body" describes him in his relation to other individuals and to other things; "mind" refers to his innermost thoughts; "flesh," to his mortality and fragility; "heart," to the seat of his intentions, thoughts, and affections; "soul" (*psyche*), to the individual life that ends in death; "spirit" (*pneuma*) to the breath of life that the Creator breathed "into his nostrils" (Gen 2:7):

> Lend me a looking-glass;
> If that her breath will mist or stain the stone,
> Why, then she lives. (*King Lear*)

This is the reason why the resurrection occupies such a central position both in Paul's theology and his anthropology. The Christian's *only* hope of life after death is resurrection from the dead to eternal life. To forget this basic truth, to get caught up in the endless philosophical debates on the "immortality of the soul," to wander aimlessly in the labyrinth of vain speculation about the dead, is, ultimately, to render Paul's anthropology incomprehensible, and his insistence on the resurrection of our "mortal bodies" (Rom 8:11, 23) superfluous:

If the Spirit of him who raised Jesus from the dead dwells in you, he who raised Christ Jesus from the dead will give life to your mortal bodies also through his Spirit which dwells in you (Rom 8:11).

Thus, "body" describes the individual in his relationship to others, that by which and through which he has contact with others. Death, of course, is the definitive termination of all these relationships with others, even with God himself:

For in death there is no remembrance of thee (Ps 6:5).

Death cannot praise thee (Is 38:18).

So is it any wonder that, if "there is no resurrection," "if for this life only we have hoped in Christ, we are of all men most to be pitied" (1 Cor 15:13, 19)?

The Spirit of God

Having made these preliminary remarks about Paul's anthropology, we now turn to the major use he makes of the term *pneuma* to express, as he does in the Romans 8:11 passage above, the dynamic reality behind the redemptive act and its permanent power. In other words, we turn from the "spirit of man" to the "Spirit of God" (see 1 Cor 2:11). If we keep in mind what was said above about the *pneuma* as force and power, we can more readily see two principal modes of speaking about the divine *pneuma* in Paul: the first in its contrast with *sarx* (flesh), and the second in its relation to God's work of salvation in Christ Jesus.

A. When Paul contrasts spirit (*pneuma*) with flesh (*sarx*), as he does for example in Romans 8:12–14 ("according to the flesh . . . by the Spirit") and Galatians 5:19–26 ("the works of the flesh . . . the fruit of the Spirit"), then he is setting in opposition two distinct forces, two irreconcilable spheres of influence. This is not—as we are likely to imagine, and to imagine quite wrongly—a contrast between what we mean nowadays by "spiritual" and "material"; far less is it a contrast between "lofty spirit" and "crass sexuality." The contrast is

rather between two opposing forces in tension ("you are not
in the flesh, you are in the Spirit"—Rom 8:9; see 7:14—"spiritual . . . carnal"), two antithetical modes of existence: "living
in the flesh" and "the new life of the Spirit" (Rom 7:5, 6):

> For those who live according to the flesh set their minds
> on the things of the flesh, but those who live according to
> the Spirit set their minds on the things of the Spirit (Rom
> 8:5).

Perhaps it will make this contrast a bit clearer if we recall
that *sarx*, like *pneuma*, has several meanings in the New Testament. There is, for example, the use of *sarx* (flesh) in "flesh
and blood," a biblical expression for a mortal human being in
all his limitations (Gal 1:16; Mt 16:17; 1 Cor 15:50; Eph 6:12).
"Flesh" is principally the mode of reference to the human
condition in its fragility and vulnerability. "Man" *is* flesh, not
has flesh. "The Word became flesh" (Jn 1:14). Thus, the RSV
rightly translates the Greek "all flesh" in Romans 3:20 as "human beings," and, similarly, it renders the Greek "life in the
flesh" in 2 Corinthians 10:3 as "life in the world" (compare
Phil 1:22).

But *sarx* has another, more dynamic, sense. It expresses
all that is not God, who is "spirit" (Jn 4:24; compare 2 Cor
3:17), all that in the creature and in its "boasting" (see 1 Cor
1:29) and sinfulness stands opposed to God:

> With my flesh I serve the law of sin (Rom 7:25; see 7:14,
> 18; 8:5);

> Those who are in the flesh cannot please God (Rom 8:8).

This sinful aspect of "flesh" is not known to the Old Testament, where the term is used rather in its neuter sense to
mean "all living creatures," to refer to the frailty and impotence of the creature. There it is also used in the more obvious
sense of "eating flesh," "sacrificing flesh," or "flesh and
bones":

> All flesh is grass, and all its beauty is like the flower of the
> field (Is 40:6; Ps 103:15).

He remembered that they were but flesh, a wind that
passes and comes not again (Ps 78:39).

The Old Testament does know, however, the contrast be-
tween the flesh of the creature and the spirit of the living
God, as is evident from Isaiah's parallelism of men-flesh and
God-spirit:

The Egyptians are men, and not God; and their horses
are flesh, and not spirit (Is 31:3).

But Paul pushes this antithesis further, making of "flesh" a
dynamic sphere of force that is in constant opposition to and
tension with the sphere of "spirit." Thus, he sets up the opposition between "spirit" and "flesh," equating the former
with "hearing with faith," and the latter with "works of the
law" (Gal 3:1–5). The whole life of the believer is seen as a
constant tension between walking and living "according to the
flesh" and walking and living "according to the Spirit" (Rom
8:4–5; Gal 5:16, 18, 25).

  B. The antitheses which Paul thus sets up between flesh
and spirit are the result of his understanding of the role of
the Spirit in the Christ event. This role moreover has to be
understood against its background in the Old Testament
prophecies. The promise of the advent in the last days of the
Spirit of God, the Holy Spirit, finds its ultimate fulfillment in
the coming of Jesus Christ:

And the Spirit of the Lord shall rest upon him (Is 11:2;
42:1; 61:1; see Lk 4:18–21; Acts 2:17–21).

The time of salvation is, therefore, the time of the Spirit,
"when I pour out my Spirit upon the house of Israel, says the
Lord God" (Ez 39:29; see Acts 2:33).

  Consequently, the definition of the gospel with which the
Epistle to the Romans opens, apart from the fact that the formula itself is pre-Pauline, reflects a truth fundamental to the
Christian faith in Jesus Christ, and not merely its Pauline peculiarity:

> The gospel concerning his Son, who was descended from
> David according to the flesh and designated Son of God
> in power according to the Spirit of holiness by his resur-
> rection from the dead, Jesus Christ our Lord (Rom 1:3–
> 4).

The "Spirit of holiness" is, in all likelihood, a Semitism, a
common Hebrew mode of saying what the Greek would nor-
mally express by an adjective: the "holy Spirit" (see, e.g., Acts
9:15, where Paul is referred to as an "instrument of election,"
meaning of course "a chosen instrument"). This Spirit is
"holy" because it is the Spirit of God. Therefore, it is divine.
But there is a long way to go before you say simply that it is
God. There is, after all, a great difference between "God is
spirit" (Jn 4:24) and "the Spirit is God." Nevertheless, there
never was in the early history of dogma any protracted debate
about the divinity of the Holy Spirit as there was, for centuries, about the divinity of the Son. What took some five or six
centuries to clarify was, of course, the relation of the three
"persons" to one another. If in John's Gospel the Spirit Par-
aclete is spoken of as a "person" (see, e.g., Jn 14:16), this is
not so evidently the case when Paul speaks of the Holy Spirit
in his letters.

In Paul's letters the Spirit is referred to as the Spirit of
God (Rom 8:14; 1 Cor 2:11; 12:3), "the Spirit which is from
God" (1 Cor 2:12), the Holy Spirit (Rom 15:13; 1 Cor 12:3; 2
Cor 13:14), the Spirit of the Lord (2 Cor 3:17; compare "the
Lord who is the Spirit" in 2 Cor 3:18), the Spirit of his Son
(Gal 4:6), the Spirit of (Jesus) Christ" (Rom 8:9; Phil 1:19), or
simply "the Spirit" (Rom 8:5, 27; 1 Cor 2:10). Such designa-
tions would, in themselves, indicate a relationship that exists
between God and the Spirit, and between Jesus Christ and the
Spirit.

It is God "who gives his Holy Spirit" to us (1 Thess 4:8;
1 Cor 6:19; 2 Cor 1:22; Gal 3:5); and because it is God's gift,
the Spirit is divine and, therefore, holy. This Holy Spirit is
given to us as God's agent of revelation:

> God has revealed to us through the Spirit (1 Cor 2:10).

This revelation is made by the same Spirit who spoke "in the mouth of his holy prophets from of old" (see Acts 3:21; Rom 1:2; compare 1 Cor 12:3). What his Spirit reveals is, of course, what the author of Ephesians calls the "mystery of Christ" (Eph 3:4),

> which was not made known to the sons of men in other generations as it has now been revealed to his holy apostles and prophets by the Spirit (Eph 3:5).

Spirit and Community

But the Spirit of the Lord, who spoke the mystery of God to his people in the Old Testament, assumes a new and distinguishing mark in the New Testament. It is now specifically the Spirit of Christ. Just as God is revealed in the New Testament as the Father of Jesus Christ, so too the Spirit of God is revealed as the Spirit of Jesus Christ. This new attribution is the obvious result of the Spirit's role in the work of redemption. The one and the same Spirit of God who "was moving over the face of the waters" (Gen 1:2) is the agent of the new creation. For every creation is a redemption: the first, from the chaos and darkness of matter; the second, from the worse chaos and darkness of sin and death.

The descent of the Holy Spirit in the Synoptic accounts of Jesus' baptism (Mk 1:9–11 and parallels) is a more graphic way of expressing the gospel of the Son who was "designated Son of God in power according to the Spirit of holiness" (Rom 1:4). The Spirit is the power of God (1 Cor 2:4–5; Rom 15:19; 1 Thess 1:5) revealed in the life and the ministry of Christ (see especially the Gospel of Luke, e.g., Lk 1:35; 4:18; etc.), as also in his resurrection from the dead (Rom 1:4). Thus, the Spirit in the New Testament is eminently "the Spirit of him who raised Jesus from the dead" (Rom 8:11; compare 1 Cor 6:14). Therefore, the resurrection of Jesus from the dead is but the inauguration of the new role of the Spirit in the work of redemption.

This is the reason why the acclamation of Jesus as Lord by the community of believers is exclusively the work of the Spirit:

> No one can say "Jesus is Lord" except by the Holy Spirit
> (1 Cor 12:3).

So too all the functions of the Christian community, both ordinary and extraordinary, are the work of the same Spirit.
For the abiding Lordship of the risen Jesus over the community of believers is exercised through the Spirit of the
Lord. This fact, we should recall, is what the author of Acts
so memorably portrays in the account of Pentecost (Acts 2:1–
4). This fact too is what Paul tries to express in that puzzling
section in 2 Corinthians:

> Now the Lord is the Spirit, and where the Spirit of the
> Lord is, there is freedom. And we all, with unveiled face,
> beholding the glory of the Lord, are being changed into
> his likeness from one degree of glory to another; for this
> comes from the Lord who is the Spirit (2 Cor 3:17–18).

The Spirit of the Lord is "the manner in which the *kyrios* is
present to the community" (E. Schweizer, *T.D.N.T.*, vol. VI,
p. 434).

But the Spirit is more than the mere presence of the Lord
to the community. The *pneuma* is, as was indicated above, essentially force, power. The Spirit of the Lord is the way in
which the Lordship of Christ, his reign and dominion, is exercised over the community. It is, in other words, the power
of the abiding presence of the risen Lord in the community
of believers. This is why Paul reminds them that the "new life
of the Spirit" (Rom 7:6) is the result of their redemption in
Christ Jesus. It is a new life because of the Spirit who now
dwells within them:

> Do you not know that you are God's temple and that God's
> Spirit dwells in you? (1 Cor 3:16).

> God's love has been poured into our hearts through the
> Holy Spirit which has been given to us (Rom 5:5).

While we are "still in this tent," while we wait to have "what is
mortal swallowed up by life," we know that here and now

[God] has put his seal upon us and given us his Spirit in our hearts as a guarantee (2 Cor 1:22; 5:4–5).

The Spirit, moreover, not only dwells in the believers but leads them:

For all who are led by the Spirit of God are sons of God (Rom 8:14).

And it is precisely this "sonship" which is our true title to freedom:

For you did not receive the spirit of slavery to fall back into fear, but you have received the spirit of sonship. When we cry, "Abba! Father!" it is the Spirit himself bearing witness with our spirit that we are children of God (Rom 8:15–16; Gal 4:6–7; Eph 1:5).

Indeed, the Christian's vocation to freedom (Gal 5:13) is the work of this same Spirit:

Where the Spirit of the Lord is, there is freedom (2 Cor 3:17).

As we have had occasion to note, both in the discussion of redemption (No. 32) and in that of freedom (No. 24), the Christian's true liberty derives from the death and resurrection of Christ:

If the Spirit of him who raised Jesus from the dead dwells in you, he who raised Christ Jesus from the dead will give life to your mortal bodies through his Spirit which dwells in you" (Rom 8:11).

The Spirit, then, is the permanent "guarantee" (2 Cor 5:4–5) of God's free gift to us, which is "eternal life in Christ Jesus our Lord" (Rom 6:23b).

This possession of the Spirit is a present reality and not a merely future hope. Those who possess this gift can "walk in the Spirit" (Gal 5:16). They have, in other words, the freedom of living, "not according to the flesh," but "according to the Spirit" (Rom 8:5). Moreover:

> To set the mind on the flesh is death, but to set the mind on the Spirit is life and peace. For the mind that is set on the flesh is hostile to God; it does not submit to God's law, indeed it cannot; and those who are in the flesh cannot please God (Rom 8:6–8).

The life of those who have the Spirit of God, therefore the life of those who "belong to Christ" (Rom 8:9–10), is a life that not only knows but also manifests "the fruit of the Spirit":

> Love, joy, peace, patience, kindness, goodness, faithfulness, gentleness, self-control (Gal 5:22–23).

It seems hardly necessary for Paul to add, as he does, that "against such there is no law" (Gal 5:23). This statement will not sit very well with the lugubrious lamenters of their lot in the Church, the proclaimers of freedom who are in thrall to one another's good opinion and shackled to the current fashions in the clichés of theological revolution. Yet, there is no escaping the injunction:

> If we live by the Spirit, let us also walk by the Spirit (Gal 5:25).

The reverse, of course, is equally true. Walking in the Spirit is the only way anyone can find out whether we do actually have the life of the Spirit, which is a life with genuine "love, joy, peace, kindness, goodness, faithfulness, gentleness, and self-control."

Thus, Paul sees the life of the Spirit in the individual Christian, as well as the Christian's life in the Spirit, within the total context of salvation history:

> But when the time had fully come, God sent forth his Son, born of woman, born under the law, so that we might receive adoption as sons. And because you are sons, God has

sent the Spirit of his Son into our hearts, crying "Abba!
Father!" So through God you are no longer a slave but a
son, and if a son then an heir (Gal 4:4–7).

As has already been remarked above (No. 31), and as this passage from Galatians illustrates well, Paul associates God, his
Son and the Spirit in the work of redemption. He can do so
because "their encounter with the believer is one and the
same event" (E. Schweizer, *T.D.N.T.*, vol. VI, p. 437):

> Now there are varieties of gifts, but the same Spirit; and
> there are varieties of service, but the same Lord; and
> there are varieties of working, but it is the same God who
> inspires them all in every one (1 Cor 12:4–6).

How this "encounter" takes place is what we finally have
to consider.

34. "If You Believe . . ."

There is no theory, wrote Paul Valéry, that is not a carefully prepared fragment of an autobiography. Valéry's observation is no less true of the theologian than it is of the man
of letters. It is no less true of Paul than it is of the prophet
Jeremiah or of Saint Augustine. Everything Paul wrote bears
the mark of his own encounter with God, or rather of God's
encounter with him:

> But when he who had set me apart before I was born, and
> had called me through his grace, was pleased to reveal his
> Son to/in me, in order that I might preach him among the
> Gentiles . . . (Gal 1:15–16).

However you may wish to describe it, such an encounter with
God had to be, somehow or other, an encounter with "the gospel of God" (Rom 1:1), with the proclamation of the good
news about Jesus Christ the Lord:

> But how are men to call upon him in whom they have not
> believed? And how are they to believe in him of whom

they have never heard? And how are they to hear without
a preacher? (Rom 10:14).

Having heard the proclamation of the good news, you
can do one of three things: accept it, reject it, or be utterly
indifferent to it. The Athenians' "We will hear you again
about [the resurrection]" (Acts 17:32) is the attitude of indifference which, not infrequently, marks those who find religion "most interesting." Paul "breathing threats and murder"
(Acts 9:1) against the new religion is the attitude of rejection
which underlies the element of intolerance that accompanies—*pace* the would-be ecumenists!—every true religion.
And, of course, the whole extant epistolary output of Paul
stands as a monument to the totality of his acceptance of the
gospel, that is to say, to his faith.

Therefore it comes as no surprise that "faith" (*pistis*) and
"to believe" (*pisteuein*) occupy such a prominent place in the
vocabulary employed by Paul to proclaim his gospel:

> the power of God for salvation to everyone who has faith
> (Rom 1:16),

to elaborate his Christology:

> Because, if you confess with your lips that Jesus is Lord
> and believe in your heart that God raised him from the
> dead, you will be saved (Rom 10:9),

to formulate his soteriology:

> Since all have sinned and fall short of the glory of God,
> they are justified by his grace as a gift, through the re-
> demption which is in Christ Jesus, whom God put for-
> ward as an expiation by his blood, to be received by faith
> (Rom 3:23–25),

to express his pneumatology:

> For all who are led by the Spirit of God are sons of God.
> For you did not receive the spirit of slavery to fall back

into fear, but you have received the spirit of sonship.
When we cry, "Abba! Father!" it is the Spirit himself bearing witness with our spirit that we are children of God,
and if children, then heirs, heirs of God and fellow heirs
with Christ (Rom 8:14–17),

and to expound his theology:

But now the righteousness of God has been manifested
apart from the law, although the law and the prophets
bear witness to it, the righteousness of God through faith
in Jesus Christ for all who believe (Rom 3:21–22).

In "the law and the prophets" of which Paul speaks, the
belief in God is expressed by a variety of terms deriving from
a common triliteral Hebrew root *amn* (whence our "amen").
It was not only because the Greek *pisteuein* (to believe) and *pistis* (faith) are in fact terms most frequently used by the Septuagint translators to render *amn* and its cognates, but also
because of Paul's own Jewish, Old Testament background
and faith in the God who gave Israel "the glory, the covenants, the law, the worship and the promises" (Rom 9:4) that
we need to look at what the Old Testament understood faith
and its object to be before we turn to Paul's own writings.
    The first thing to be said about it is that "faith" in the Old
Testament expresses an attitude of the creature to the Creator. The God whom Israel worshiped was a "hidden God":

Truly, thou art a God who hidest thyself, O God of Israel,
the Savior (Is 45:15; see 8:17).

This God, "who created the heavens" (Is 45:18), revealed
himself and spoke to his people the mystery of his redeeming
love for them in the law which he gave them:

I am the Lord your God, who brought you out of the land
of Egypt, out of the house of bondage (Ex 20:2),

as well as through the prophets he sent them:

Go and say to this people . . . (Is 6:9).

Go and proclaim in the hearing of Jerusalem, Thus says
the Lord . . . (Jer 2:2).

Israel's response to this revelation was a faith that both
acknowledged a relationship of dependence and expressed
an attitude of obedience, not only by its confession of belief
in God's mighty deeds, but also by a life that reflected this belief in worship and in the keeping of his law, in Israel's trust
in and reliance on his "steadfast love," and in its hope in his
fidelity to his promises:

> The Lord, the Lord, a God merciful and gracious, slow to
> anger, and abounding in steadfast love and faithfulness,
> keeping steadfast love for thousands, forgiving iniquity
> and transgression and sin, but who will by no means clear
> the guilty, visiting the iniquity of the fathers upon the chil-
> dren and the children's children, to the third and the
> fourth generation (Ex 34:6–7).

Thus, Israel's faith in its God is, above all, a firm and un-
shakable trust in him and in his promises:

> If you will not believe, surely you shall not be established
> (Is 7:9).

This trust rested on God's past mercies to Israel: his unfailing
aid in time of trouble, his coming to their rescue in time of
need, and principally on their deliverance from the house of
bondage, by the Lord's "mighty hand and outstretched arm"
(Dt 4:34; see 4:32–40).

But, as catastrophe followed on catastrophe, as the God
of Israel hid "his face from the house of Jacob" (Is 8:17), the
elements of hope and trust came to predominate in Israel's
faith. Israel's faith became increasingly a faith that hoped in
God's future salvation and trusted in his faithfulness to his
promises. The hope and trust of God's people rested on their
knowledge of his past deeds of deliverance "by trials, by signs,
by wonders, and by war, by a mighty hand and outstretched

arm, and by great terrors, according to all that the Lord your God did for you in Egypt before your eyes" (Dt 4:34). Indeed, the Hebrew of the Old Testament hardly possesses a technical term for "hope." Israel's faith is its hope in the God who has saved and who will therefore save.

"Faith" in the New Testament

The New Testament, of course, conserves most of the characteristics that mark faith in the Old Testament, but it does so with modifications made necessary by the event of Jesus Christ. Thus it is immediately evident that, whereas the object of faith in the Old Testament was the word of God, the "oracles of God" (Rom 3:2), in the New Testament it is "the gospel of God . . . concerning his Son" (Rom 1:1, 3). But this modification implied a radical alteration in the believer's attitude to God. For, as in the past Israel trusted in God's future deliverance *because* of the marvelous deeds he had done, now the Christian believes *that* God has already wrought that deliverance in Jesus Christ.

In other words, "to believe" in the New Testament is to accept the fact that in the death and resurrection of Jesus Christ we do have God's final and definitive act of salvation. This salvation is a possession here and now, and not the object of a hope in some certain but indeterminate future deliverance:

> But now the righteousness of God has been manifested . . . the righteousness of God through faith in Jesus Christ for all who believe (Rom 3:21–22).

This is the good news of the gospel. To accept it is to accept the simple given: "that Jesus is Lord . . . that God raised him from the dead," and that to confess this is to be saved (Rom 10:9–10):

> Therefore, since we are justified by faith, we have peace with God through our Lord Jesus Christ. Through him we have obtained access to this grace in which we stand, and we rejoice in our hope of sharing the glory of God (Rom 5:1–2).

This justification by faith is not a contingent but an outright gift of grace given on God's own and sole initiative. To believe in the present possession of salvation, therefore, allows a sharper distinction to emerge between this faith and the hope (*elpis*) of "sharing the glory of God" in the future:

> knowing that he who raised the Lord Jesus will raise us also with Jesus and bring us with you into his presence (2 Cor 4:14).

Consequently, because of its object, faith in the New Testament is distinct from, though inseparably linked with, hope. The hope is in the future perfect realization of what is already a present possession:

> The free gift of God is eternal life in Christ Jesus our Lord (Rom 6:23; 5:18; 8:10);

> There is therefore now no condemnation for those who are in Christ Jesus (Rom 8:1; see 6:4).

Nor is the gift given us in Christ an ordinary gift, but one which sets us free here and now from all the shackles that bind the unredeemed:

> For the law of the Spirit of life in Christ Jesus has set me free from the law of sin and death (Rom 8:2).

The Obedience of Faith

The acceptance of the gospel, then, is not just the notional acquiescence in an enunciable: "that Christ died for our sins . . . that he was raised on the third day" (1 Cor 15:3–4), but the practical, lived realization of what that fact must mean for me the believer. Jesus' death and resurrection for us means more than the cancellation of "the bond which stood against us . . . nailing it to the cross" (Col 2:14). It means a "newness of life" (Rom 6:4), the "new life of the Spirit" (Rom 7:6), which is a life of genuine freedom, not just from sin and guilt and punishment, but from the law and from death itself.

This is why faith in the New Testament is not only a

confession but also—as it is in the Old Testament—an obedience. But it is not the obedience to a law whose fulfillment is the condition of salvation; rather it is the obedience to the way of salvation revealed in the cross of Jesus Christ. Faith accepts the salvation offered me, a sinner, an enemy of God (Rom 5:6–11), as a free gift of grace, without any possibility of merit on my part. The "obedience of faith" (Rom 1:5; 16:26) is the obedience to salvation by the way of the cross, which is the emptying out of self of all claims to imagined rewards, merits, or achievements:

> Indeed I count everything as loss because of the surpassing worth of knowing Christ Jesus my Lord. For his sake I have suffered the loss of all things, and count them as refuse, in order that I may gain Christ and be found in him, not having a righteousness of my own, based on law, but that which is through faith in Christ, the righteousness from God that depends on faith; that I may know him and the power of his resurrection, and may share his sufferings, becoming like him in his death, that if possible I may attain the resurrection from the dead (Phil 3:8–11).

Thus it is that the faith professed by the Christian has to accept, unconditionally and without possible exception or qualification, all grace as unearned, unmerited and undeserved gift. In so doing this faith acknowledges that the death of Christ on the cross is the only source of "our wisdom, our righteousness and sanctification and redemption" (1 Cor 1:30). That is, in the death and resurrection of Jesus, our relationship with God has been set aright once and for all, not provisionally, nor conditionally, but permanently and, henceforth, irrevocably—at least on God's part. The new covenant, unlike the old, has no conditional clause:

> And if you will obey my commandments which I command you this day . . . (Dt 11:13, 26–28; 13:18).

> But this command I gave them, "Obey my voice, and I will be your God, and you shall be my people; and walk in all the way that I command you, that it may be well with you" (Jer 7:23).

As we have already noted (see No. 28), in order that grace be really grace, three facts have to coincide—the offer, the acceptance, and the acknowledgment—failing any of which, grace, whatever its source and however sublime its nature, is not grace. Not only must God offer the gift freely and gratuitously, but the recipient must accept it and, in the very acceptance, acknowledge it as free and gratuitous, unearned, unmerited and undeserved. In the gospel proclaimed and believed the first two conditions are readily fulfilled. It is the third condition, the acknowledgement of the unearned gratuity of the gift, that is forever in jeopardy.

This is the reason why Paul has to warn the Christians:

Work out your own salvation with fear and trembling (Phil 2:12).

It is the "fear and trembling," not of a just and jealous God, but of my own self, of my insatiable desire to contribute my share, to do my part, to get some recognition, or merely to make doubly sure. It is, in other words, the fear of my succumbing to the ever-present temptation to nullify grace by denying its essential gratuity. Those who insist on seeing Paul's exhortation as a warning against the fearsome anger of a severe and exacting judge forget that this verse is part of the paraenesis that follows, and is intimately linked with, the hymn in Philippians (see above, No. 31). Put very simply, it is a needed warning against our limitless capacity to evade the consequences of the cross, to escape the total emptying of ourselves of all claims and pretenses. It is a needed warning against our inveterate tendency to evade the way of salvation chosen by God, to substitute for it our preferred variety of "cheap grace."

This aspect of the obedience of faith is all the more difficult to grasp because of the heavy mechanisms of exculpation and penance that have been built into the very life of the believer. The churches proclaim the good news; the believers readily enough accept it; but then, by an unholy connivance between one and the other, both the proclaimers and the be-

lievers manage to erect a system of laws and commandments
to rival anything the Old Testament has to offer:

> Let me ask you only this: Did you receive the Spirit by
> works of the law, or by hearing with faith? Are you so fool-
> ish? Having begun with the Spirit, are you now ending
> with the flesh? (Gal 3:2–3).

Most Christians would readily and willingly admit the utter gratuity of the gift, but most of them would feel the need
to do something to hang on to it, or at least to feel a little less
undeserving of it. We have allowed ourselves to be talked
into, or have talked ourselves into, believing that the God who
gave his Son for us while we were ungodly enemies and un-
righteous sinners will somehow or other withhold the gift if
perchance we sin. We have been led to believe that the "new
creation" is a physiological, psychological, and religious mu-
tation. Yet we know:

> That a man is not justified by works of the law but
> through faith in Jesus Christ, even we have believed in
> Christ Jesus, in order to be justified by faith in Christ, and
> not by works of the law, because by works of the law shall
> no one be justified (Gal 2:16; 3:2; Rom 3:28).

Somewhere along the line, we have hoodwinked ourselves into believing that, while the positive commandments
are "works of the law," the negative ones somehow are not.
We are reluctant to see, for example, the avoidance of sin as
possibly a "work of the law." It is no easy matter to keep constantly in mind that the gift of salvation in Christ is a grace:

> But if it is by grace, it is no longer on the basis of works;
> otherwise grace would no longer be grace (Rom 11:6).

All too conveniently do we forget that grace can be undone
by the simple denial of its total gratuity. We refuse to believe
literally that in the gospel:

The righteousness of God is revealed through faith for faith; as it is written, "He who through faith is righteous shall live" (Rom 1:17).

This is why the example of Abraham became such a rich source for Paul's elaboration of his theme of justification through and by faith in Jesus Christ ("through faith in Jesus Christ . . . by faith in Christ" (Gal 2:16):

For man believes with his heart and so is justified, and confesses with his lips and so is saved (Rom 10:10; see 10:4; 3:22; Phil 3:9).

Abraham's faith, almost like no other in the entire history of salvation, was such that he was willing to sacrifice the only possible—indeed, the only conceivable—means of having the divine promise fulfilled: his only son. This is what the author of Hebrews so admirably explains:

By faith Abraham, when he was tested, offered up Isaac, and he who had received the promises was ready to offer up his only son, of whom it was said, "Through Isaac shall your descendants be named." He considered that God was able to raise men even from the dead (Heb 11:17–19).

It is because of this readiness "to offer up his only son" that Abraham's faith "was reckoned to him as righteousness" (Rom 4:3; Gal 3:6; Jas 2:23; see Gen 15:6):

The promise to Abraham and his descendants, that they should inherit the world, did not come through the law but through the righteousness of faith (Rom 4:13).

Paul, therefore, concludes:

That is why it depends on faith (Rom 4:16).

The Life of Faith
    If this faith is the acceptance of the gospel, i.e., the acceptance of the saving grace of God to all who believe in the

death and resurrection of Christ "for us," if this faith is both the confession of Christ's Lordship—"Jesus is Lord!"—and an active obedience to it as the Lordship of him who "emptied himself . . . and became obedient unto death, even death on a cross" (Phil 2:7–8), then the inevitable, the only true response to this faith has to be more than a notional assent, far more than verbal formulae, and infinitely more than supine, passive acceptance.

"It depends on faith," says Paul (Rom 4:16), but it is faith in a crucified Lord. Therefore, this faith has to be a dual response: obedience to the way of salvation, and obedience to its specific consequence. As indicated above, the obedience to the way of salvation is the acceptance of the given grace as it is given: the acceptance of the fact that we are justified, saved, made alive, "not by works of the law but through faith in Jesus Christ" (Gal 2:16; 3:2, 24; Rom 3:28; 4:5). "Faith in Jesus Christ" requires the believer's acceptance of the cross as the sole way to resurrection and life. Those who choose to accept the gift must accept it as it is, not as they wish or imagine it to be. It is a gift given by Jesus' emptying of himself and becoming obedient unto the death on the cross. Therefore, the believer has no other option to follow but this: to empty himself by foregoing all "works of the law," by giving up all attempts at recognition and any striving after achievement or merit:

> I have been crucified with Christ; it is no longer I who live, but Christ who lives in me; and the life I now live in the flesh I live by faith in the Son of God, who loved me and gave himself for me. I do not nullify the grace of God; for if justification were through the law, then Christ died to no purpose (Gal 2:20–21).

To accept in actual practice, in all the lived-out specific details which such acceptance requires, that our salvation is a free gift of grace, that it is not "by works" but "by faith," is a daily crucifixion known only to those who let go the counterfeit securities and guarantees offered, whether by established institutions of salvation, or by preferred channels of redemption, or by proven ways of perfection. It is a crucifixion for all those who are willing to sacrifice the comforts of the "well done, good and faithful servant" of the house of ecclesiastical bondage, for all those who categorically refuse to "boast of men" (1 Cor 3:21) and so live as to glorify God by their "obedience in acknowledging the gospel of Christ" (2 Cor 9:13). If they have to boast at all, then:

> "Let him who boasts, boast of the Lord." For it is not the man who commends himself that is accepted, but the man whom the Lord commends (2 Cor 10:17–18; 1 Cor 1:31; see Jer 9:24).

The whole gospel we are called upon to accept in faith is to this one single end:

> to the glory of God the Father (Phil 2:11).

Its acceptance is an obedience to the way which God the Father chose to redeem us. Faith in this gospel is an acknowledgment that:

> He is the source of your life in Jesus Christ, whom God made our wisdom, our righteousness and sanctification and redemption (1 Cor 1:30).

It is the recognition that:

> All things are yours, whether Paul or Apollos or Cephas or the world or life or death or the present or the future, all are yours; and you are Christ's; and Christ is God's (1 Cor 3:21b–23).

The Law of the Life of Faith

Faith, as has already been said, consists of a dual response. In addition to the obedience to the way of salvation, the believer must submit to the specific demands of this way. Thus, this twofold consequence of faith is in reality a dual obedience: obedience to the way of salvation chosen by God, and obedience to the demands of the new life which this salvation confers. Here, too, not only the gratuity of the gift but its resultant freedom also is—or ought to be—fully preserved.

Therefore, *as a consequence* of this gratuitously conferred gift of grace, but certainly *not as a condition* for its bestowal, the believer must obey the law of the new life in Christ:

> Owe no one anything, except to love one another; for he who loves his neighbor has fulfilled the law. The commandments, "You shall not commit adultery, You shall not kill, You shall not steal, You shall not covet," and any other commandment, are summed up in this sentence, "You shall love your neighbor as yourself." Love does no wrong to a neighbor; therefore love is the fulfilling of the law" (Rom 13:8–10; Gal 5:14).

This, of course, is only the inevitable consequence of our confession:

> God shows his love for us in that while we were yet sinners Christ died for us (Rom 5:8).

The Christian, then, does have to fulfill a law, not because such fulfillment will earn or help him or her to secure salvation, but because the fulfillment of this law is the natural and spontaneous consequence of salvation. The faith professed by a Christian is not any kind of faith, but specifically a "faith working [effective] through love" (Gal 5:6); else it would be no more than pious hypocrisy and religious bombast:

> If I speak in the tongues of men and of angels, but have not love, I am a noisy gong or a clanging cymbal. And if I have prophetic powers, and understand all mysteries and all knowledge, and if I have all faith, so as to move mountains, but have not love, I am nothing. If I give away all I have, and if I deliver my body to be burned, but have not love, I gain nothing (1 Cor 13:1–3).

Moreover, if you truly believe that Christ loved you and gave himself for you, that his death and resurrection for you truly grants you eternal life and divine sonship, that it delivers you here and now from the bondage of sin and death and the law, then what else could you do but "most gladly spend and be spent" for the other (2 Cor 12:15)?

> For you were called to freedom . . . through love be servants of one another (Gal 5:13).

The gift of eternal life through Jesus Christ our Lord (Rom 5:21), like the gift of freedom, is given us not for ourselves but for others. Life—at least in the New Testament—is life for others:

> God's love has been poured into our hearts through the Holy Spirit which has been given to us (Rom 5:5).

God's love, by very definition, is both creative and redemptive: it created all things and redeemed all mankind; it gives us life, and it sets us free. To truly believe that God's love for us in Christ has been poured into our hearts is not to mouth words or to invent sophisticated credal formulae:

> For the kingdom of God does not consist in talk but in power (1 Cor 4:20).

It is in order to enable us to exhibit this "power" by our obedience to the command of love that God's own love has been "poured into our hearts through the Holy Spirit" (Rom 5:5). This love, therefore, is both life-giving and liberating, since its source is God the Creator and Redeemer.

Moreover, in order that God's love be truly life-giving and liberating, not just for the recipient but for the neighbor, in order that it be "genuine" (anypokritos) (Rom 12:9; 2 Cor 6:6), it must spring from (a) the faith that the Son of God "loved me and gave himself for me" (Gal 2:20), and (b) the faith that the life and the freedom that are consequently mine are pure grace. Only then can I obey the command of love with that utter forgetfulness of myself, that genuine prodigality which "counts others better" than myself (Phil 2:3), that

death to myself which is the hallmark of unselfish, uncon-
ceited, and humble service of others (Phil 2:3):

> As it is written, "For thy sake we are being killed all the
> day long . . ." (Rom 8:36; see Ps 44:22).

This dying "all the day long" is the inevitable consequence of that single commandment which is "the fulfilling
of the law" (Rom 13:10). Though by no means easy, the commandment to love ("love your neighbor as yourself"—Rom
13:9; Gal 5:14; Mt 22:39 and parallels; see Lev 19:18) is quite
simple—so simple in fact that Paul hardly feels the need to
write about it:

> But concerning love of the brethren you have no need to
> have anyone write to you, for you yourselves have been
> taught by God to love one another (1 Thess 4:9).

To love one another is, of course, something far removed
from that calculated remoteness which has given "charity"
such a bad name. The love commanded by the unique law of
the New Testament springs from the realization of the true
meaning of grace and of the freedom it confers upon us:

> What have you that you did not receive? If then you re-
> ceived it, why do you boast as if it were not a gift? (1 Cor
> 4:7).

If indeed all things are ours (1 Cor 3:21b), then we are re-
lieved of the need to boast of anything as though "it were not
a gift." We are freed to love one another without either reck-
oning the cost or counting the obstacles:

> Who shall separate us from the love of Christ? Shall trib-
> ulation, or distress, or persecution, or famine, or naked-
> ness, or peril, or sword? . . . For I am sure that neither
> death, nor life, nor angels, nor principalities, nor things

present, nor things to come, nor powers, nor height, nor depth, nor anything else in all creation, will be able to separate us from the love of God in Christ Jesus our Lord (Rom 8:35, 38–39).

The realization of the true meaning of grace makes us render thanks to God in everything. Eucharistic worship is the natural and spontaneous expression of any community of believers in the Lord Jesus. Such a community renders thanks for the faith which—it realizes upon reflection—is every bit as much a gift as the grace of salvation itself:

We have received grace and apostleship to bring about the obedience of faith for the sake of his name among all the nations, including yourselves who are called to belong to Jesus Christ (Rom 1:5–6).

Indeed, so total is the divine initiative in the work of redemption that even the faith response to it is a grace:

And those whom he predestined he also called; and those whom he called he also justified; and those whom he justified he also glorified (Rom 8:30).

The community of believers therefore renders thanks, not only by rejoicing "in our hope of sharing the glory of God" (Rom 5:2) and in the hope in which "we were saved" (Rom 8:24–25), but also by recognizing that even now we are

being changed into his likeness from one degree of glory to another; for this comes from the Lord who is the Spirit (2 Cor 3:18; see Rom 15:13).

For it is by the power of this same Holy Spirit that the community abounds in hope (Rom 15:13). This hope, moreover, is the reason why every time the community "assembles as a church" (1 Cor 11:18), every time it comes together for "the Lord's Supper" (1 Cor 11:20), it does so to hear the word:

For whatever was written in former days was written for our instruction, that by steadfastness and by the encouragement of the scriptures we might have hope (Rom 15:4).

In these same "scriptures" the community is constantly reminded of "the surpassing grace of God in you." It can therefore say over and over again:

Thanks be to God for his inexpressible gift! (2 Cor 9:14–15).

Yet, though the whole triad of faith and hope and love is destined to abide, it is love that is singled out as "the greatest" of all three (1 Cor 13:13). Its pre-eminence is due to the fact that love is the motive of God's gift of salvation in Christ (Rom 5:8) as well as the end and the purpose for which the gift itself was given:

Make love your aim (1 Cor 14:1).

Let all you do be done in love (1 Cor 16:14).

What "instruction, steadfastness, and encouragement" the Christian community finds today, it finds—in part at least—in the letters of Paul. The gospel which these letters proclaim is the genuine source of that freedom for which "Christ has set us free" (Gal 5:1). This is the reason why the hope we have "does not disappoint us" (Rom 5:5). For it is the gospel that provides us with the only permanently valid motive for our love for one another:

For the love of Christ controls us, because we are convinced that one has died for all; therefore all have died. And he died for all, that those who live might live no longer for themselves but for him who for their sake died and was raised (2 Cor 5:14–15).

In the letters of Paul we have one example of such a life. For Paul, "a slave of Jesus Christ, called to be an apostle, set apart for the gospel of God" (Rom 1:1), knew he had ample reason to say:

> Wherever I go, thank God, he makes my life a constant pageant of triumph in Christ, diffusing the perfume of his knowledge everywhere by me (2 Cor 2:14 [Moffatt]).

It is a pageant of God's triumph in Paul's conversion as in his missionary labors, in Paul's gospel as in his theology, in Paul's life as in his ministry:

> In Christ Jesus, then, I have reason to be proud of my work for God. For I will not venture to speak of anything except what Christ wrought through me . . . by word and deed . . . by the power of the Holy Spirit (Rom 15:18–19).

Bibliography of Works Cited

C.K. Barrett, *The New Testament Background: Selected Documents* (New York: Harper & Row, 1961)

Hans Dieter Betz, *Galatians* (Hermeneia; Philadelphia: Fortress Press, 1979)

Günther Bornkamm, "Lord's Supper and Church in Paul," in *Early Christian Experience* (London: SCM, 1969), pp. 123–160

F.F. Bruce, *1 and 2 Corinthians* (New Century Bible; London: Oliphants, 1971)

Rudolf Bultmann, "Christ and the End of the Law," in *Essays Philosophical and Theological* (London: SCM, 1955), pp. 36–66

————, *Theology of the New Testament,* two volumes (London/ New York: SCM/Charles Scribner's, 1952 and 1955)

Hans Conzelmann, *1 Corinthians* (Hermeneia; Philadelphia: Fortress, 1975)

Gerhard Delling, *"pleres . . . plerophoria,"* in *Theological Dictionary of the New Testament,* edited by Gerhard Kittel and Gerhard Friedrich, vol. VI (Grand Rapids: Wm. B. Eerdmans, 1968), pp. 309–311

A.-J. Festugière, *L'Enfant d'Agrigente* (Chrétienté—6; Paris: Cerf, 1941)

————, *Personal Religion among the Greeks* (Berkeley: University of California Press, 1960)

J.A. Fitzmyer, "Qumran and the Interpolated Paragraph in 2 Cor 6, 14–7, 1," *Catholic Biblical Quarterly* 23 (1961) 271–280

Werner Foerster (with Gerhard von Rad), *"eirene . . . ,"* in *Theological Dictionary of the New Testament* vol. II (1964), pp. 400–420

Ernst Haenchen, *The Acts of the Apostles: A Commentary* (Philadelphia: Westminster, 1971)

Martin Hengel, *Judaism and Hellenism: Studies in their Encounter in Palestine during the Early Hellenistic Period,* two volumes (Philadelphia: Fortress, 1974)

J. Hering, *The Second Epistle of Saint Paul to the Corinthians* (London: Epworth, 1967)

E. Käsemann, "The Pauline Doctrine of the Lord's Supper," in *Essays on New Testament Themes* (Philadelphia: Fortress, 1982), pp. 108–135

Helmut Koester, *Introduction to the New Testament,* vol. one: *History, Culture and Religion of the Hellenistic Age;* vol. two: *History and Literature of Early Christianity* (Philadelphia: Fortress, 1982)

Werner Georg Kümmel, *Introduction to the New Testament,* revised edition (Nashville: Abingdon, 1975)

Eduard Lohse, *Colossians and Philemon* (Hermeneia; Philadelphia: Fortress, 1971)

Wayne A. Meeks, *The First Urban Christians: The Social World of the Apostle Paul* (New Haven: Yale University Press, 1983)

Jerome Murphy-O'Connor, *1 Corinthians* (New Testament Message—10; Wilmington, 1979)

Albrecht Oepke, *"parousia . . . ,"* *Theological Dictionary of the New Testament,* vol. V (1967), pp. 858–871

Heinrich Schlier, *"eleutheros . . . eleutheria,"* *Theological Dictionary of the New Testament,* vol. II (1964), pp. 487–502

Eduard Schweizer and others, *"pneuma . . . ,"* *Theological Dictionary of the New Testament,* vol. VI (1968), pp. 332–451

Vatican II, *Dei Verbum* (Dogmatic Constitution on Divine Revelation) in *The Documents of Vatican II,* edited by Walter M. Abbott and Joseph Gallagher (New York: Guild Press, 1966)

Konrad Weiss, *"phero . . . symphero,"* *Theological Dictionary of the New Testament,* vol. IX (1974), pp. 69–78

For Further Reading

J. Christiaan Beker, *Paul the Apostle: The Triumph of God in Life and Thought* (Philadelphia: Fortress, 1980)

———, *Paul's Apocalyptic Gospel: The Coming Triumph of God* (Philadelphia: Fortress, 1982)

Günther Bornkamm, *Paul* (New York: Harper and Row, 1971)

Rudolf Bultmann, "Paul," in *Twentieth Century Theology in the Making,* edited by Jaroslav Pelikan, vol. 1: *Themes of Biblical Theology* (The Fontana Library; London: Collins, 1969)

Lucien Cerfaux, *Christ in the Theology of St. Paul* (New York: Herder & Herder, 1959);

———, *The Christian in the Theology of St. Paul* (New York: Herder & Herder, 1967)

———, *The Church in the Theology of St. Paul* (New York: Herder & Herder, 1955)

———, *The Spiritual Journey of Saint Paul* (New York: Sheed & Ward, 1968)

Hans Conzelmann, *An Outline of the Theology of the New Testament* (London: SCM, 1969)

Nils Alstrup Dahl, *Studies in Paul: Theology for the Early Christian Mission* (Minneapolis: Augsburg, 1977)

W.D. Davies, *Paul and Rabbinic Judaism: Some Rabbinic Elements in Pauline Theology* (London: S.P.C.K., 1965)

Martin Dibelius, *Paul,* edited and completed by Werner Georg Kümmel (London: Longmans, 1953)

C.H. Dodd, *The Meaning of Paul for Today* (Fontana Books; London: Collins, 1958)

Joseph A. Fitzmyer, *Essays on the Semitic Background of the NT* (London: Geoffrey Chapman, 1971) [which contains, pp. 205–217, the *C.B.Q.* article cited in the bibliography]

————, *Pauline Theology: A Brief Sketch* (Englewood Cliffs: Prentice-Hall, 1967) [an extract from *The Jerome Biblical Commentary* (Prentice-Hall, 1968), #79, pp. 800–827]

Victor Paul Furnish, *Theology and Ethics in Paul* (Nashville: Abingdon, 1968)

Morna D. Hooker, *A Preface to Paul* (New York: Oxford University Press, 1980)

Ernst Käsemann, *New Testament Questions of Today* (London: SCM, 1969)

————, *Perspectives on Paul* (Philadelphia: Fortress, 1971)

Werner Georg Kümmel, *The Theology of the New Testament* (Nashville: Abingdon, 1973)

Ralph P. Martin, *Reconciliation: A Study of Paul's Theology* (Atlanta: John Knox, 1981)

Wayne A. Meeks, ed., *The Writings of St. Paul* (Norton Critical Edition; New York; W.W. Norton, 1972)

Johannes Munck, *Christ and Israel: An Interpretation of Romans 9–11* (Philadelphia: Fortress, 1967)

Jerome Murphy-O'Connor, *St. Paul's Corinth: Texts and Archaeology* (Good News Studies—6; Wilmington: Michael Glazier, 1983)

E.P. Sanders, *Paul and Palestinian Judaism: A Comparison of Patterns of Religion* (Philadelphia: Fortress, 1977)

————, *Paul, the Law, and the Jewish People* (Philadelphia: Fortress, 1983)

Hans Joachim Schoeps, *Paul: The Theology of the Apostle in the Light of Jewish Religious History* (Philadelphia: Westminster, 1961)

Donald Senior and Carroll Stuhlmueller, *The Biblical Foundations for Mission* (Maryknoll: Orbis Books, 1983) [chapter 7, "The Mission Theology of Paul," pp. 161–190]

Krister Stendahl, *Paul among Jews and Gentiles and Other Essays* (Philadelphia: Fortress, 1976)

Michael J. Taylor, ed., *A Companion to Paul: Readings in Pauline Theology* (New York: Alba House, 1975)

D.E.H. Whiteley, *The Theology of St. Paul* (Philadelphia: Fortress, 1964)

J.A. Ziesler, *Pauline Christianity* (New York: Oxford University Press, 1983)

Index

Scriptural Index

Genesis		Deuteronomy	
1:2	235	4:1, 6, 8	92
1:26	201	4:34	242, 243
2:7	230	11:13	245
2:17	224	16:3	146
2:24	127	30:15	211
3:3, 19	210, 224	30:19–20	93, 211
3:5	94, 201	32:39	211
6:17	226	33:2	79
17:5	5		
22:1–2	21	Judges	
25:26	5	3:10	227
31:11–13	21	14:6	227
32:28	5		
46:2–3	21, 22	1 Samuel	
		3:4–14	21
Exodus		10:6	227
3:4, 10	21, 22		
12:14	146	2 Samuel	
20:2	241	23:2	227
20:6	93		
24:12	92	Nehemiah	
31:3	227	8:8	19
34:6–7	242		
		Job	
Numbers		4:15	226
11:25	227	32:8	226
16:22	226		

269

Mark		1:20–21	161
1:1	191	1:21–22	27, 162
1:9–11	235	2:1–4	236
1:14–15	188	2:9–11	84
7:13	94	2:23	160
8:29	188	4:32	88
9:35	202	7:58	23, 24
10:11–12	127	8:1	23, 24
10:45	218	9:1–19	21–22, 24, 27, 30
14:22–24	146	9:1	240
14:62	80	9:3–6	162
15:34	222, 223	9:15	21, 234
16:6	160	9:18	137
		9:19–21	43
Luke		9:23–35	43
1:6	35	9:26	25, 45
1:43	191	9:27	26
16:18	127	10:21	21
16:31	163	11:26	222
18:11–12	96	12:2	161
22:15–20	146	13:9	7
23:46	229	13:47	72
24:13–31	165	15:1–29	89
24:26	201	15:2	20
24:27	164, 165, 189	15:28	84
24:34	161, 189	17:23	14
24:41	162	17:32	240
24:51	162	18:1–3	67
		18:12	47
John		20:33–34	67
1:1	192	21:37	19
1:14	232	21:39	8, 17
1:18	164, 199	21:40	19
4:24	232, 234	22:2	19
5:44	64	22:3–16	21–22, 24, 27, 30
14:16	234	22:3	17, 19
		22:20	23, 24
Acts of the Apostles		22:28	8
1:11	79	22:30	27